GEOGRAPHIC INFLUENCES
IN AMERICAN HISTORY

KENNIKAT PRESS SCHOLARLY REPRINTS

Dr. Ralph Adams Brown, Senior Editor

Series on

MAN AND HIS ENVIRONMENT

Under the General Editorial Supervision of
Dr. Roger C. Heppell
Professor of Geography, State University of New York

Forefathers' Rock, Plymouth

GEOGRAPHIC INFLUENCES
IN AMERICAN HISTORY

BY

ALBERT PERRY BRIGHAM, A.M., F.G.S.A., 1855-1932

KENNIKAT PRESS
Port Washington, N. Y./London

GEOGRAPHIC INFLUENCES IN AMERICAN HISTORY

First published in 1903
Reissued in 1970 by Kennikat Press
Library of Congress Catalog Card No: 72-113280
ISBN 0-8046-1318-4

Manufactured by Taylor Publishing Company   Dallas, Texas

KENNIKAT SERIES ON MAN AND HIS ENVIRONMENT

IN MEMORY OF MY SON

CHARLES WINEGAR BRIGHAM

A LOVER OF TRUTH AND BEAUTY, AN ARDENT READER
OF AMERICAN HISTORY, WHO PASSED FROM THIS
LIFE TOO SOON TO FULFIL THE PROMISE OF
HIS YOUTH, THIS VOLUME IS INSCRIBED

CONTENTS

PREFACE

In the chapters which follow, an attempt has been made to combine the materials of American history and geography. One must invent a method as he can, for models in this field can scarcely be said to exist. The plan chosen is geographic, as might be expected from a student of earth science. Each division of the book deals with a region which is more or less distinct in its physical development, and which often shows in the end a good measure of historical unity.

Parkman and Fiske have been among the most useful historical authorities; also McMaster, and the "Winning of the West," by Theodore Roosevelt, who, as an official and as a private citizen, has shown an unfailing appreciation of the physical features of our country.

Prof. Charles Worthen Spencer of Colgate University has kindly read the manuscript of the volume and has made valuable suggestions. It should be stated that parts of Chapter I have previously appeared in the *Geographical Journal* of London, and a few paragraphs of Chapter VIII were originally prepared for the Bulletin of the American Geographical Society.

Many have generously aided me in securing the illustrations. A considerable number have been drawn from the collections of Mr. William H. Rau, Philadelphia. I am also indebted to Dr. F. J. H. Merrill, State Geologist, Albany; Rev. A. K. Fuller, Newburg; Prof. J. T. Draper, Holyoke; Prof. Arthur M. Miller and Prof. H. Garman, State College of Kentucky; Prof. W. B. Clarke, Johns Hopkins University; Prof. Edward M. Lehnerts, Winona, Minn.; Prof. Samuel Calvin, State Geologist of Iowa; Mr. G. K. Gilbert, United States Geological Survey; President Benjamin Ide Wheeler of the University of California; Secretary S. P. Langley of the Smithsonian Institution; Prof. R. S. Tarr of Cornell University; Assistant Principal Frank Carney of the Ithaca High School; and various bureaus of the Department of Agriculture.

Both the physiographer and the historian may often regret omissions or brevity of treatment, but such limits are imperative when a vast and twofold theme is undertaken in a small volume.

ALBERT PERRY BRIGHAM.

COLGATE UNIVERSITY,
    May, 1903.

LIST OF ILLUSTRATIONS

xi

LIST OF MAPS

Copyright, 1895, by A. E. Frye. Used by permission

RELIEF MAP OF THE UNITED STATES

GEOGRAPHIC INFLUENCES IN AMERICAN HISTORY

CHAPTER I

THE EASTERN GATEWAY OF THE UNITED STATES

COLUMBUS did not search for a new continent. He sought a new path to an old world. If he had sailed due west from Palos, he would have touched the eastern shore of North America where the Chesapeake Bay opens upon the Atlantic Ocean. But he turned his prows southward to the Canary Islands, that thence he might run due west along the 28th parallel, to the north end of Japan, which, under the name of Cipango, he found upon a map of his time. This point was twelve thousand miles distant, but reckoning the size of the globe too small, and the extent of Asia too great, he counted only upon a voyage of twenty-five hundred miles. Sailing westward from the Canaries, he found himself wafted by the trade-winds. Hence he daily reported to his officers and sailors a smaller number of miles than were really traversed, that they might not be scared by their fearful progress over the Sea of Darkness.

Thus, unwittingly, the discoverers of America were heading toward the West Indies. The Spaniard stumbled in at the Mediterranean portal of our continent; for the great seas which we know as the Caribbean and the Gulf of Mexico lie between the great lands, and are as truly a Mediterranean as those waters that wash the shores of Europe and Africa. Thus the West Indies, Florida, the mouths of the Mississippi, and the coastal plain about Vera Cruz became forever associated with the Spaniard. His power has gone, but he has sprinkled island and shore with geographic names which live.

As early as 1500, European craft began to visit the cod banks of Newfoundland, starting an industry which has been plied until the present time. Among these fishermen were French navigators, and it was not many years before Cartier entered the Gulf of St. Lawrence, sailed up the great river, looked upward upon the promontory where Quebec was to stand, and called at an Indian village at the foot of a small but rugged mountain of volcanic origin, which he named Mount Royal. The Indian village has given way to a great city, and Cartier's name has become Montreal. He is the first of those illustrious Frenchmen who made the map of the Great Lakes, and explored the Mississippi River to its mouth. Champlain, La Salle, Joliet, Marquette, Frontenac, — these are the names: Belle Isle, Montreal, Detroit, Prairie du Chien, St. Louis, Baton Rouge, — such are the memorials of French heroism and French occupation. The gateway was the St. Lawrence and the Lakes.

Meantime, in 1587, Drake had sailed into the harbor of Cadiz, and "singed the king of Spain's beard." In 1588 the sea-dogs of England joined with wind and storm and sunk the Spanish Armada, strewing the shores of the North Sea and of the Atlantic with the wrecks of Castilian greatness. Drake and Hawkins scoured the sea for Spanish treasure. Their hands were harsh, but in no other way could English shipping keep afloat, or English settlements survive in any land. The breaking of Spanish power opened the way to English colonies in America.

Where would the Englishman come upon American shores? The Spaniard held the islands and seas of the south; the French occupied the St. Lawrence; from the St. Lawrence almost to the Gulf stretches a system of mountains; they are not lofty, but they are continuous; they stand back a little from the sea. In the north the hills of southeastern New England lie between the mountains and the Atlantic. From central New Jersey to Georgia we find a flat or gently rolling coastal plain. Behind, everywhere, is the barrier, a low wall, rugged, however, and broad, — the Appalachian Mountains.

The narrow strip of lowland between the mountains and the sea was left to the Englishman. He made his home about Massachusetts Bay, on the Delaware, the Chesapeake, by the rivers of Virginia, and on the low coasts of the Carolinas to the Savannah. He forged the colonies into a chain, and began to push over the mountain barrier and through its passes until he had occupied Tennessee, Kentucky, and Ohio, and driven out the French. Then he swept across the prairies, adopted the Western mountains as his own, and planted great cities by the harbors of the Pacific.

Conquering the Dutch, who had anticipated him in possessing the best Atlantic harbor of North America, he found a narrow but open and easy road, through the Appalachian wall, between the seaboard and the prairies of the Mississippi. The Eastern Gateway of the United States is the valley of the Hudson and Mohawk rivers.

The history of the Empire State gathers about this gateway. When the voyager from the Old World approaches the chief city of the New, he sees the southern shore of Long Island, and the line of Atlantic Highlands converging toward the Lower Bay. Then he passes the Narrows and enters New York Harbor. Leaving the East River on his right and continuing northward, he enters the lower waters of the Hudson. He may follow its valley for a hundred and fifty miles, and at every point the rise and fall of the tide will remind him of the ocean which he has left behind.

Eastern New York is occupied by a narrow belt of low mountains. In some places these mountains rise to moderate heights, and in others they are worn to their roots and form a region of hills and rocky ledges. These mountain ridges run north-northeast by south-southwest and are a part of the great Appalachian system. The Hudson cuts across them in a long diagonal, in its southward course from Albany to New York. This is most plainly seen in the Highlands. This range, built of hard and ancient

FIG. 1. The Palisades of the Hudson opposite Spuyten Duyvil.

crystalline rocks, enters New York from the northeast and leaves the state to the southwest, where it
becomes the Highlands of New Jersey. Through
it is cut the gorge of the Highlands, barely wide
enough to carry the river, with steep slopes rising
to the summits of Storm King, Crow's Nest, and
Anthony's Nose.

If Hendrik Hudson had an eye for landscape, he
did not lack for variety after he sailed the *Half Moon*
through the Narrows. The forested flats and low
hills of Manhattan on the east lay in contrast to the
precipitous wall of the Palisades that followed him on
his left for nearly forty miles. He doubtless did not
recognize in their huge columns the outcropping of
massive beds of ancient lava. When he reached
Haverstraw Bay and saw the river broaden to three
miles, we may safely think that his spirits quickened
with the hope that the passage to Cathay had been
found. But he was doomed to doubt as he began to
thread the Highland gorge. When he emerged on
the north the river was wide again, and its valley
more spacious than he had seen it before. Going
northward, the Catskills would fill his vision as he
looked westward over a few miles of low country to
the strong profile that ruled the horizon far along his
course. Eastward he would see rough and rising
land, but he could not see that here are the foothills
of the mountains of New England. As the voyager
passed the hundred-mile limit from the sea, he would
find shoal water and many islands, and begin to sus-
pect, what a few more miles of journeying would
prove, that he was following a river toward its source,

and that he must turn back and seek in regions yet unknown a passage to the far East.

It remained for others to learn what lay beyond the site of Albany. Succeeding explorers climbed the slopes on which Albany is built, and thence for nearly twenty miles traversed a region of half-sterile sands to the Mohawk River bottoms, where Schenectady now stands. Looking westward, there appears a deep V-shaped gap in the uplands. Through this gap the river pours from the west. By this channel, in the closing times of the Ice Age, flowed the waters of the Great Lakes, depositing in the Hudson Valley the great body of sands that lies west of Albany.

The Mohawk Valley, or that part of it which now interests us, is a trench nearly one hundred miles long, extending from Schenectady westward to Rome, in central New York. Easterly it opens into the Hudson lowlands, westerly it widens into the plains of Iroquois, in other words, the flat bottoms of the greater glacial ancestor of Lake Ontario. Viewed from near the river, the valley appears to be about 500 feet deep, with an average width of flood-plain of a half mile. Seen more truly from the bordering plateau, it is a vast gap, 1500 to 2000 feet deep, its upper slopes several miles apart, lying between the great uplands on either hand. The parting of the waters is at Rome. From that point the streams enter Lake Ontario. Once pass this gateway, and the path is clear across the lake plains and over the prairies and plains to the Rocky Mountains.

South of the Mohawk are the uplands of New York, stretching from the Hudson Valley to Lake

Erie. On the east we know them as the Catskill
Mountains. But these are only lofty hills with rolling
tops, and descending by a precipitous slope, or escarpment, on the east. Seen from the east, along the
Hudson River, this slope, with its crest, appears like
a mountain range. It is really the edge, or end, of a
plateau. This plateau, which is 3000 feet or more
in altitude in parts of the Catskills, falls to an average of 2000 feet in central and western New York.
The Mohawk gap lies north of the plateau, or may be
said to be cut through the plateau along its northern
edge.

North of the Mohawk Valley the land rises, at first
moderately, and then more boldly, to the slopes and
summits of the Adirondack Mountains. While these
mountains, like the Highlands of the Hudson, are
ancient and much denuded, they preserve a series of
bold northeast by southwest ranges, so that there is
no line or avenue, north of the Mohawk, along which
a railway could be well constructed. Except for local
traffic, the mountains are a perfect barrier to commerce and travel.

The physiographer can look back to an era when
no Mohawk Valley existed, when the drainage of the
southern Adirondacks crossed the state to the Pennsylvania region, and he can see that there is a Mohawk
Valley because a belt of soft and destructible rocks,
known as the Utica and Hudson shales, extends from
the region of Albany westward, between areas of
harder rock on either hand. The valley has a long
and intricate physical history which cannot here be
told. It must suffice to say that in ancient days there

FIG. 2.   Adirondack Mountains about Clear Lake.

was no such valley, that its presence is due to a belt
of destructible rocks disintegrating for long periods,
that the ice sheet entered it and overrode it, that the
waters of the Great Lakes poured through it for a
time, until they were diverted to their present course,
leaving the valley to become in due time the channel
of human intercourse.

As the traveler, going up the valley, passes Rome,
the bordering slopes recede on either hand and on
the north are soon lost to view. On the south, however, he sees bold hills, to Syracuse and beyond. These
form the northern slope of the Catskill-Alleghany
plateau. The railway traverses a flat country, the
bed of Lake Iroquois. This plain, studded between
Syracuse and Rochester with elongated glacial hills,
continues through western New York, south of Lake
Ontario. It is a region of high fertility, and is now
one of the garden spots of the United States.

The explorers and settlers of this part of New
York found established here several powerful Indian tribes, — the Iroquois. A few generations before
the white man came they banded themselves in a
close alliance known as the Confederacy of the
Five Nations. They called their country the " Long
House." The Mohawks were the most easterly of
the tribes, calling their fair valley the eastern gateway of the Long House, and they were its keepers.
All the tribes, including Oneidas, Onondagas, Sene-
cas, and Cayugas, were in a comparatively advanced
state. They practiced agriculture extensively, lived
in neat and comfortable cabins, possessed considerable industrial skill, were eloquent in public counsel,

and were the objects of widespread fear through their prowess in war. Whatever their progress, they were still savages, delighting in torture and given to occasional cannibalism.

Good camping grounds and natural highways have usually been found out by savage tribes, and often by wild animals, long before civilized man appears. Thus the Iroquois had made their own what Fiske calls the "most commanding military position in eastern North America." How far their power was due to qualities which they had inherited and brought with them, and to what measure it came from their environment and opportunity, is a question which neither the geographer nor the ethnologist is yet ready to answer. Whatever be the answer, the European immigrant met these sturdy aborigines, and found himself in alliance or at war. One avenue of approach to the Long House was by ascent of the Hudson and Mohawk rivers. A second was through the Champlain Valley from the St. Lawrence. A third lay along the eastern shore of Lake Ontario. Thus, from the first, the rippling waters and bordering flood-plains of the Mohawk were a frequented path, traversed by French, Dutch, and English in various contact of war and peace with the natives of the land. Of these the French were the first to invade the Mohawk country. Not far away, at Ticonderoga, Champlain, the first white actor on this stage, had aided the Hurons against the Five Nations, and had thus, by the enmity aroused, determined for the English the ultimate control of the region. A later invasion was made by the French along the shore of

Lake Ontario, but they were defeated and forced to retire. There were peaceful invasions also, for in the valley captive missionaries endured torture and sometimes death. Most heroic and famous of these is Father Jogues, whose fate has recently been commemorated by a shrine of his church, erected where he perished, on the edge of a glacial terrace south of the river. The final failure of the French to dislodge or convert the natives of the valley was fraught with weighty results in the history of the new continent. Had they won this great highway, they might in later years have maintained themselves on the St. Lawrence, and might now hold the keys of the New World.

It was the Hudson-Mohawk Valley which early guided the Dutch in their effort to carve a slice from the new continent. Under an English commander, Hendrik Hudson, they sailed up the river which bears his name. At the limit of navigation the Dutch later built Fort Nassau below the site of Albany and concluded a treaty with the Mohawk Indians. Its object was trade, and it went far to prevent French control of the valley. They built Fort Orange in 1622, and thus laid the foundations of Albany. In 1642 Arendt van Curler entered the Mohawk country, reported its lands as "the most beautiful that eye ever saw," and was later authorized to buy the "Great Flats," where Schenectady now stands. The old town and family names of the lower Mohawk still bear proud testimony to this wave of immigration, in the ever present Fondas, Schuylers, Sprakers, Sammonses, Van der Veers, and Yosts of the river country.

The first white settlement in the upper stretches of the valley was made by the Palatines in 1723. Following the devastating wars of Louis XIV, thousands of these stricken people left their homes on the Rhine and took refuge in England. Some of these were sent to America under a compact to reimburse the English government for their passage and for the allotment of lands. After a period of great suffering, first on the Hudson and then on the lower Mohawk, a final removal brought them to the German Flats Patent, between Little Falls and Utica. Here each family received a liberal allowance of the rich alluvium and adjacent uplands of the valley, and their descendants have been powerful in the history of the state and nation.

The next wave of immigration which swept up the valley was English. In 1784 Hugh White passed the Hollanders of Schenectady and the High Dutch settlement of German Flats, and founded Whitestown on the upper river. His coming was the signal for a lively movement from the stony slopes of New England to the inviting fields of the Long House, to which the Mohawk was the only road. Then came the stream of emigrant wagons, bearing the names of Ohio and Indiana, then in the far distant West.

These successive invasions are vividly recorded in the layers of geographic names that are spread over New York. Manhattan, New Amsterdam, New York, — this is a sample of the record. But in this case one of the names is now only a historical relic. The Indian tribal names have attached themselves to river, lake, town, and county. The student of the ice invasion gives the name of the Indian confederacy to the earlier and greater Ontario. Ontario itself is one of many melodious aboriginal names beginning and ending in *o* : Owasco, Otisco, Otego, Owego, Oswego, and Otsego. Happily these musical primitive names stay with many of our streams : Chittenango, Chenango, Unadilla, Genesee, Chemung, and Susquehanna.

The Dutch invasion has left plentiful memorials: Harlem, Tappan Zee, Kaaterskill, Stuyvesant, Rensselaer, or in the Mohawk Valley, Schenectady, Amsterdam, Fonda, and Schoharie. Palatine, Minden, Manheim, and Herkimer, are memorials of the refugees from the Rhine, settling in the Mohawk country. The Englishman marked his presence by names from the mother country, though this habit is by no means so common as in New England, where the first settlers had come, with fresh memories, direct from the old home. Still, we have such names as New York, Westchester, Albany, and Rochester. Then come the records of the pioneer, or prominent citizen : such are Dobbs Ferry, Wappingers Falls, and, in greater numbers as we go west, Whitestown, Gilbertsville, Sangerfield, Smithville, Binghamton, or Cooperstown. Another stratum is composed of names great in our history, as Washington, Madison, Hamilton, Clinton, Steuben, or Fulton. And finally we discover that a curious shower of classical names fell in early days on central New York, the memorials of men who, in a pioneer region, revered the ancient culture. They may be counted by scores : Utica, Rome, Syracuse, Ithaca, Homer, Tully, Virgil, and many more.

The stream of travel has never ceased to flow, but has rather become thousand fold in the century which has passed. Before considering the Mohawk and Hudson valleys as a modern highway, however, it will be well to observe that they were the theatre of important military events in colonial times. English forts had been erected on the upper Hudson by the year 1709, and before the year 1712 the chain had been extended up the Mohawk to Fort Hunter, forty miles from Albany. In 1720, through the influence of William Burnet, son of Bishop Burnet and governor of New York, forts were built at Oswego and farther west at Irondequoit Bay. About the time of the French War, a number were built near the present city of Rome, or in the vicinity of the Oneida carrying-place. "These, and similar efforts on the part of the English, served to divert from the French into English channels a large Indian trade, and to make the route *via* Mohawk River and Oneida Lake, the shorter one between Albany and Canada, the one most generally travelled." The Mohawk and Champlain became thus the great highways trodden by hostile forces in the French and Indian Wars, until the French rule came to its end in Canada in 1760. Local histories are filled with exciting records of midnight attack, weary marches in captivity, and all the terrors of border warfare. Here, too, was fought one of the less-known but most pivotal battles in the struggle between the colonies and the mother country, the battle of Oriskany. On the south slope of the valley, a few miles west of Utica, the Dutch farmers rallied under Nicholas Herkimer, and defeated the

English and the Indians, who would otherwise have gone down the valley and supported Burgoyne in his campaign on the Hudson. The contestants on each side numbered but a few hundred, but the result is thought by many to have been decisive of the main issue of the war.

The control of the Hudson was far more vital to both Americans and British than the holding of the Mohawk. By its connection with the Champlain Valley it became the focus of strategy in the Revolution. While the colonial forces were still about Boston, Arnold had advised Dr. Warren that Ticonderoga and Crown Point be seized, both because they contained military stores and because they stood in the gateway of the north. Before the British army evacuated Boston, it was suspected that New York would be the point of attack, and General Lee, on his urgent request from Washington, was permitted to prepare for the defence of the city and the Hudson. No one can know what might have happened, if Clinton, hovering in the harbor, had not found that Lee was in New York, ready to defend it. To have gained the Hudson at that early day would have cut off New England from the Southern colonies and put to risk the independence of all. Plans for fortification went on after Clinton disappeared. The East River near Hell Gate, the Brooklyn Heights, and the Highlands to the north were included in the scheme.

When the British forces under Howe did make their appearance, in June, 1776, they were not to find the lower Hudson an easy conquest. They could drive Washington out of Long Island, and they could

FIG. 3. The Hudson Valley and the Catskills shown in Relief.

sail past Putnam's obstructions of the North River and win at Fort Washington and Fort Lee, but they could not get possession of the upper Highlands. When Sir Henry Clinton, in 1777, failed to subjugate the Hudson and make connection with Burgoyne, coming from the north, the most promising device of British strategy fell to the ground. American victory at Oriskany and Bemis Heights, and British failure on the Hudson, left the great highways of New York in the possession of the colonies. It was four years later, at Dobbs Ferry, on the lower Hudson, that Washington planned the Yorktown campaign. In the same old house, occupied as his headquarters, Washington and Carleton, in 1783, arranged for the departure of the British from American soil. Here the French allies had been received in 1781, and here in 1783, two days after the conference with Carleton, a British warship fired seventeen guns in honor of the American commander. These facts are now inscribed on this old mansion, and typify the importance of the Hudson Highlands throughout the long struggle.

In the pioneer days the Mohawk was considered a navigable stream, and immigrants and freight were conveyed over its waters in boats propelled by poles. Several breaks were, however, necessary; a first beyond Albany, because of the abrupt fall of seventy feet at Cohoes, a second at Little Falls, on account of impassable rapids over the barrier of hard rocks which the stream there encounters, and a third of two miles at the Oneida carrying-place, where the Mohawk is left to the east, and the winding course of Wood Creek is followed to Oneida Lake. Early legislative authority was given for improving navigation at these points, and soon after 1791 a canal, three miles long, with five locks, was constructed at Little Falls, and a further canal conducted boats across the Oneida carrying-place. We read that the enlarged boats, with five men, could transport, between the terminal points of navigation on the river, twelve tons in twelve days. Long lines of wagons and stages also traversed the bottom-lands, making the valley a busy highway between the East and the expanding West.

A continuous waterway, from the tidal waters of the Hudson to the blue expanse of the Laurentian lakes, became now the subject of serious discussion. Enough of the geography was known to suggest the possibility of such communication, but the following order, issued to a commander on Lake Ontario, in 1814, shows also the extent of the ignorance that prevailed. "Take the *Lady of the Lake* and proceed to Onondaga, and take in at Nicholas Mickle's furnace a load of ball and shot, and proceed at once to Buffalo." "That means," said the perplexed officer, "that I am to go over Oswego Falls and up the river to Onondaga Lake, thence ten miles into the country by land to the furnace, and returning to Oswego, proceed to the Niagara, and up and over Niagara Falls to Buffalo!"

The demand for a water-route was strengthened by the danger that the growing commerce of the Genesee country would be diverted, either down the St. Lawrence to Montreal and Quebec, or by the Susquehanna to Philadelphia. It is difficult to assign credit for the suggestion of an Erie Canal. Probably the idea was conceived independently in several thoughtful minds. Such a prediction is said to have been made by Captain Joseph Carver in 1776. Elkanah Watson, describing a westward journey in 1788, voiced his "strong presentiment that a canal communication will be opened sooner or later from the Great Lakes to the Hudson." Gouverneur Morris is reported to have said, in 1803, "Lake Erie must be tapped and the waters carried across the country to the Hudson." He thought there should be a uniform declivity between the two, not taking account of locks and summit supplies of water. The legislature took up the matter in 1808, a survey was made, and in 1810 a commission was appointed. The project then fell into abeyance until revived by De Witt Clinton in 1817. Navigation was finally opened between Lake Erie and the Hudson on October 26, 1825. The price of transportation from Albany to Buffalo, about three hundred miles, gradually declined during the twenty-six years after the opening of the canal, from $88 to $5.98 per ton. Later, railway competition became effective, and transportation from Buffalo to New York, in 1885, was but $1.57 per ton. Of the vicinity of Rochester it was said, upon completion of the canal, that her timber found market and floated away. Wheat quadrupled in price. The mud dried up, the mosquitoes, the ague and fever, and the bears left the country, and prosperity came in on every hand. In like manner the salt, gypsum, lime, and grain of Onondaga, where is now the great city of Syracuse,

FIG. 4.   Down the Mohawk River from Palatine Bridge ; the Four Tracks of the New York Central Railway on the left ; the Erie Canal on the right.

found ready market.   But it is not enough to cite
these comparatively local results.   The meaning of
the Mohawk Valley is that the entire region of the
Great Lakes and the vast prairie and mountain
regions of the West became tributary to the rising
metropolis on Manhattan Island.

A similar story has now to be told of railway communication through this valley.   There was no railroad in America prior to 1826.   In that year a horse
railway, four miles long, was built at Quincy, Mass.,
for the transportation of granite from the quarries.
In the same year the legislature of the state of New
York granted a charter to the Mohawk and Hudson
River Railway Company to build a road from Albany
on the Hudson to Schenectady on the Mohawk, a distance of eighteen miles.   This was the first chartered
railroad in America.   It was completed October 31,
1826, and at once carried four hundred passengers
daily.   This, it will be remembered, was soon after
through traffic began on the Erie Canal.   In 1833 a
charter was granted for a road to extend from
Schenectady up the river to Utica, a distance of
nearly eighty miles.   This division was in running
order in 1836.   A further link in the westward series,
between Syracuse and Auburn, was finished in 1837,
and from Utica to Syracuse in 1839.   A curious
argument was urged for a break in the chain of
roads at Utica; namely, that otherwise it would become a mere way-station on a great line and its
business would fail to develop.   The discussion shows
that the consolidation of the future was forecast at
an early time.   Gradually the line was completed

from New York to Buffalo, 450 miles, and became known as the New York Central and Hudson River Railway, or more commonly as the New York Central, one of the greatest railways of the world. Four tracks lie side by side from Albany to Buffalo, two being used for passenger traffic and two for the conveyance of freight. Owing to the abrupt descent of the valley slopes to the river, but two tracks lead from Albany down to New York. A great number of minor railways pour their tribute into this artery of transportation, and it is hardly true to call Buffalo a terminal point, since many solid trains each day push on without change both south of the lakes and across Niagara, through Canada, five hundred miles farther, to Chicago. Except at West Albany there is not a difficult grade or an embankment or trestle of any importance between New York and Buffalo, and with slight exception this holds good from Buffalo to the Rocky Mountains. Two thousand miles of splendid country are thus made tributary to the harbor of New York through the river gateway which we have described.

About twenty-five years ago a competing line with two tracks was constructed and called the West Shore Railway. It extends up the Hudson on the west side, along the Mohawk on the south side, and then closely parallel to the Central Railway to Buffalo. For the most part the same towns are served by the two lines, and the newer has now become an integral part of the older system, so that the New York Central virtually crosses the Empire State with a line of six parallel tracks. It should be added that the second telegraph line in America joined Albany and Utica along the Mohawk Valley, being finished on January 31, 1846. A short line between Baltimore and Washington preceded it by two years.

To sum up, the valley is now threaded by the ancient highways, the Erie Canal, six railway tracks, and innumerable telegraphs and long distance telephones by which New York converses with Detroit, Indianapolis, Chicago, and other Western cities. The passing up and down, day and night, of men, of thoughts, of commodities, is like the ebb and flow of tidal waves, whose course is only stayed as traffic rests on the docks of Europe and of more distant continents.

But it must not be thought that the Mohawk is the only road which has been sought out to the West. It is only a broader gate with a lower threshold. There are other great railways, but none of them passes the Appalachian belt at an altitude, as at Rome, of 445 feet. A brief comparison will be instructive. Take first the roads which traverse the Empire State from the seaboard. Much English capital was invested in the Erie Railway. Perhaps the flow of money would have been less free had its sinuosity and heavy grades been known. At 75 miles from New York it must attain a height of 870 feet to pass the Kittatinny Mountains. At Port Jervis the altitude is 442 feet; at Deposit, 1008 feet; near Elmira, 799 feet; and at Castile, 1401 feet, with some large embankments and difficult bridges. Likewise the New York, Ontario, and Western Railway, running to Oswego and the West, crosses difficult

divides, and rises and falls between low altitudes
and heights of nearly 1800 feet. The Delaware,
Lackawana, and Western Railway rises to 1932 feet
at Tobyhanna, Pa., and in 27 miles descends to 745
feet at Scranton. Thence it passes into New York,
where it varies between 846 feet and 1359 feet.

Of the roads which cross the Appalachians south
of New York, the conditions are similar. The Lehigh
Valley road from Philadelphia maintains a course
below 700 feet for 100 miles, then in 30 miles climbs
to its summit, 1728 feet, and in 20 miles more drops
to 549 feet at Wilkesbarre. The Pennsylvania, one of
the finest roads in America, is obliged to make at one
point an altitude of 2161 feet, and has one section of
five miles whose grade is 80 feet per mile. The Baltimore and Ohio road has its summit at 2620 feet.
Farther south the facts are yet more striking, and it
is less than twenty years since a railway first crossed
the southern Appalachians.

An old writing, dating from 1634, makes reference
to a company which bought from its Indian owners
"the island of Manhattan, situated at the entrance of
said river, and there laid the foundations of a city."
Here were available lowlands lying by a secure haven,
and they were seized instinctively as the home of a
new community. As the inland waterways and passes
became known, they showed that Manhattan Island
was at one end of a natural highway. A great terminal
city has grown up because of the unrivaled combination of harborage and lines of interior communication.

New York could be no other than the chief city of
the Western Hemisphere. Such a center must be on

the Atlantic shore, in the north temperate zone, for
there commerce is most favored between America
and the great nations of Europe. Manhattan Island
has on either side many miles of water front, at whose
piers the largest vessels can lie. A similar frontage
is afforded across the North River by the New Jersey
shore. Miles of wharfage stretch along the Long
Island side of the East River. That tidal avenue
leads to the protected waters of Long Island Sound,
which carry the coastwise trade with New England.
Southward the inner harbor leads by a narrow passage down to the Lower Bay, Raritan Bay, and Sandy
Hook Bay. When New York shall have become the
first city of the world instead of the second, she will
still have ample room for the shipping of all nations
to rest in her quiet waters.

The perfection of her harbor might not, however,
have made her the metropolis but for the inland ways
to north and west. Down to the completion of the
Erie Canal she was surpassed by Boston and Philadelphia. The latter was the largest shipping point
in North America. But when the grain and other
products of the West began to float down the Hudson,
the race was won for New York. Ships could come
to her from foreign shores and get a return cargo on
her docks. This was true of no other city. Philadelphia and Baltimore have no such favorable openings into the Mississippi Valley. Boston lies behind
the Berkshire barrier. About half of all the foreign
trade of the United States passes through the port
of New York. If imports are considered, two-thirds
enter this gateway.

The human history of the last three centuries was possible through the geographical unfoldings of the later geological periods. Imagine the northeastern United States as standing several hundred feet higher than now. There would be no water in the Hudson channel except what falls in the Adirondacks and on the nearer lands, and runs seaward. The sea border itself would be nearly a hundred miles southeast of New York. Raritan River would join the Hudson from the west. A land stream would come from the northeast, along the line of the East River. There would be no harbor; there might be a modest town at the confluence of the rivers. Now suppose the eastern edge of the continent sinks slowly down to its present position in reference to the surface of the sea. Eighty miles of lowland would be buried by the waters. The fresh water of the rivers would be checked and mingled with the brine of the Atlantic. The tide would ebb and flow among the bays and coves around Manhattan, and its pulse would be felt within the pass of the Highlands and far beyond. Such was the history, long before man, even the savage, appeared. The region was elevated and dissected by the streams. Long courses of rock decay wore down the crystalline masses of New York island to a lowland, only that they might be more fiercely attacked by the drill and dynamite of modern days. The softer rocks that lay over and behind the Palisades lava were disintegrated and swept away. Then came the long submergence and the "drowning" of the streams, giving deep waters for ships. And the tides going in and out serve as a broom to sweep the channel. And, where the tidal scour is not enough, man anchors a scow and drives a steam shovel through the slime, aiding nature.

We may add another short chapter. At the close of the glacial time the sinking of the land had gone farther than at present. Much of Manhattan was covered with water. The Hudson estuary was deeper and wider than now. In these deeper and broader waters, at many sheltered points, fine muds settled between the present sites of New York and Albany. These muds are often clays, fine, massive, and blue, which make the Hudson Valley the greatest brick-making district in the world. The connection is simple, — unlimited clay, a tidal river, and a metropolis to be built. The muds are not all clays. Often they are coarse and should not be called muds but sands and gravels laid down in deltas, where the Croton, Fishkill, Catskill, Mohawk, and Hoosick discharged into the long body of tidal waters. We read the record again : uplift, and long denudation and valley-making; submergence, greater than now, with soft deposits along the valley; a moderate uplift, bringing in present conditions and followed by the advent of man.

If clay were not enough, a peculiar limestone is found at Rondout, which, when ground, affords the finest cement. The marbles of Tuckahoe, the brownstone of the Connecticut Valley, and the granites of New England are not far away, and, perhaps most important of all, a half-dozen trunk railways bring the anthracite coal by easy hauls to the docks of the North River. A great city was inevitable.

FIG. 5. Roseton Clay Beds and Brickyards, on the Hudson. The Terraces are due to the cutting of the Clay to Successive Levels. Photograph by H. Ries, in "Bulletin of New York State Museum."

The development of human life along the Hudson and Mohawk highway has been parallel to that of New York. Of forty-one communities, having the rank of a city in the state of New York, eleven are on the Hudson and six are on the Mohawk. If we extend our view from New York to Buffalo, four-fifths of the population and nine-tenths of the wealth of the Empire State are found within the counties bordered or crossed by the Hudson River and the Erie Canal. The east bank of the Hudson is almost a continuous suburb of New York up to the Highlands. Newburg is at the north gate of the Highlands, and Kingston has grown up at the mouth of the Wallkill, a tidal branch of the Hudson, whose valley offers a natural road from the coal region. The Hudson Valley, about the entrance of the Mohawk, forms a natural center of population. Here is the head of navigation, and an open road to the west and to the north. These conditions centered here the lines of travel from New England. There is no good gate opening eastward, but the Westfield and Deerfield valleys of the Berkshires find their best western outlet here. A fall of water due to blockades of glacial origin has given rise to Cohoes, while shipping lines the river borders of Albany and Troy.

The half-dozen cities of the Mohawk are good illustrations of physiographic control. Cohoes has been named. Schenectady, with thirty thousand people, lies on the great flats, where the river issues from the uplands upon the old estuary ground of the Hudson. The river itself has dug away the sands of its ancient delta and smoothed out a few square miles of alluvial floor. Farther up is Amsterdam, with twenty thousand people, a center for the manufacture of knit goods and carpets. Little Falls, a small but busy city, developed from an ancient carrying-place, and by reason of its water-power, the primal cause being a dislocation of the rocks, which here crosses the river from south to north. The harder, older, and deeper rocks were brought up, and the river has not yet finished its task of grading its valley bottom : hence the "little falls." Utica, a city of sixty thousand people, is determined by an old fording-place, and receives tribute from south and north by railway lines which reach New York across the uplands, and open to the St. Lawrence through the Adirondacks or along the Ontario lowlands. Rome is built at the old Oneida carrying-place, where little cargoes were borne over from the Mohawk and sent down the sluggish waters of Wood Creek toward Oswego.

Going westward, Syracuse originated by reason of the brines found by boring to the underlying gravels, but has other reasons for her growth, among which is her position along the great highway from east to west. A like word may be said of Rochester, while Buffalo finds assured greatness in being the point of transshipment at the foot of Great Lake navigation. Erie in Pennsylvania is the natural correlative of Philadelphia, as Buffalo is of New York. But Erie is small and Buffalo is great. The explanation is the Mohawk-Hudson Valley. So far as Philadelphia has a natural gateway to the west, therefore, it is not Erie but Pittsburg.

If we consider the commonwealths which represent the thirteen colonies, New York, more truly than Pennsylvania, is the " Keystone " state. On the one hand is New England, which, as we shall see in the following chapter, stands in many ways by itself. On the other, Pennsylvania is an Appalachian state and is closely related to Maryland and Virginia. New York, with its harbor, its artery of travel, and its frontage on the Lakes and the St. Lawrence, is the key to the West and the North. She is not hampered by the mountain barriers of the South, nor is her traffic hindered by the Falls of Niagara, nor by the rapids and the winter ice of the St. Lawrence.

We do not yet know how much physical environment molds mental and spiritual life. We cannot trace geographical influences in a complete way, but we gather hints of their power. The Hudson country could not fail to be richer in tradition and riper in its harvest of thought than some other portions of the commonwealth in which it lies. For geographic reasons it has an older civilization than the interior. The old Dutch life was followed by an incoming from England. These elements reacted on each other, as both had felt the shock of migration across an ocean. Their social and their physical environment was new.

Dwellers on the lower Hudson must ever feel a more or less conscious relation to the sea and have a sense of neighborhood to its farther shores. The ebb and flow of the tides and the passing of ships are tokens of a larger life. More tangible in its effects, perhaps, is the near metropolis. Commercial opportunity has brought wealth. In some measure, homes

Fɪɢ. 6. Looking into the North Gateway of the Highlands from a Point near Newburg, N.Y.

on the Hudson may show how wealth has conspired with the higher tastes to find serene living where nature is beautiful. It would be presuming to assign nature's share in the literary unfoldings of the valley, but its literature cannot be less than a natural growth from soil and atmosphere. The breath of the sea is here. Cities and villages are old enough to have traditions. Mountains, too rugged to bear but a scanty forest, rise from the borders of the river. But a few miles away are the mysterious gorges and untrodden woods of the higher Catskills.

Unless one is plying the river for trade, Irving is the best guide to the Hudson. No other has so fully given speech to her life. We do not know the measure of intimate influence that comes on a writer from his surroundings, but Irving assuredly laid hold upon the traditions and the history of the region, and embodied, or shall we say created, the typical spirit of the great river. Did he not in some measure do both? His birth was in the year in which the British troops left the city of New York not to return. As a youth he voyaged up the Hudson, and made many journeys along the Hudson and Mohawk in the years that followed. In the satires of the Knickerbocker story he reveals his knowledge of every phase of local history and every nook of the Hudson country. His tales of humble domestic scenes in the "Legend of Sleepy Hollow" are pictures, and the woods in which Rip Van Winkle slept are the living forests of the Catskills. The real Hudson becomes more real because idealized and seen through the serener atmosphere of the older time. Not far from the Hudson

lived Andrew Jackson Downing, the landscape archi-
tect, forerunner of a generation that is to increase,
of men who are to enter into the heart of nature and
preserve her freshness and beauty, while subduing
her to the uses of man.

The poet has not been forgetful of the river.
Halleck's lines in praise of Weehawken may have
a strange sound, in the light of modern changes, but
Drake's "Culprit Fay" can hardly pass out of date
so long as the imagination touches human feeling.
This, perhaps, is the poem of the Hudson River, but
we turn rather to Bryant. His "Night Journey of a
River" must have been inspired by the river of his
home, and nothing could better express the subtle ties
that bind the river and its greatest city than these lines
from "A Scene on the Hudson" : —

> "River! in this still hour thou hast
>   Too much of heaven on earth to last;
>   Nor long may thy still waters lie,
>   An image of the glorious sky.
>   Thy fate and mine are not repose,
>   And, ere another evening close,
>   Thou to thy tides shalt turn again,
>   And I to seek the crowd of men."

Within the domain of the Hudson, also, for many
years John Burroughs has lived in his cottage, and
gone forth, in winter and in summer, to share and
interpret the life of her birds and forests. Curtis
made his home where river passes into ocean. He
was a lover of the Hudson, and voices his loyalty, if
such it may be called, to his own land in his fine parallel between the Hudson and the Rhine. "Its

spacious and stately character, its varied and magnificent outline, from the Palisades to the Catskills, are
as epical as the loveliness of the Rhine is lyrical. The
Hudson implies a continent behind. For vineyards it
has forests. For a belt of water, a majestic stream.
For graceful and grain-goldened heights it has imposing mountains. There is no littleness about the Hudson, but there is in the Rhine. . . . The Danube has,
in parts, glimpses of such grandeur. The Elbe has
sometimes such delicately pencilled effects. But no
European river is so lordly in its bearing, none flows
in such state to the sea."

CHAPTER II

SHORE–LINE AND HILLTOP IN NEW ENGLAND

New England is a geographical province. The Berkshire barrier runs from southern Connecticut to its culmination in the Green Mountains of northern Vermont and divides New England from New York and the West. Northward, the St. Lawrence is the natural boundary, though its lowlands belong to another political division. On the east and the south is the sea.

It has, however, other elements of geographic unity. It is, with small exceptions, a very ancient land, as the geologist counts time. Some of its areas have a rocky foundation which is among the oldest known, comparing with the Adirondacks, the Piedmont and Blue Ridge of the South, the core of the Black Hills, or the ancient lands between the Great Lakes and Hudson Bay. Other parts of New England have a less but still incomprehensible antiquity ; such are most of the Green Mountain and Berkshire region and the districts about Boston and the Narragansett. The rocks of the Connecticut Valley in Massachusetts and Connecticut are much younger, yet their age must be reckoned in millions of years. Geologically youthful are parts of Cape Cod, the larger islands, and the barrier beaches and marshes of the southeast.

It may be a more useful description, if we say that about all of New England has felt the disturbing forces that build mountains. Most or all of the region was once a sea bottom, receiving waste from other lands. These sea floors became land by uplift, and by powerful folding of the sheets of rock, forming mountains, of which the Green and White Mountains are but remnants. But these were not the only regions roughened by elevation. If we study the rocks of Rhode Island, or about Boston or Worcester, we shall find them as much disturbed and tangled as on the slopes of Greylock or Mansfield. And they are usually crystalline, for by crushing, by the action of water, and in some cases of heat, they have been changed from their original condition. The limestones have become marbles in Vermont and along the Housatonic; the sandstones, made from waste of still older rocks, have turned into schists, and the muds have become shales or slates.

If such has been the change within, the change of outer form has been as great. A land of bold mountains has become a region of rough hills. This is one of the ways in which the great age of the land might be determined. Southern Maine and New Hampshire, eastern Massachusetts, southern Connecticut, and all of Rhode Island, are a rough lowland. Northern and western New England may originally have been higher than the south and east, — we cannot know, — but all was lofty and perhaps Alpine. Time enough has passed to make the beds of rock, transform them

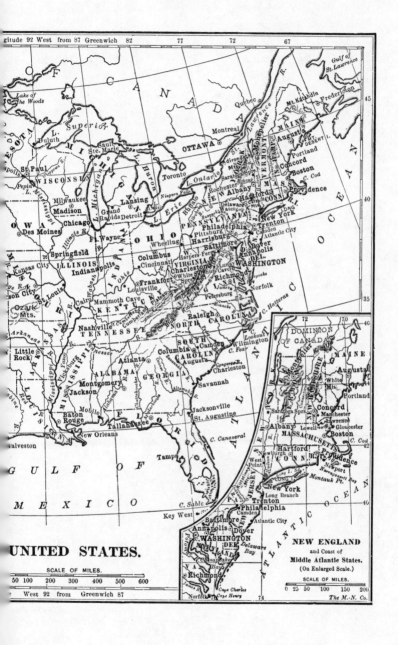

UNITED STATES.

SCALE OF MILES.

50 100   200   300   400   500   600

West 92 from Greenwich 87

NEW ENGLAND
and Coast of
Middle Atlantic States,
(On Enlarged Scale.)

SCALE OF MILES.

0 25 50   100   150   200

The M.-N. Co.

into mountain ranges, and wear them down nearly to the level of the sea.

At some epochs of this history volcanic fires were active, lavas were poured out, and explosive eruptions, like those of Krakatoa and Pelée, sent forth clouds of gases and spread sheets of ash over land and water. Cones were built, which have been long destroyed. Their roots may be found at many points along the rocky shores and far inland. Sheets of ash and lava still bear testimony to these days of fierce changes when New England was an unstable region like the Caribbean and Mediterranean.

The reliefs of northern New England are not so well known as those of Massachusetts and the region to the south. The three more southern states have been completely covered with mapping by the system of contours, while in the northern states only patches here and there have been thus surveyed. In northern New England we find the Green Mountains. On the one hand are valleys and lowlands leading to the Champlain and Hudson, and on the other are the slopes and narrow, fertile terraces and flood plains of the Connecticut. Rising to the heights of the White Mountains, we pass on to the moderate elevations of central and northern Maine, culminating in Katahdin ; southern Maine and New Hampshire are like southern New England.

Through Massachusetts and its southern neighbors the crests of the uplands fall in with one another so well that we may call the general surface a plateau. Viewed from the uplands in western Massachusetts, the surrounding uplands have an even sky-line, and we may imagine a continuous surface, which has later been broken by cutting valleys through it. We can thus think of an upland passing from the Berkshires across the present Connecticut Valley, merging with the lower region, where Worcester stands and from which Wachusett rises. Then we can picture the upland slanting still farther down, east through Massachusetts, and southward through Connecticut and Rhode Island, to the sea. In other words, if we could fill up all the valleys, we should have a plateau descending from the Vermont and New York border to the sea. It would be about two thousand feet above the sea in western Massachusetts, about one thousand feet around Worcester and in eastern Connecticut, and of less altitude toward the Atlantic and the Sound. Physiographers have given attention to this slanting land surface. Not seeing how it could otherwise have been formed, many think that the ancient mountains were worn nearly to sea-level, that the resulting lowland was uplifted, and more to the northwest, and that the Connecticut, Westfield, Housatonic, and other valleys have since been sunk into it. Whatever be the truth, this conception helps us to see geographic forms truly, and to avoid supposing that southern New England is an orderless jumble of rugged lands.

Interesting results follow from these contrasts between northern and southern New England. Forests prevail in one and homes in the other. Maine has the size of the other five states combined, but only one in eight of the inhabitants. Vermont has two towns of more than ten thousand people; Rhode Island has eight. Maine has seven such centers; Massachusetts has forty-seven; while New York has but forty-five. Northern New England has no city of sixty thousand people, and southern New England has fourteen such communities.

The chief drainage systems have a common direction — the greater rivers flow southward. They are mainly longitudinal streams, by which geographers mean that they follow the lines of mountain foldings. Parallel ridges and troughs result from such disturbances, and such troughs controlled the ancient streams. These may have slowly shifted their courses in the ages of their development, but they have not departed from parallelism with the mountain ranges. All the great streams are tidal at their mouths, but some have sunk their inland valleys more effectively than others. Thus the Connecticut has graded its course close to sea-level across Massachusetts, while the bed of the Housatonic at Pittsfield is a thousand feet above the tide.

In another way New England has geographic unity; it was all invaded by land ice in the Glacial Period. For detailed accounts of the Ice Age, the reader should look to special works; it is within our province here to see in a general way the changes wrought on the face of the land. The chief movement was from the north and northwest, down upon the Sound and the Atlantic. That the ice was thick, we know, because it overswept Katahdin, Washington, and Mansfield. And we have more startling proof in the fact that it disregarded the southern trend of the western mountains and valleys, and flowed freely across them on a diagonal. Many years ago this was shown by Sir Charles Lyell and others, who observed trains of boulders near Richmond, Mass., which were carried and distributed in this manner.

We know that the enveloping mantle crossed the place of the present Long Island Sound, and heaped its parallel belts of moraine in Long Island. These moraines run from east to west, and similar belts are found in southern Rhode Island, from Point Judith to Watch Hill; along the southern part of Cape Cod, from Buzzard's Bay to Nauset Beach; and along the shores of Martha's Vineyard and Nantucket. These and others are the terminal moraines of the New England ice sheet. More full of meaning in our present study is the heavy scoring which the surfaces of soil and rock everywhere sustained. In a country which has not been plowed by the ice, soils develop by the wasting of the rocks for long periods. Hence, below the proper soils, the surface rocks are discolored or half-disintegrated. Nearly everywhere in New England these old soils and corroded rocks were pared away, and a new cover of "drift" laid upon the freshly exposed and unchanged bed-rock. This drift was formed by mingling, in and under the glacier, the rock fragments eroded by the ice, and the preglacial soils lying to the north and northwest. We are not to understand that this new and mixed material had been pushed for long distances. Some of it was far-traveled, as we know by boulders from remote ledges, but most of it came to rest again within a few miles of the place of its origin.

The records of this scoring are often to be seen

FIG. 7. Crawford Notch, White Mountains.

when the bed-rock is stripped. They are the glacial grooves, or striæ, and also the rounded or elliptically carved crests of exposed rocky hills, which were attacked and polished into their present forms by the overriding ice. We are not to suppose that the glacier removed a large thickness of the rock from the general surface. But exposed and narrow elevations may have been planed away for many feet, and valleys may have been deepened where powerful ice masses occupied them for a long time. Thus the complexion of the country was changed not a little by giving the surface rocks and soils a hard push and a new distribution.

Much of the drift consists of clay and stones of various size, promiscuously mingled and spread, sometimes evenly, over the land. Moraine heaps and the smoother cover of this stony clay are often thickly sprinkled with the great boulders which are so common a feature in the landscape of New England. Sometimes these great stones are delicately perched, and some are known as rocking-stones, whose many tons may be swayed by the push of a hand. Professor Shaler has ingeniously shown, from these, that no violent earthquake could have visited New England since the Glacial Period, else would these stones have rolled over and assumed a more stable position.

There are other sorts of glacial accumulation of land waste. Glacialists give the name drumlin to hills of curving crest, parallel to each other and trending in the direction in which the ice moved. Such are the islands of Boston Harbor, though their curves have been marred, as sea waves have trimmed the outer edges of these half-submerged glacial hills. They abound, unaltered, however, about Boston and Worcester and along the lower Merrimac. Such a hill is a mass of the boulder clay, or "till," modified in form by the ice moving over it. It was formed under the ice, therefore, while the moraines gather chiefly about its edge. Long gravel ridges occur in some parts of New England ; they often have steep slopes, a sharp crest, and are serpentine in their curves ; they may be flanked by swamps, and thus the crest line has not seldom been adopted as the line of a roadway ; ridges of astonishing length are found in southern Maine. They were usually deposited in the beds of streams coursing in tunnels under the ice sheet.

Interruption of the direct flow of surface waters to the sea is a most striking result of ice work. Sections of old valleys were clogged with drift. Lakes formed behind the dam, and in sinking new outlet courses, rapids and waterfalls have been formed. In a variety of other ways lakes came into existence, and thus to the glacier we must attribute the thousands of lakes or tiny ponds that form the eye of the landscape everywhere and minister in many ways to the needs of man.

Thus two sorts of geological events have affected New England everywhere, — the ancient mountain building and the recent invasion of the ice. These have deeply influenced human life in the few centuries in which civilized men have dwelt here. The rocks are, as a rule, profoundly changed by disturbing forces, or they are deep-seated masses brought to the surface by denudation. Hence granites, marbles, and slates abound and furnish the best building materials. As early as 1737 the Boston builders began to gather and dress granite boulders. The walls of King's Chapel in Tremont Street grew thus out of the fields. In 1825 the quarries at Quincy were opened, the chief occasion being the building of the memorial on Bunker Hill. Then the use of granite began to be general, until every New England state opened its stores of this rock, soon to appear in every eastern city and burial ground. Great excitement was aroused, when, in 1697, some one found limestone at Newbury, in Massachusetts. Thirty teams a day were soon hauling it from the newly opened quarries, for heretofore the colonists had depended on the shells of the seashore for their lime. But most of New England limestone is in the form of marble and lies along her western border, in Connecticut, Massachusetts, and Vermont. Another product of geologic change is the beds of slate, made from ancient deposits of clay. As Vermont leads all the states in marble, so it is second only to Pennsylvania in this product, while a few quarries are open in Maine and Massachusetts. Isolated mineral industries are afforded by the mica deposits of Grafton County in New Hampshire and the corundum of Chester, Mass.

The soils are the waste of these ancient rocks, stirred by the glacier and mingled with the products of plant decay. It is not merely a modern notion that New England soils are somewhat barren. An old writing on Virginia, dating from London in 1649, says of the Northern colony, " Except for the fishing there is not much in that land, which in respect of frost and snow is as Scotland compared with England, and so barren withal that, except a herring be put into the hole that you set the corn or maize in, it will not come up." This would scarcely appeal to the gardeners about Boston, and doubtless the writer had not looked upon the lands that were to become the tobacco fields and peach orchards of the Connecticut Valley.

Yet it is true that the uplands predominate, and the soils of the uplands are not rich. Much of the fine soil material of the preglacial time has been washed into the sea by the streams that flowed forth from the ice sheet. The drift, from which the true surface soil is derived, contains a large proportion of coarse waste, broken mechanically from the bed-rock by the plucking and grinding of the ice, and thus the minerals are not ready for the nutrition of plants. The soils are often thin, or lie on steep and bouldery slopes, and the range of crops is limited by the shorter summer and severer cold of the winter months. The decline of general agriculture has been a central feature in the later history of New England. No end of writing has found here a theme, and a few of the writers have viewed the change with cheerfulness, but more with despair. It is not inspiring to see family mansions decay, farms abandoned, and untended roadways furrowed with incipient ravines, or to find villages in stagnation, with churches neglected, ancient academies abandoned, and the ambitious children of the fathers gone to the cities, the prairies, and the Pacific coast. But the history could not be different in the geographic unfolding of the United States.

While a compact people of English birth were held together on this first American ground, they forced a living from the soil, and built at last the New England of fifty and a hundred years ago. But the prairies and the great Northwest have settled the case for the farmer in New England. He must change his occupation or give himself to special forms of tillage, and while there is hardship and pathos in the change, the end is not to be deplored. There are weights to be thrown into the other side of the balance. Shaler has shown how the very coarseness of the soil elements insures permanence: these minute, pebbly fragments of rock will gradually disintegrate and yield, in soluble form, the elements needed by plants, and the soils may continue to have moderate fertility long after the soils of the Mississippi Valley are exhausted, or begin to require large use of fertilizers. And it is wholly to be desired that much New England upland should relapse into forest. Mountainous and glacial conditions have combined to fit these lands for trees and for nothing else.

In some neighborhoods new methods of tillage, carried on with greater intelligence, and often involving special crops, for which the soil is fit or for which there is local demand, are beginning to change the face of rural New England. New and better roads will bring into contact with the general life many corners that have been smothered by their isolation. As population grows, the swamp lands, of which there are some thousands of square miles, will begin to be reclaimed. They are in patches in the interior and along the shore-lines, and are either glacial or tidal in origin. They will be largely re-claimed and become as productive lands as anywhere lie under the plow.

Nature, as we have seen, invites the permanence of the forest in New England, and man has not yet completed his defiance of her will. Fifty years ago it was thought impossible to exhaust the pine forests of Maine; by 1880, however, the Pine Tree State was importing white pine from Michigan and Canada, and her lumbering was mainly upon the spruce, which in early days was left almost untouched. Still, the white pine was not destroyed; for in many areas the second growth has been spared, forest fires have been restrained, and the beginnings of rational for-estry are practiced. Intelligence is growing and conviction is deepening in New England, and there is hope that the lumberman's ravages in the White Mountains may be stayed, keeping the crown of glory on the uplands, and saving the valleys from destruction by floods of water and by the hillside waste which devastates the fields of the riverside.

Even Connecticut is a much forested state. Her stirring towns, growing cities, and farms of the low-lands appeal first to our thought; but a forest map of Connecticut carries the green, used as a symbol of the woodland, widely over the state. Such a map seems more green than white, and points to wide areas on the east and west of the central river suited only to the growth of trees.

A recent writer has drawn a picture of the neigh-

boring state,—its western half, — "In Wildest Rhode
Island." A strange title is this for the smallest and
most densely peopled of our states, and one of the
most ancient, centering in great towns and busy
villages with humming spindles, on the waters of
Narragansett. But draw a line from north to south,
dividing the little commonwealth into halves. West
of the line are ten back townships and less than six
per cent of the population of Rhode Island. Here
are some of the well-worn mountains of New England. Rightly do we call them hills, for they show
but a few hundred feet of relief. In five of these
townships, during the last century, there was a loss of
one-third to more than one-half of the people. All
the features of New England rural decline are here;
and whether forests, and estates of the rich, or truck
farms, towns, and electric railways will cover these
lands in future days is a question unanswered.

Yet another persistent thread of New England history began to take form in glacial times. Before
these days the streams had flowed so long in their
courses that they had smoothed their channels and
made easy grades to the sea. When the ice finally
disappeared, these old valleys were often left in a
condition of blockade. Banks and massive piles of
drift lay where the waters had run, and they forced the
renewed streams to seek other courses. In a short
distance, commonly, the old valley would be resumed,
but in passing around the barrier the river would
sink its channel upon the rocks, forming waterfalls, or rapids. This concentration of descent has
created the available water-power of New England

FIG. 8.   The Great Dam at Holyoke ; 35 Feet High, about 1000 Feet Long, and with 12 Feet of Water on the Crest.

and determined the sites of many of her towns and cities.

The Rev. Samuel Peters, who, being a Tory, took refuge in London in Revolutionary days, had visited the Connecticut Valley, and described the river as flowing fast enough at a certain point to float iron crowbars. Here grew up Bellows Falls, with its factories; and the visitor may read more sure proofs of the river's power in the pot-holes that pierce the rocky bed, and in the terraces that rise like stairs on the slopes above the town.

Several inland cities have a similar origin. Such are Lewiston in Maine, Manchester in New Hampshire, and Lowell, Lawrence, and Holyoke in Massachusetts. Lowell is a splendid example, founded three-quarters of a century ago, and having now nearly one hundred thousand people and about one thousand factories and mills of various kinds. This great center of production was located by a physiographic feature, —the falls of the Merrimac. For a similar reason Holyoke has grown up on the Connecticut River, with its great granite dam, its spacious raceways, and its enormous business, in which, as well as in population, it has become a rival of its near neighbor, Springfield.

Some cities combine the advantages of water-power and tidal highways. In other words, the falls or rapids of glacial origin occur at the head of tidewater, and cities would naturally follow, — such as Pawtucket, Norwich, Fall River, and Augusta. It is to be remembered that in many cases, as notably at Fall River, water-power has been largely supplemented by steam, since, once established, a manufacturing industry is likely to develop in a center made famous by it far beyond the limits of the available power.

The state of Maine has about 230 miles of shore-line, reckoned in a direct line from Kittery to the St. Croix River. But if one should follow the border of all its bays and headlands, and encircle all the islands, he would traverse more than two thousand miles of beach, so intricate is the labyrinth of the Pine Tree State's ocean border. For the most part it is a rugged shore. Rocky headlands stand out to sea, and meshes of landlocked waters extend inland from ten to forty miles. The only part of the shore-line that is not thus broken is between Kittery and Portland, at the southwest. All the rivers have tidal mouths, and illustrate in their cities, in a small way, the conditions of London, Bristol, and Liverpool. These deep valleys are commonly explained as due to river work when the land was higher than now, with submergence following. It is the same story as that of the Hudson, but we do not know how much the channels were deepened by glacial ice. Glacier, river, and the sinking of the lands may have joined with the sea in fashioning such a shore-line.

Massachusetts has also a rough shore-line, but with more variety than in Maine. Long strips of sandy beach alternate with coves and deep and spacious bays. Cape Ann is a well-worn but still jagged headland, thrust out among the breakers of the Atlantic. Tipped with granite and girded with volcanic dikes, this land is not easily overcome by the onset of the waves. On the south a secure haven has led to the growth of Gloucester; but to the north

are the long, smooth curves of Plum Island and Salis-
bury Beach, kept apart only by the outflow of the
Merrimac. These are low and sandy barrier beaches,
built and shaped by wave and wind, and backed by
salt marshes and quiet bays, south and north of
Newburyport.

FIG. 9.   A Rocky Shore, Marblehead Neck.

South of the Cape is Boston Bay, with a ragged
shore, but not so broken as in more ancient days.
The work of waves and currents tells its own story,
if we study a large-scale map.   Low and narrow
beaches have been built, joining former rocky islands
to the mainland, giving us Marblehead Neck and
Nahant.   The drumlins are wave-worn and have
helped to furnish the lines of waste that now offer
a continuous succession of curved shores from Point
Shirley to Point of Pines. Such is the story of Nan-

tasket Beach from Long Beach Rock to Point Aller-
ton. These beaches and the islands that lie between
seclude Boston Harbor from Boston Bay and protect
the shipping from Atlantic storms. The Mystic,
Charles, and Neponset rivers have shallowed the
fringes of the harbor, and man has contributed his
own large share to create dry lands for the Eastern
metropolis.

Then Cape Cod sends its magnificent curve into
the Atlantic and incloses the waters of Massachusetts Bay. Here the hard rocks give way, and lands
of modest altitude are composed of youthful strata
mantled with glacial drift and shifting sand-dunes.
Lakes and swamps abound, and smooth shore-lines
rule from Buzzards Bay around to Provincetown, and,
indeed, nearly everywhere, also, on the inner shore of
the Cape. The narrow eastern arm of the Cape was
once wider than now, but the waves, attacking from
the east, have trimmed the shore-line, and the resulting land waste has been swept up 'and down the
shore, or drifted out into deeper waters. Southward,
Nauset Beach and Monomoy Island have been
formed. Northward, the sands have been carried
around to the west and south, building the hooked
spit that incloses Provincetown Harbor. Sparse
population, little towns, and limited tillage of the
soil, — such is the law that nature lays upon this frail
and exposed foreland.

Much that may be said of Cape Cod is true of
Marthas Vineyard and Nantucket. The eye needs
but little training to mark the moulding of waves and
currents on these shores. Nantucket is a crescent,

with its concave shore fronting the mainland, trimmed here and built out there, until the lines are smooth and flowing. In old days many shallow bays pierced the southern lowlands of Marthas Vineyard. Every intervening headland, built of yielding materials, has been shortened in, and the eroded material swept across the openings of the bays, making them into lakes.

Turning again to the mainland, we may contrast the ragged outline of Buzzards Bay with the smooth borders of Cape Cod. To the westward, the edge of the lands resembles that of Maine, but is not so continuously irregular. Narragansett waters are, however, deeply landlocked, and represent a " drowned " trunk stream, whose chief branches were the Taunton, Blackstone, and Pawtuxet. Here we have the great physiographic feature of Rhode Island, and it is hardly too much to say that the existence of the state as an independent commonwealth hinges upon it.

In Connecticut a dozen large towns and cities line the waters of bays or stand near the mouths of tidal streams. The Mystic, Thames, Niantic, Connecticut, Quinnipiac, Housatonic, and Norwalk are the tidal rivers, great and small, that enter the sound. The Thames is followed by the tides to Norwich, fifteen miles, and the Connecticut to Hartford, more than forty miles. The fading out of the uplands makes a shore-line railway possible, and the protected waters of Long Island Sound offer a parallel highway for coastwise communication.

New England has been compared with Northern Europe. These regions are alike in important ways, —

in their low and ancient mountains, in the prevalence of the glacial ice, and in their broken shores. Every city of the sea border has a story well worth the telling, and none of more variety and fascination than peaceful and ancient Salem, with its decaying wharves, which no more receive consignments from the remotest lands. As with New York, so in a less striking way here, the lines of inland communication have turned the balance. Boston has a more spacious harbor than Salem, and from Boston the great railways lead out westward. Where the railways meet the shipping gathers also, and Boston is the one great port of New England. Portland, Providence, and New London must be content with coastwise shipping because Boston is the New England link between foreign lands and the interior of our own. But the records of the past may well remind us that Salem once led the shipping of the United States, and Providence sent more vessels from her harbor than set sail from the piers of New York.

Many New England coast towns have seen their life transformed through the decline of fishing. Several causes have led to this decay. Canadian catches have been admitted on more favorable terms; the Chesapeake, the Great Lakes, and the salmon of the Pacific have come into competition; other marine foods have grown in favor; and preservation in various ways has made the rivalry of remote regions effective. Hence the houses of Marblehead may be as quaint and her streets as narrow as they were, but shoes have taken the place of the fisherman's schooner and the sailor's yarns. Yet New England has her

calling from the sea and can never turn her face alone
to the land. Even fishing thrives, but centers itself
at a few places, as at Gloucester, after the more effective fashion of modern times. Many a fisherman has
turned to lobster-catching, which saves him from long
and dangerous absences from home, or he fully with-

Fig. 10. The Sea from Burial Hill, Plymouth.

draws himself from gathering sea food, and makes his
village, his home, and his skill with oar and sail minister to seekers of rest from the cities.

Like the St. Lawrence country and the Carolinas,
New England was discovered from the sea. For our
present study it does not matter whether the Vikings
came to this shore, or whether "Vinland" was their
name for a part of southern New England. The
real discoverers are more modern. Fifteen years

before the Pilgrims came, Champlain had sailed from the North and coasted along the shores; he named Mount Desert and entered the Penobscot; the peaks of the White Mountains caught his eye from the northwest, and rounding Cape Ann, he recognized a good harbor, where Gloucester now is, for he called it Beauport. Later he found safety in Plymouth Harbor, and doubling the greater cape, made his farthest south in Nauset Harbor. Three years earlier, Gosnold was exploring the southern shores and gave names to the Elizabeth Islands, Marthas Vineyard, and Cape Cod.

When we study the first occupation and earliest migrations by New England colonists, the broad fact appears that drainage lines did not control. There are no such waves of movement up a river as we see along the Hudson and Mohawk. Had the *Mayflower* come to land in the mouth of the Connecticut River, the history might have been different; but the lines of human movement were transverse rather than longitudinal. Plymouth, Boston, and Salem were natural points of approach, and there history begins. Roger Williams and his followers went across the low hills from the Massachusetts colonies and found a natural resting-place in the first great valley and at the head of Narragansett. The next wave of population crossed the low plateau to the westward and found the fertile lands of the Connecticut Valley; beyond rose the Berkshire barrier, and life gathered along the river, clearings grew, towns rose, and there was a forecast of the home of men, of industry, and of education, which now lies between

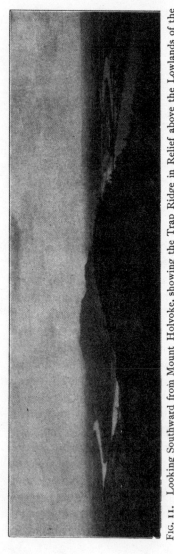

FIG. 11. Looking Southward from Mount Holyoke, showing the Trap Ridge in Relief above the Lowlands of the Connecticut Valley. Mount Tom and the Great Ox Bow are across the River.

Long Island Sound and the north border of Massachusetts. Here are at least six institutions of higher learning, a network of railways, mills without number, and scenery, not Alpine, but in its own way magnificent. Let one stand on Mount Holyoke and look into the geologic past; go far back in the record which lies about and below, and there will be a spacious gulf between lofty uplands on either hand and leading down to the sea; the tides go in and out, and streams bear in waste from east and west, — ancestors of the Westfield, Deerfield, and Chicopee rivers. Curious reptiles throng the mud-flats when the tide is out and leave their tracks to be uncovered in later times, and sometimes volcanic eruptions cover the muddy bottoms with sheets of lava. As time passes, the lands are elevated, the muds are hardened, the resulting shales and sandstones and sandwiched beds of lava are tipped to the eastward and south-eastward. Then the softer sands and shales are etched away by long processes of weathering and stream work, and the western edges of the thick, hard lavas form mountain ridges, the hanging hills of Meriden, or Mount Tom, steep and columnar on the west and sloping on the east. Curving to the east, where the Connecticut cuts the range, we have Mount Holyoke, which disappears southward from Amherst. The glacial ice, the glacial floods, the terraces, flood plains, and ox-bows of the river, — these represent the later history, leading to man's advent.

The aborigines also regarded the Berkshires as a barrier, protecting them in some measure from the fiercer savages of the Long House. But as now, so then, the wall was not impassable, for sometimes the elders of the Iroquois came across to collect their tributes of wampum. The massacres of the valley mark its lowlands as then a border country, and from that time until late in the last century we have had a migrating frontier, something which belongs only to a young and expanding nation.

The early colonists may well have felt surprise, if not dismay, at the severity of the winters that greeted them. They had come from a mild climate in latitude 52°; and here in latitude 42°, ten degrees nearer the equator, they met the keen cold and fierce changes of New England winter. We must not forget the differences, however, between north and south in this region. The Northmen might have found soft winter weather south of Cape Cod; for even the waters show a difference of temperature, and bluefish and some other marine creatures abound south of the Cape and are absent from more northern seas.

New England could not be the key of Eastern America in war. Her valleys do not lead to the heart of the continent, but northward into rugged lands by the St. Lawrence. On the west is a mountain barrier which has never been crossed by a large body of armed men. Causes that lay in the people, and not in their land, gave to New England the opening events of the American Revolution. In that first short act certain geographic features came into the settings of the stage. Among these were the drumlins; such are Breed's Hill and Bunker Hill; and it was the modest heights of Dorchester whose fortification by Washington made Boston untenable for the enemy. After the latter withdrew to New York, New England was almost a stranger to military operations.

We have already discovered some of the trends of New England life and have seen how they flow from her physiographic conditions. The decline of the old agriculture was inevitable and need not be regretted. The sons and daughters of the farmers have gone to the factory, to business in the cities, to the prairies. Boulder fences have fallen down, houses are deserted, and fields grown with saplings; but population has increased, towns and cities are everywhere, railways and trolley roads and better highways thread the country, and much of New England

FIG. 12. Bar Harbor, from Bar Island.

will become suburban. The forests will be fostered, and the willing immigrant will subdue again the farms that have not already become the summer homes of urban people. The decline of New England is temporary, and the hardships and losses belong only to the period of transition.

The center of cotton manufacture is shifting from New England to the South. In the southern Appalachians and along the streams that flow from them, King Cotton will widen his sway from the fields of the Gulf plains. There is the cotton, the coal, the water-power, and the iron, and short hauls bring the one to the other. New England cotton mills cannot long meet such conditions as the rising South affords; but wool can take the place of cotton, and the shoes and brass and paper of New England will not suffer.

If fishing has lost its relative place, and lumbering also, the stores of granite, marble, slate, and brownstone are limitless, and the wealth of the cities pours into the mountains and along the shores, during the heat of summer and the bright days of autumn. We see the process of final adjustment to geographic conditions. There is stress in the changes, but higher development and a richer civilization in the end.

" Man is what he eats; " " Character is a function of latitude; " " History is nothing more than an echo of the operation of geographic laws; " such are some of the sweeping affirmations that have been made about man's relation to the earth. They are too strong, and sure to confuse rather than to guide.

That environment influences character need not be asserted; but we cannot be sure in weighing this influence. Did the lands about the North Sea shape Teutonic character from time immemorial? And were some of these Teutons transplanted to a similar geographic province in the New World only to have the type perfected? But suppose the Puritan had gone not to New England but to Virginia. Would he not as easily have made the New England type of civilization in a more genial climate and with a more generous soil? Thus may physical features find limits to their efficiency; and none may so wisely recognize this as those who seek to trace the lines of physiographic control. The first New Englanders were picked men; the average man did not leave the eastern shires of Britain, but those who would have founded a state anywhere.

Now we may freely concede what nature has done, so far as we can read it, for New England life. If sturdy men could have been tempted to indolence, the short summers and rough fields left them no opportunity for such indulgence. Whether the climate is more a breeder of sturdy constitutions, or of consumption, may be left an unanswered question; but none can doubt that the geographic features of this province are pronounced and that they have colored all the life of her people, and have been in a large way the channel of its expression. We have seen how her works and days, her products and her industries, have hinged upon her shore-lines, her streams and waterfalls, her soils and forests. And beyond this, the garb, at least, of New England feeling and thought, is woven in the loom of her fields and skies.

This we can trace in her literature. And yet we do not think that nature is a mere cloak, put on and off at will by the New England writers. The appreciation that we mean, whether found in her prose or verse, is essentially poetic. The best example of this is Emerson, a prose poet everywhere, and nowhere more truly than in his "Nature." If deepest sympathy with the outer world be our test, Emerson is the poet of New England. In the forest "is sanctity which shames our religions, and reality which discredits our heroes." "The mind loves its old home; as water to our thirst, so is the rock, the ground, to our eyes, and hands, and feet." "We nestle in nature and draw our living as parasites from her roots and grains." "The fall of snowflakes in a still air, the blowing of sleet over a wide sheet of water, the reflections of trees and flowers in glassy lakes, the crackling and sporting of hemlock in the flames,— these are the music and pictures of the most ancient religion." These are flash-lights upon New England, but her fields and woods and storms are deep with meaning.

We may leave to the critics Emerson's rank in poetry, pass his faults of meter, and call him "a great man who wrote poetry"; but this, at least, we shall find, — the transcendentalist was not lifted off his native soil, and "the secret of the land was in the poet." None can mistake the coming of New England spring in May-day or feel himself in any other land when —

> "Announced by all the trumpets of the sky,
> Arrives the snow, and, driving o'er the fields,
> Seems nowhere to alight; the whited air
> Hides hills and woods, the river, and the heaven."

A poet of the prairies would scarcely personify the sea, thundering on its border : —

> "I drive my wedges home,
> And carve the coastwise mountain into caves," —

nor would he seek the deep and rocky forest : —

> "The watercourses were my guide;
> They led me through the thicket damp,
> Through brake and fern, the beaver's camp,
> Through beds of granite cut my road."

The physiographer has adopted Monadnock as the name of a typical form of land; and here our poet has also found a song : —

> "Every morn I lift my head,
> See New England underspread
> Anchored fast for many an age,
> I await the bard and sage."

Less intuitional and prophetic, but more simple and full in his pictures of the New England country, is Whittier. His biographer has made him tell of his early suffering from the fierce winter cold; and he has given us further proof of the tardy and difficult fashion in which the New England fathers adapted or failed to adapt themselves to a severer climate, "toughening themselves and their children sitting in cold churches, and deeming flannel garments no necessity."

He, too, has immortalized the winter snows, but in
a tale of domestic life, and tells of the uncle : —

> " Himself to Nature's heart so near
> That all her voices in his ear
> Of beast or bird had meanings clear."

Whittier, too, has his : —

> "Monadnock lifting from his night of pines
> His rosy forehead to the evening star."

He sees it from Wachusett, and here also draws a
sweet story of human faithfulness. He could not,
living on its banks, fail to touch the Merrimac with
his fancy. Other rivers he had seen, the Potomac,
the Hudson, and —

> " Have seen along his valley gleam
> The Mohawk's softly winding stream ;
> Yet wheresoe'er his step might be,
> Thy wandering child looked back to thee."

To a blue water in New England belongs his
" Summer by the Lakeside." Here is the same
refuge in nature that we found in Bryant by the
Hudson ; and in the closing lines we have a double
picture, — the landscape and the deep seriousness of
the old New England life.

Thoreau was a poet also in keen vision and strong-
lined reflection of his native fields and woods. His
" Week on the Concord and Merrimac rivers " will
surely leave one remembrance in the reader's mind, —
the still, scarcely flowing waters of the lesser stream.
He lived too soon and was too little systematic to

know or care that this little stream belongs to a group
of north-flowing rivers in Massachusetts, or the "still
rivers" of Connecticut, which are sluggish because,
since their valleys were excavated, the lands have
tilted a little to the south, impeding their flow, and
sending with a rush to the sea their south-flowing
neighbors. But Thoreau could see, with eyes often
lacking to the geographer, deep into the mystic meaning of out-of-door New England, and he who would
know the land should go with him, " half college
graduate, half Algonquin, the Robinson Crusoe of
Walden Pond," to his hut in the woods, or walk with
him down the soft sands of Cape Cod to Provincetown, or beneath the green arches of the Maine
woods.

CHAPTER III

THE APPALACHIAN BARRIER

WE are still to view the stage on which the scenes of early American history were enacted. As with New England, we look out upon it from the sea. The floor of the stage is the Atlantic lowland. Behind it are painted the crags and woodland slopes of the Appalachian Mountains. But the foreground is not the same in the South as in the North: in New England it is worn mountain land, in the South it is coastal plain. The one is a country of hills, the other a land of smoother aspect, flat or gently rolling, and showing low platforms alternating with shallow stream valleys. In one the rocks are of fabulous age, toughened in fiber and gnarly in face. In the other they consist of scarcely cemented land waste spread out in even sheets, often bearing marine shells, and thus giving proof of their recent emergence out of the sea. These beds of sand, gravel, marl, and clay slant gently toward the sea border and continue far beneath its waters, as would appear if we could remove the covering waves and dig valleys to reveal the structure. If the eastern part of our continent should come up a hundred feet, there would only be more of this flat country. And if it should go down a hundred feet, the ocean would only be conquering again a part of its former domain. Such a coastal plain is not alone a feature of our land but borders parts of many continents. And in central New York or Wisconsin the geologist finds proofs of ancient coastal plains, now lifted and roughened beyond recognition, except to the initiated.

In typical form this lowland does not begin until we go south of New York Harbor and enter New Jersey. Of that state it makes the central and southern parts. Then it includes all of Delaware and most of Maryland, except where the latter state reaches a long and slender arm out across the ridges and valleys of the Appalachians. And here are all the low-lying plantations of Virginia, alone rivaling New England in its harvests of colonial record and tradition. Going south, we find it still, a hundred miles or more in width in North Carolina ; and at this distance from the sea it has attained a height of but three hundred feet, or a little more, above the ocean level. The rivers are tidal far within the shore-line, and merge into sounds, as Albemarle and Pamlico. Outside of the sounds are long barrier beaches, theaters of wave and wind, protecting the waters within, and opening here and there for communication with the outer seas. So flat are parts of the coastal plain that " the Wilmington and Weldon Railroad has a stretch of 40 miles, where there is neither curve, excavation, nor embankment."

South Carolina tells the same story, only the coastal plain is wider, about 150 miles. So low and flat is this region that swamps abound, especially along the streams and shore-line. The alligators are at home in the rivers, and the names of the forest trees have a tropical sound. The old story of tidal rivers is told again, and the towns — Charleston, Port Royal, Beaufort — remind one in this respect, at least, of New London, New York, or Philadelphia.

The mountains do not rise at once from the plain. Lying between, in Maryland, Virginia, and the Carolinas, is a belt of hilly country, a little more than plain in some parts and a little less than mountain in others. In North Carolina this strip is two hundred miles wide, and begins to rise abruptly from the coastal plain on the east. Falls, or swift reaches, amounting to two hundred feet of descent, mark the eastward passages of the streams across this boundary, which physiographers have long called the Fall Line. The line runs southward into Georgia and northward to the Delaware. Up to this limit on the east, the rivers are sluggish, if not tidal. Down to this limit on the west, they are swift of flow. The hilly belt has also its physiographic name, — it is the Piedmont region, lying at the foot of the Blue Ridge. It is well-worn mountain land and is much like southeastern New England. If we could lift the New England region and expose her sea bottom it would be like the South Atlantic country; it would have a coastal plain, a Piedmont region, and its mountain ranges.

"Tide-water" Virginia and Maryland lie between the Fall Line and the sea. Within this region is the Chesapeake with its tributary waters. As in Maine, or on the Narragansett, or the Hudson, we are dealing now with a "drowned" river system. Perhaps the Chesapeake is the finest example, and on any map it looks like a swollen river with over-

FIG. 13. View from Wildcat Point, Maryland, showing Gorge and Islands of the Susquehanna River, a Short Distance South of the Pennsylvania Line. It is the Region of the Piedmont Plateau.

widened branches.   Raise the land, and see how the
salt waters would retire, and how the Potomac, York,
and James would join the lengthened Susquehanna
and enter the Atlantic somewhere to the east of Norfolk.   But things were as they are long before the
memory of man; and when the early navigators entered the gateway of Cape Charles and Cape Henry,
a wilderness of quiet waters was before them, and
they could make long voyages within sight of green
shores, and for hundreds of miles thread narrow, tidal
inlets shadowed by the overhanging forests.   Captain
John Smith gave the summer of 1608 to such voyages of exploration, going up the bay and entering the Susquehanna, Patapsco, and Potomac rivers.
" Chesapeake Bay is a bay in most respects scarce
to be outdone by the universe, having so many large
and spacious rivers, spreading themselves to immeas-
urable creeks and coves, admirably carved out and
contrived by the omnipotent hand of our wise Creator,
for the advantage and conveniency of its inhabitants."   Good as this is, Fiske, who quotes the above
from an old writer, has drawn a picture in yet stronger
lines.   "The country known as 'tidewater Virginia'
is a kind of sylvan Venice.   Into the depths of the
shaggy woodland, for many miles on either side of
the great bay, the salt tide ebbs and flows.   One can
go surprisingly far inland on seafaring craft, while
with a boat there are but few plantations on the old
York peninsula to which one cannot approach very
near."   So easy and convenient were these ready-
made highways as to retard the making of roadways
across the lands and through the woods.

No single influence molded the life of the colony of Virginia. The beginnings in a wilderness are never easy. But this was no such land to struggle with as the Puritan found. Its climate was genial, its virgin soils were rich, and the battle with the winter's cold did not consume the energies that were sorely needed in other ways. If there had been no other differences, tobacco was enough. The world was calling for the new-found weed. The soils were suited to it. It was good currency when there was little other, and it was raised in fields that were washed by navigable waters. Direct to many plantations came the ships that loaded it for London. Or, if not, it was small trouble to raft it down the more shallow inlets to wharves that ocean-going sails could reach.

Plantations developed rather than towns. The prevalence of tobacco, the introduction of slave labor, the absence of land roads, and the facility of the waterways, — all favored the scattered, rural life. But no more here than in New England are geographic causes all; for the Cavalier, and not the Puritan, came to Virginia. The one was proud, given to amusement, an aristocrat, building a mansion, and surrounding himself with a landed estate like those of his native England. The other worked with his hands, had Yankee curiosity and invention, was frugal, and lived with his fellows in towns or on small neighborly farms. Each could understand the other's defects better than he could his points of excellence; and these two unlike men came into singularly contrasting environments to found a home across

the seas.   Where the two lived were the two foci of
colonial history, and the causes of the unfolding
might baffle a complete analysis, either by the geographer or the historian.

Such is a glimpse of the tide-water country, the
coastal plain.   We must have such a view that we
may know the meaning of the barrier that looms behind.   Not all the lowland life is rural, though country is more than city as one goes farther south.   But
at the inner edge of the coastal plain, at the head
of navigation, close by water-power, at the Fall Line,
— here cities could but grow.   Here, then, is the seaboard rival of New York, seated by the estuary of
the Delaware.   And here is the fourth of the great
Atlantic quartette of cities, on the Chesapeake.   And
then come Washington, below the falls of the Potomac, Fredericksburg, Richmond, and Petersburg in
Virginia, and Raleigh, Camden, and Columbia in the
Carolinas.   Narrow lowlands everywhere, and cities
grown up by the side of short, tidal rivers, — such is
the Atlantic border of the United States.

The barrier itself is not a single elevation, nor is it
a disorderly group of heights, but has, as all mountain systems have, a plan that can be analyzed.   It is
indeed a mountain *system*.   The shortest description
of it is that it consists of parallel ridges and valleys
which, as a group, but not as individuals, reach from
eastern New York into Alabama.   As in New England, so here, the downwear has been great.   The
ridges are not in relief because they have been elevated relatively to the valley bottoms, but because the
valleys have been dug between them.

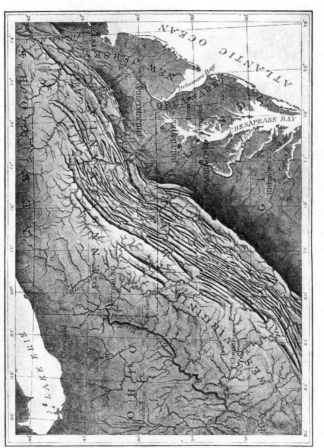

RELIEF MAP OF THE NORTHERN APPALACHIAN REGION

With the Coastal plain on the southeast and the Allegheny plateau and the Lake plains on the northwest

These very general statements will be clear if we look more specially at the barrier in three regions, — first in Pennsylvania, then in Virginia, and finally in North Carolina and Tennessee. We will note the elements in a profile of the country seen by one who goes from Philadelphia to Erie or Pittsburg. We go across the lowlands to Harrisburg. Here we are in a broad and fertile valley which runs far to northeast and to southwest. In New York it is the Wallkill Valley. In Pennsylvania, Easton, Bethlehem, Allentown, Reading, Lebanon, Harrisburg, Carlisle, and Chambersburg lie in it. Toward the Maryland line it is called the Cumberland Valley. In Maryland, Hagerstown is in it, and in Virginia it is the Shenandoah Valley. It is not the trench of a master river; for the rivers commonly flow across and not through it. It is often a dozen miles or more wide. It is due to the etching out of softer shales and limestones, leaving harder masses on either hand as mountains. Because the rocks are shales and limestones, the soils are rich, the farms are productive, towns are many, and railways cross and thread the valley everywhere. Physiographers know it as the Appalachian Valley.

To call it a valley will not puzzle the traveler who looks north from Allentown or Harrisburg. The even crest of Blue Mountain follows the horizon as far as he can see, ranging from twelve hundred to nearly two thousand feet above the ocean. On the southeast the mountain range that should bound the valley is in places worn away, but it appears in South Mountain, east of Chambersburg. It is worth our while to remem-

ber this name, for this modest elevation grows and rises
southward until it becomes the Blue Ridge, and at
last includes the strong and lofty mountain masses of
the Carolinas. To the northeast it reappears again
also, and becomes the Highlands of New Jersey, and
the Highland Range of New York, cut by the Hudson. If even this were all, we should not have a
barrier of historic importance. But, returning now to
Pennsylvania, beyond the Blue Mountain are other
ridges like itself, following it in long parallel walls,
and separated from each other by longitudinal valleys.
As a rule, the small streams run along these valleys and
enter at right angles larger rivers which cut boldly
across or through the mountains. Such are the Delaware, Lehigh, Schuylkill, and Susquehanna. Sometimes a large stream runs between ridges, as the east
branch of the Susquehanna from Scranton to Northumberland, or the west branch past Williamsport.
Such an arrangement of streams gives a rectangular
or trellised pattern to the drainage. How it comes to
be so is too long a story to be told here.

The Susquehanna crosses all ·the ridges. Why,
then, is not its valley as good a doorway to the interior as the Hudson offers? Because the river is
shallow, and beyond the mountains its head waters
fringe out and are lost in the heights of the Alleghany
plateau. To this we must turn to try to correct a
most persistent misunderstanding about the land
forms of Pennsylvania. Here are meant the unnum-
bered references to the "Alleghany Mountains," as
though there was, in Pennsylvania, a range of that
name, rugged, and thousands of feet in height.

FIG. 14.   Delaware Water-gap.   Photograph by W. H. Rau, Philadelphia.

From near Williamsport, far to the southwest, runs the Bald Eagle Valley. It is narrow and slightly curved to the southeast. On this southeast side it is flanked by a mountain ridge. The rocks are disturbed and tilted, and it is in all respects like the other ridges of the region. On the northwest rises a wall of equal height, about one thousand feet from the bed of the stream, but the rocks in it are not disturbed; they are piled one on the other in horizontal beds. This great wall, or escarpment, is made rugged by weathering and gashed by ravines. Follow up one of these and we come, not upon a mountain crest, but upon the eastern edge of the plateau which makes western Pennsylvania a surface about two thousand feet above sea, only lower in its valleys and where, at the northwest, it slopes down to Lake Erie. The "Alleghany Mountains" are nothing but this rough and steep wall that faces the southeast, and it seemed like another mountain range to those that came to it from the seaboard. If we follow the Alleghany escarpment northeast, it becomes obscure in that part of Pennsylvania, but reappears in New York, where it is known as the Catskills. Neither Catskill nor Alleghany, therefore, is the name of real mountains, but both, of the edge of a plateau, and the drainage, not being controlled by upturned beds of rock, is arranged like the branches of a tree. If we follow the Alleghany front southeast, we shall find it in West Virginia, Virginia, and Tennessee; and here again this long wall, facing southeast, has long been called the Cumberland Mountains, but ought to be called, and is becoming known as, the Cumberland escarpment. If the reader will remember that this wall, whether it be steep slope or sheer cliff, extends from the Hudson River into Alabama; that the rocks are horizontal and form a plateau back of it, while all the proper mountains of the Atlantic seaboard are southeast of it, — he will have a key to the form and structure of the Appalachian region.

Returning for a moment to Pennsylvania, the barrier embraces South Mountain, the ridges from Blue Mountain to Bald Eagle Valley, the Alleghany escarpment, and the uplands of western Pennsylvania. The meaning of it will be somewhat appreciated if the path of the Pennsylvania Railroad be carefully traced from Philadelphia to Pittsburg.

Let us place ourselves at Harpers Ferry in Virginia. A river flows by us to the southeast. It is north of the town and is the Potomac. Barely east of the village it passes through a gorge, and in two miles comes out upon lowlands again. It has passed the Blue Ridge, whose severed heights rise in strong slopes nearly a thousand feet on either hand. Harpers Ferry is barely within the Blue Ridge on the west. From the southwest another river flows along the western base of the Blue Ridge and joins the Potomac at the east end of the town, which lies in the fork. It is the Shenandoah, and this is the Shenandoah Valley. To the north and east we should cross Maryland and come up to Harrisburg. To the southwest we should follow a broad and rich vale to the head waters of the Shenandoah beyond Staunton. It is a part again of the Appalachian Valley. As in Pennsylvania, it has towns, railroads, and fertile fields,

82 GEOGRAPHIC INFLUENCES

and the Potomac, like the Susquehanna, crosses it.
Like the Susquehanna, too, it gathers its waters in
longitudinal streams among the mountain ridges, and,
turning, crosses them and the Shenandoah Valley
to the southeast. Unlike the Susquehanna, however,
the Potomac does not gather tribute from far over
the plateau, for there the Monongahela holds sway.

Fig. 15. Characteristic Forested Slopes in the Southern Appalachians.
Linville Gorge.

The great barrier, then, in Virginia, is the Blue
Ridge, the Appalachian ridges, the Alleghany escarpment, and the plateau, and we may appreciate it
by tracing again the line of a railway, the Baltimore
and Ohio, which, like the Pennsylvania, starts on a
tidal bay, crosses the Atlantic lowlands, the several
parts of the Appalachian barrier, and comes down
into the Ohio Valley.

Let us place ourselves at Knoxville in Tennessee.

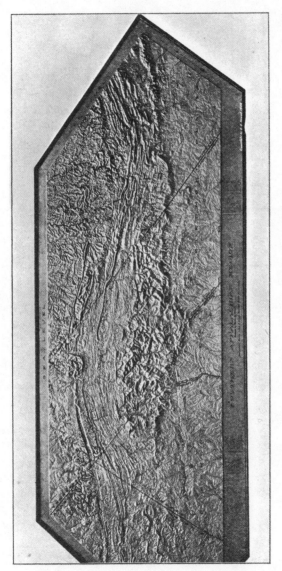

RELIEF MAP OF SOUTHERN APPALACHIAN REGION

From model by Edwin E. Howell

A few miles to the southeast bold mountains rise and lie well over into North Carolina. It is a rudely triangular tangle of ridges, peaks, and high, intermontane valleys. More peaks than can be counted on the fingers of a hand rise above six thousand feet, and Mount Mitchell passes that limit by more than seven hundred feet. It is more than four hundred feet loftier than Mount Washington, and is the highest point of the United States east of the Rocky Mountains. These heights are built of the ancient crystalline rocks and are the southern continuation of the Blue Ridge. But the ridge so easily passed by the Potomac River has become a geographical province, broad and high. Locally the name Blue Ridge is used of the eastern range of the group, and the western range is the Unakas, and here are the loftiest peaks. But both together and all between connect through Virginia with the old New York Highlands. Atmospheric effects tell their story here, for in the distance the ridge is "Blue," and in poem and story, as in the common speech, the Unakas become the Great Smoky Mountains.

But not forgetting that we are at Knoxville, we travel to the northwest a few miles, and we are at the foot of the Cumberland escarpment. We may climb it and wander across the upland and come down to Nashville or into Kentucky. If we follow the foot of the wall north to the Tennessee-Kentucky line, we can ascend to the uplands through the historic Cumberland Gap.

Up and down the great valley past Knoxville extend the Appalachian ridges, but they are not so

high or persistent as in Pennsylvania. Going between some of these ridges to the north, we may
follow the Holston or Clinch rivers to their head
waters in Virginia. To the southwest we go down
the Tennessee. At Chattanooga the river leaves the
valley and winds through a trench in the plateau,
later to make its curious swing to the north and to
the Ohio. But if we pass Chattanooga and Lookout
Mountain on our right, we shall be still in a broad
valley, whose walls begin to fade, and we come upon
the waters of the Coosa, which would take us southward to the Gulf.

The Clinch and Holston do not alone contribute to
the trunk river. These follow longitudinal valleys;
but from the southeast, out of the mountains, come
most of the waters of Hiwassee, Little Tennessee,
and the French Broad. And these streams reach
across the higher Unakas far to the east, and bring
the waters from the Blue Ridge as well. Taking the
Tennessee system, therefore, even with the important
longitudinal flow above and below Knoxville, its general flow is westward, like the Kanawha farther north.
The southern Appalachians have westward drainage.
The northern Appalachians drain eastward.

In the South the barrier consists of crystalline
mountains, ancient and massive, a series of ridges
alternating with valleys, an escarpment, and a plateau. Comparing the north, middle, and south parts,
the general profile is the same, but there are many
differences. The Blue Ridge is worn out opposite
Harrisburg, it is conspicuous at Harpers Ferry, it is
high and wide in the south. The younger but yet

FIG. 16. Spruce Forest near the Summit of White Top Mountain, Virginia. Photograph by U.S. Bureau of Forestry.

ancient ridges between the Blue Ridge and the plateau are high and persistent in Pennsylvania and Virginia, but weaken at Knoxville and disappear southward. It may yet be added that the long, wide belt of ridge and valley land between the Blue Ridge and the Alleghany-Cumberland escarpment is known to physiographers as the " Greater Appalachian Valley."

We have dwelt upon the physiographic aspects of the Appalachian region because they are usually left by historical writers to the reader's imagination. Those writers, unfortunately, do not all have Parkman's appreciation of geographic setting or the artistic skill with which he makes pictures of the land rise in perspective and color out of his pages.

This great rampart of the East does not seem difficult now, when the forests have been so largely cut away, when engineers have found reasonable grades for steam passage, and when electricity bids defiance to grades of every degree. But the greatest influence of the barrier goes back to the time when the forest was everywhere, when the wilderness was nearly unknown, and when even a country highway belonged to the future. The explorer, finding a gap, might encounter another mountain in front of him, for the ridges often "break joints," like bricks in a wall. And if he hit on the Susquehanna or the Potomac, it would lead him to the mazy wilderness of the Alleghany plateau. In addition to the physical difficulties of entering the mountain belt from the Atlantic plain, the pioneer must be ready for the prowling savage and count on the hostility of the French garrisons as he neared the Ohio River. Only the adventurer, or the man with a serious public errand, would be likely to leave the fertile fields of Penn's country, or the tidal lowlands of the Chesapeake, for the hard trails and doubtful goals of the Appalachian wilderness. It has required more than two centuries to clear the forests, lay the roads, and open the regions fully to civilized man. Even down to 1880, there was a stretch of 350 miles, from the Roanoke southward, that had never been crossed by a railway.

If, without a mountain barrier, the Atlantic plains had merged into a land like the prairies, it would be hard to say how American history would have shaped itself. If the fierce aborigines of the Southwest and the Northwest had been in the same relative positions, the new colonies would have been for them a more easy prey. And the colonists would have scattered, seeking the best lands, tending to individual rather than community life. This, in a medley population drawn from all the nations of Northwestern Europe, would have kept civilization back, and deferred the founding of coherent states. But the new Americans were pressed between the sea and the base of the mountains, forced to be neighborly, to assimilate each other's ideas, provide for common defense, and build up common institutions. Kept on the sea border, the centers of life were maritime, and there was, for those old days of slow-going ships, active interchange of ideas and products between the Old World and the New. The education of the mountains and forest came later. Now the people were held somewhat to their ancestral tutor, — the wide sea.

If the unity thus enforced was useful, so also was
the diversity fostered by physical conditions. The
Atlantic strip of colonial land was cold-temperate
at the north and subtropical at the south. Boston
and Charleston could not be the same. And almost
every colony had a natural home differentiating it
from the rest. Massachusetts Bay, Narragansett,
Hudson, Delaware, Chesapeake, — these need no
comment. With Roundhead, Dutchman, Quaker,
Romanist, and Cavalier, other diversities came in,
and came in so strongly that final unity for the colonies was by no means to be taken for granted. There
was portentous uncertainty as to how New York and
Pennsylvania would go in the Revolution. But the
barrier held the colonies together in the first flush
of individualism, when, escaping one yoke, they were
unduly afraid of putting their heads into another.
It has been said that even in 1700, barely three-
fourths of a century after American ground began
to be occupied in New England and Virginia, one
could go from Portland to the Potomac and sleep
every night in a "considerable village." The people
had to live close enough to each other to insure
organic life for each of the colonies, and in the end,
for all, moving surely on to what Fiske calls a "continental state of things."

No English settlements had been made beyond
the central and southern Appalachians at the beginning of the Revolution. A century and a half had
been spent in building the states by the Atlantic.
Thirty years later the president of the Republic
would send Lewis and Clark to the mouth of the

Columbia River. Within eighty years a half-dozen railway surveys would be run from the Mississippi River to the Pacific Ocean. In a century and a quarter great cities would stand by the Golden Gate and by the bays of the Northwest. The public men of the colonies did not much appreciate the country beyond the mountains. But we need not wonder, for it was to them unknown. They had, indeed, heard of the Lakes and the French forts, and may have served in frontier wars, but they never dreamed that the destinies of the nation were there. There were exceptional men who saw more than others. Such was Spotswood of Virginia, who, in 1716, crossed the Blue Ridge in central Virginia, and thus wrote, "We should attempt to make some settlements on ye lakes, and at the same time possess ourselves of those passes of the great mountains, which are necessary to preserve a communication with such settlements."

This was the call of a clear trumpet, but no one was aroused by it. The Virginia colonists had too much to do and to be interested in nearer home, and two generations were to pass before there would be a nation. It was not the fault of the colonists that when they awoke to it they did not find another great nation across the mountains. Great movements work out in the silent chemistry of events. Neither individuals nor peoples plan their greatest deeds. This has nowhere been more true than in "the winning of the West."

How the Appalachian barrier was crossed, we must now inquire. Most physiographers think that an

ancient river system had its head waters in West
Virginia, its middle course in Pennsylvania, and discharged into a great valley, where Lake Erie now
lies. By the strange changes of the ice invasion,
the system was so broken up and rearranged that
two broad streams, the Allegheny from the north,
and the Monongahela from the south, coming together
at a sharp angle, form the Ohio, and carry many
waters of West Virginia and southwestern New
York to the Gulf of Mexico. Covering the narrow
point between the rivers, and stretching along their
banks and eastward over the uplands, is Pittsburg,
the "Gateway of the West." Washington had
prophetic visions of the meaning of this place, but
the French were too strong. Fort Duquesne, Braddock, Fort Pitt, — these are the early chapters. A
permanent settlement was made in 1773, and the
tides of life began to flow. A million people now
belong to the city and its environs. No more powerful geographic causes can be found in any land
than group themselves here, — navigation on three
rivers, valleys inviting railways, and mineral products
close at hand, making this the North American
metropolis of petroleum, of natural gas, of bituminous
coal, and of iron.

But we wish most to see how the overflow from
the East centered upon Pittsburg and passed down
the Ohio River. From the head of the Delaware
and Chesapeake bays paths were sought between
the Potomac and the upper waters of the Susquehanna, or in the belt of country now lying between
the Pennsylvania and the Baltimore and Ohio Rail-

FIG. 17.   Pittsburg : Union of the Allegheny and the Monongahela forming the Ohio River.

ways. Such paths must lead across the Hagerstown-Harrisburg Valley, across the Appalachian ridges, and over the plateau east of the Monongahela River. But there is no natural highway. The Mohawk route was a steady menace to the trade of Philadelphia during the early decades of the nineteenth century. An Albany firm, as told by McMaster, owned a Hudson River line of packets, and offered to carry freight from New York to Pittsburg for six dollars a ton, while wagon lines from Philadelphia, with tiresome efforts, could scarcely meet the price. To go around and come down the Allegheny River, or up the streams from Lake Erie, was easier than to come over the barrier. The New Yorkers, at the same time, insured the goods and gave easier terms of payment. Thus they held the advantage and looked forward to even better days, for the Erie Canal was under way.

The men of Philadelphia in those days thought that they held the geographic key to the inland trade. By one scheme they would go on rivers, lakes, and short canals, by Elmira and Seneca Lake, to Lake Ontario. Or they were going by the Susquehanna to the Allegheny, the Conewango, and Lake Erie, or by the Juniata to the Allegheny and the Ohio. But why wonder that they saw visions of fleets on shallow rivers and obscure creeks, when Washington himself had visited, years before, the Oneida carrying-place, and had considered the pass from Otsego Lake to the Mohawk, and had grown eloquent upon the navigable waters of central New York.

FIG. 18. Valley of the Allegheny, sunk below the Even Surface of the Alleghany Plateau. Oil Refinery at Franklin, Pennsylvania.

While New York and Philadelphia strove, danger for both loomed in the far Southwest. Would not the farmers and traders of the new West send their goods to New Orleans? What was to prevent the Southern town, lying between the prairies and the sea, from winning in the race? Sugar and cotton had already come to the seaboard by way of Pittsburg. Thus the call grew loud for roads and canals across the mountains; and the statesmen joined in, for they said, we cannot form into a compact nation lands that are divorced in trade and have scant intercourse with each other. "State after state heard the cry, and an era of internal improvements opened, which did far more to cement the Union and join the East and West inseparably than did the Constitution and the laws." [1]

That the old roadways from Philadelphia and the Chesapeake country to the Ohio River were so various shows that nature offered no commanding route. There was a northern highway, if we may so dignify it, leading from Philadelphia almost directly westward. It ran at no great distance from the future field of Gettysburg, crossed the Appalachian Valley at Shippenburg, passed out of the mountain belt beyond Bedford, and, bearing more to the north, led down into the muddy hamlet of Pittsburg; but in the years following the Revolution it guided multitudes to the west. The other routes were farther south, and led along the Potomac in western Maryland, then up into Pennsylvania to the Youghiogheny, and down by this river and the Monongahela to Pittsburg. Such were

[1] McMaster, "History of the People of the United States," IV, 397.

FIG. 19. Cumberland and the Narrows of Wills Mountain, Maryland. Wills Creek has cut a Typical Appalachian Water-gap, and enters the Potomac here. At this Point was the Old Fort Cumberland, on the Natural Road between Virginia and the West.

Washington's road and Braddock's road, which often
followed a still older Indian trail. Washington, too,
was watching New Orleans, and was anxious to tap
the Ohio Valley for the Potomac and the James. For
this a road across the mountains was needed, a true
highway, and not the difficult path which he himself
had so often trod. Not long after his death the national government undertook the building of the Cumberland Road. We have described its general course,
and often it was identical with the roads that Washington had known. It was opened in 1818; and in a few
years more the Chesapeake and Ohio Canal was finished, doing thus what was possible to concentrate the
streams of commerce and immigration in this region.

Thus along many lines, in Virginia, Maryland, and
Pennsylvania, the westward migration went on. The
mountains were like a sieve, with openings enough,
though small; and everything that went through centered, as if in a funnel, in the upper Ohio Valley.
Here, as we have seen, was Pittsburg, which had become a city a few years before the Cumberland Road
was finished. She had already begun to dig the coal
from her neighboring hills and drive her smoking furnaces. The puff of the steam whistle was heard on
the waters of the Ohio, and goods and men went
down the valley as freely as did the waters gathered
from the Alleghany plateau. But multitudes had not
waited for steam. They had been going for a generation, from the close of the Revolution, in canoes,
scows, and on rafts, bound for Kentucky or the settlements north of the Ohio.

We have now seen how the white man went west-

ward by the Mohawk Valley. How great this avenue
was will appear again when we follow the shores of
the Great Lakes and look out over the prairies. We
have seen, too, that the Ohio Valley was a door to the
West; but we have yet to follow another stream of
migration along natural highways that open farther
to the south. Through these highways went the men
who founded Kentucky and Tennessee and shaped
the destinies of the Southwest.

We may now recall the longitudinal valleys of the
Appalachians, of which the greatest is that which leads
by Harrisburg and Hagerstown up the Shenandoah.
When the early settlers had occupied these fertile
lands in Pennsylvania, and the stream of life must
flow farther, it was easier to follow the valleys to the
southwest than to cross the ranges and to come out
on the west. Hence before the rush toward Pittsburg
began, there had been for many decades a longitudinal
movement into Virginia, and then beyond to the head
waters of the Tennessee, the Watauga, the Holston,
and the French Broad. Among those who thus went
southwest were the Scotch-Irish, a people to whom
American historians are now beginning to render
justice. In great numbers these people, English in
speech, Scotch in blood, Irish by adoption, Presbyterian in faith, came to America. Philadelphia and
the Pennsylvania lowlands were full of them. Prince-
ton University is their memorial in New Jersey. They
entered the Appalachian valleys, largely populated
West Virginia, and were the backbone of the young
commonwealth that sprang up on the Tennessee and
the Cumberland. "They formed the kernel of the

distinctively and intensely American stock who were the pioneers of our people in their march westward, the vanguard of the army of fighting settlers who, with ax and rifle, won their way from the Alleghanies to the Rio Grande and the Pacific." [1]

Southwestern Virginia lies for a hundred miles along the northern boundary of Tennessee.   This boundary is purely arbitrary, for the valleys, the mountain ridges, and the streams cross it.   In one of the valleys runs the Norfolk and Western Railway, leading up to Roanoke, and thence east, across the Blue Ridge, to the sea, or one may continue northeast through the Shenandoah Valley.   The head waters of the Holston are in Virginia.   We must remember that what is now Tennessee was in early days a part of North Carolina, an ultramontane country.   Now we can understand how the backwoodsmen of Virginia went down the Holston, built their cabins, girdled the big trees, felled the little ones, planted corn, fought the savages, and thought they were still in Virginia.   When they learned their mistake, they sought to be taken under the wing of the North Carolina government; and their wish was granted, perhaps with reluctance, for they had a name worse than their deserts.   They were the makers of a new commonwealth; they had wives to support; they had no time to wear gloves or to consume in deciding what to do with Tories who stirred up the red men.   Thus they founded the Holston, or, as sometimes called, the Watauga settlements, one of the two early seed grounds of the state of Tennessee.

The Holston community was also the nursery for

<hr>

[1] Theodore Roosevelt, "Winning of the West," I, 134.

another commonwealth, long to anticipate Tennessee in becoming a member of the Union, — the state of Kentucky. On the north this state has a natural boundary, the Ohio River. On the south she is geographically one with Tennessee; and the Cumberland River, rising in the more northern state, passes south of the boundary by a long bend, and returns again toward the Ohio River. If the two form a single province, their history likewise begins with the same people, the same fierce battles with savages, the same heroic endurance of a wilderness more remote than other American colonists had known. To the settlements on the Atlantic, Europe was almost neighborly in comparison.

The eastern boundary of Kentucky, for a considerable distance, is formed by the Cumberland escarpment. Eastern Kentucky is plateau, and it overlooks the valleys of Virginia. Just where the three states now come together — Virginia, North Carolina, and Tennessee — is one of the most famous points in early American history. There is a break in the escarpment, — it is the Cumberland Gap. By it, in 1775, Daniel Boone and his companions climbed out of the Appalachian Valley from the settlements on the Holston and began to blaze an equally famous highway, — the Wilderness Road. They pushed their way through the forest, had a preliminary skirmish or two with the red men, and founded the state of Kentucky. Having carried the American frontier well down upon the Ohio River on the very eve of the Revolution, the ground was American at its close, and was the outpost of freedom in the struggle for the

West that followed.   Boone was more than a hunter;
he was one of the builders of a new nation.

By the close of the war the new colony was well
established.   It is not within our purpose to describe
its growth or character, but rather to follow the strong
lines drawn by nature, along which the migrating
hosts passed.   For hosts they were, when the cessa-
tion of hostilities left the people free to turn to the
pursuits of peace.   Then a never ending procession
of boats floated down the Ohio from Pittsburg, and
a perpetual caravan of men, women, and children, of
packhorses and cattle, filed under the rocky cliffs
of the Cumberland Gap and followed the blazed trees
and now worn path of the Wilderness Road.   In
1769, six years before he planted the permanent
settlement, Boone had made his first journey through
this gap to the valley of the Kentucky River.   He
was returning, therefore, to a land which he knew, a
land whose richness and beauty has won all behold-
ers from that day to this.   Open prairie and shaded
woodland were there then as they are to-day.   But
there were uncounted buffalo also, and elk and deer,
as well as wild creatures of fiercer kinds.   In a few
years the buffalo ceased to visit the salt licks, and
the settlers came and availed themselves of the salt,
— a product that in those days had to be carried far
and was costly.   It is not her grains and fruits that
distinguish Kentucky from other states, but the
meadows and pastures of the "Blue-grass region."
Says Professor Garman, writing in an agricultural bulletin, "The phrase, 'down in Old Kentucky,' con-
veys to the wandering Kentuckian a picture in which

FIG. 20. A Blue-grass Meadow in Kentucky. Photograph by Professor H. Garman.

are sunny slopes of soft, green grass; grazing horses and cattle, sleek and beautiful. . . . Blue-grass Kentucky is a delightful bit of the world in May and June. . . . And it is largely the result of the profusion with which the little plant, blue-grass, grows in her limestone soil." The same writer proceeds to say that a bulletin on forage plants would be little needed if all Kentucky were like this favored fifth around Lexington. The student will find no better illustration of geographic control — agricultural, social, and even political — than this famous region.

The reader of "In the Tennessee Mountains," or of "The Prophet of the Great Smoky Mountains," finds true pictures of the forests and hazy mountain slopes of the southern Appalachians. But he finds also a human type not to be met elsewhere in the United States. He is farmer, hunter, blacksmith, shopkeeper, or rude preacher. He is courageous, original, reads the sky and forest in lieu of books, and is little troubled by the outside world. He could not raise cotton, he did not own slaves, and his sympathies were with the North rather than with the South in the Civil War. His family lives as his great-grandfather's family lived, for change is almost unknown. Division of labor has little place in such a society, where homespun still prevails. These men are the descendants of the backwoodsmen, who came from the Old World, from Pennsylvania, from Virginia, and the Carolinas, to the Holston, the French Broad, the Kentucky, and the Cumberland. Retired from all the world, they reveal the effects of a stable environment in a remote region.

There is peculiar continuity of conditions throughout the long range of the southern Appalachians. There run valleys and forested ridges from Virginia into Alabama. There an archaic and almost fossil type of life has come into being. A temperate climate prevails far southward, run in like a wedge between the hot lowlands of the Carolinas and the Mississippi Valley. The isothermal lines of the weather map will sometimes run from New York to Alabama on the eastern slope of the Blue Ridge, and then double and return direct northward to southern Michigan, where they turn off again westward. Mountain, valley, forest, and climate form a realm of upland within lowlands, with strongest industrial, social, and political contrasts. There are counties in North Carolina that do not contain a single negro. But within this land are noble and modern cities, — Knoxville, where the Tennessee is formed by confluent streams, and Chattanooga, where the same river leaves the great valley and goes out through the Cumberland plateau. We shall have occasion, in the chapter on the Civil War, to return to Chattanooga and describe its surroundings with care, but these cities shall now stand for the great industrial unfolding of the last generation in this gateway of the South. From Virginia to Alabama plentiful coal and iron lie close to each other, sometimes "at pistol range." There is limestone also for flux, and thus the conditions for the making of iron are perfect. There is water-power in many mountain streams, and the cotton belt is not far away. Just outside the gate is Atlanta, predestined by its situation to be a metropolis. The

new life of the South is gradually penetrating the
wilds, bringing education and modern invention
into the most distant corners of this Southern world,
and the sternest commands of nature are in the end
softened, if not defied, by man.

CHAPTER IV

THE GREAT LAKES AND AMERICAN COMMERCE

NORTH AMERICA has its mountain systems on the east and west. Between them is a vast lowland, wider at the north, narrower at the south, but spacious everywhere. One may follow the Mississippi, the Minnesota, and the Red River of the North, pass Lake Winnipeg and Hudson Bay, and come out on the Arctic Sea. Nowhere in his journey must he be more than one thousand feet above the ocean level. If the great mountains had been massed in the central parts of the continent, their uplands might have been as arid and remote and their inhabitants as strange and averse to intrusion as among the plateaus of central Asia. But North America has the continental type of Europe or South America, with mountain borders and central plains. In South America these plains are threaded by rivers; in Europe sea-waters pierce the heart of the lands; but North America has both, and more, — the Hudson Bay, the Mississippi and Mackenzie, and the fresh-water seas of the St. Lawrence. Suppose there had been no Great Lakes; perhaps, before the glacial time, there were none. Suppose there was only a larger St. Lawrence, with many branches, flowing from the region of Superior and Michigan; such, very likely,

there was. Or, suppose the waters of the Lake region
had found no gap across the eastern mountains and
had become tributary to the Ohio. If we look at
a relief map of North America, this seems an easy
alternative.

What, in any case, would American history have
been? Where would the Frenchman have planted
himself, and would there have been a French and
Indian War, and where would the battle-ground be
found? These are idle questions if we look for
answers; but they may mean much if they fix our
eyes on the lakes and make us see how large a place
they have in the life of man on this continent.

Various European nations were sending vessels
to the cod banks of Newfoundland about the beginning of the sixteenth century. There is, according
to Parkman, some evidence that Europeans began
to fish in these waters before 1497, the year of Cabot's
voyage. At all events, the French had learned the
road, and it was but little more for them to sail between Cape North and Cape Ray and find themselves
within the Gulf of St. Lawrence, with its ample
waters and its varied shores. It was Jacques Cartier
who, in 1534, had sailed from St. Malo that he might
search the unknown regions beyond the fishing-banks.
He did not, however, take the broader gateway to
the south of Newfoundland, but went up by the east
shore and threaded the straits of Belle Isle.

In the year following he was again fitted out that
he might ascend the St. Lawrence. He went up
to the Indian village of Hochelaga, where now is
Montreal. Though he made a later voyage, he did

not succeed in planting a colony on the river — this
was left to successors who were more daring, or more
enduring, than he. But for us his first voyage is full
of meaning. He entered the continent by its northern gateway, and he found the two natural centers
of human population on the great rivers; for in
selecting a site on which to plant a town, the instincts
of the savage were as sure as those of the white man.

Among the later and greater men was Champlain.
We have seen him on the New England coast, but
his name is written in the St. Lawrence country and
in the waters that divide New York and New England; and it was left for others to make known the
country of the Lakes. His first project suggests a
striking feature of the map of North America. Follow the estuary and river of the St. Lawrence, Lake
Ontario, Lake Erie, the Ohio River, and the Mississippi. Almost in a straight line do these waters join
the Gulf of St. Lawrence and the Gulf of Mexico.
La Salle was at La Chien, above Montreal. The
Indians had told him of the Ohio River, and he set
out to explore it. His story is rehearsed by the historians, and we may only see how geographic features
shaped his courses. To go up the St. Lawrence was
inevitable, and they reached the lake, " like a great
sea with no land beyond it," writes the pious father
who accompanied him.

A few miles east of Rochester, Irondequoit Bay
penetrates several miles into the lands of western
New York. It is almost shut off from the lake by
a sand bar, over which the railway now passes.
Through this depression it is believed that the pre-

glacial Genesee entered the valley where Lake Ontario now is. But with the river shifted to the west this landlocked bay invited entrance; and here La Salle found the Seneca Indians, from whom he hoped to secure a guide to the Ohio. This plan did not mature, and he later went to the western end of Lake Ontario, near the present city of Hamilton, where he met Joliet, who had returned from the upper lakes. They did not remain long together, and Joliet and his companions were soon threading the waters of Detroit, and La Salle, as is believed by some, was accomplishing his exploration of the Ohio River. Later he went to the greater lakes, voyaged up Huron, passed Mackinac, and landed at the south end of Lake Michigan. He made the easy pass to the Illinois, but how far he descended it is not known. His planting of a settlement on the Illinois and his voyage down the Mississippi to the Gulf belong to a later period. It was left for Joliet and Marquette to enter Green Bay, pass from the Fox River to the Wisconsin, discover the Mississippi, and float with its current to a point but seven hundred miles from the Gulf.

Few spots in America have so much historic color as Niagara. And the physiographer sees the short centuries of human occupation against the background of ages of physical evolution. Savage, explorer, colonist, soldier, and man of science have gathered here, and now the place seems likely to become the industrial center of the continent; but man's part can hardly be so dramatic and wonderful as the story of Niagara in more ancient days.

When La Salle was, for the time, drawn away from

FIG. 21.   After the Waters have been used.   Niagara Falls Hydraulic Power and Manufacturing Company.

the Ohio River and went along the lake shore with Joliet, he crossed the lower Niagara, where, a commonplace stream, it flows over the Ontario plain between Lewiston and the lake. He must have heard the roar of the falls and perhaps wondered at the origin of the solemn and pervasive music, but he was not to discover the cataract. It was Hennepin who passed up the left bank of the river, looked down upon the Whirlpool Rapids, and made with his pencil the picture whose conventional rows of trees, and towering Goat Island rocks, have given the ancient priest an immortality which the master of landscape would sigh for in vain.

In 1679 La Salle joined his name to Niagara. Here, above the falls, was built the *Griffon*, a little vessel of forty-five tons, and here she was moored until her master should return with supplies from Fort Frontenac. These necessaries had to be carried up the Lewiston Heights, among them the anchor, requiring four men, as Parkman relates, "well stimulated with brandy," to bring it to the plateau above. The *Griffon* went to Green Bay, La Salle went on into the wilderness, and the ship setting out to return, loaded with furs, was lost.

Thus Niagara took its place in the human world. It was a goal, and it was a point of departure. Follow the Lakes, for exploration, for commerce, for war, and you must take account of it. Try to learn the story of the Lakes, to know their beginnings and their history, and a score of geologists must center their studies on Niagara, so large is her part in the making of things.

If there were no rapids above Montreal and no winter ice in the St. Lawrence, would Buffalo be more than a modest town? Rather would not the railways from the west, passing Detroit, cross Ontario and center upon Hamilton, there to load ships for Liverpool, Glasgow, and Hamburg? Possibly, because the mouth of the St. Lawrence is so far north, an Erie Canal might have saved something for Buffalo and New York. Or we will suppose the St. Lawrence as it is, but no Niagara, and a perfect waterway from Erie to Ontario. Would not the interior metropolis of New York then be Oswego? Here would be the eastern limit of navigation and the point of reshipment for the Mohawk Valley. Niagara makes the difference, and hence it is that Lake Erie is swept by the great vessels of the upper lakes, and Ontario is in comparison a lonely water. It is hers to bear a modest freight, a few lines of tourist steamers, and spend the rest of her energies carving cliffs in the massive glacial drift that often borders her shores. The story of her future commerce, however, is not written.

Reference has been made to the Ontario Lake plain, crossed by the lower Niagara; to the cliffs at Lewiston; to the gorge, and to the Niagara plateau. For the reader who has not visited the region, it will be useful to explain more fully the geographical surroundings of the Falls. In an earlier chapter, the lake plains of western New York were distinguished from the Alleghany plateau. But there are really two lake plains. Lake Erie lies in the upper one, which slopes abruptly up into the Alleghany plateau, beyond Dunkirk and Chautauqua, but stretches smoothly eastward from Buffalo for many miles. Lake Ontario lies in the lower plain, and the difference of altitude between the two lake surfaces is nearly three hundred feet. About half of this vertical interval is accounted for by the bluffs at Lewiston. These face north and are known as the Niagara escarpment. This wall runs west, far through Ontario, and east toward Rochester. The famous series of locks at Lockport carries the Erie Canal from the upper to the lower plain. The upper surface, viewed in reference to Lake Erie, is a lake plain, and was formerly flooded with lake waters. Viewed in reference to Ontário, it is the Niagara plateau. Its smooth top is formed upon the flat Niagara limestone, and the escarpment is chiefly the north or exposed edge of this formation. When Niagara began to flow, it fell over the bluff at Lewiston. Cutting away the limestone under the brink, the fall has receded until it is now seven miles south, and the Niagara Gorge is seven miles long — a history which seems simple, and is, in this, its great feature, but in many other ways is an intricate story and difficult to decipher.

On Lake Erie we are 573 feet above the sea. If we go up through the Detroit and St. Clair rivers, upon Lake Huron or Michigan, we are but 8 feet higher. And if we ascend through the locks of the "Soo" to Lake Superior, we add but 21 feet more, and our altitude is 602 feet. A little help from man, therefore, turns the four upper lakes into a single sea, with free navigation between remotest points. Thus, too, we can see how the cutting of the Chicago Drain-

FIG. 22.   Harbor of Duluth and Superior, seen from Duluth.   See page 137.

age Canal might become a matter of concern, not merely to St. Louis, for fear of sewage, but to Cleveland or Buffalo, if a considerable portion of Niagara should be diverted to the Mississippi. If this be speculation, it serves at least to point out the delicate balance of the lake waters. They are a great sea, and the southwest pass is so low that "tidal waves arising in Lake Michigan sometimes overflowed the dividing ridge. The early explorers of the Great Lakes are known to have passed, during the spring freshets, in their canoes from one valley to the other, by that route which enables the modern Chicago to discharge its sewage into the Gulf of Mexico instead of the Gulf of St. Lawrence."[1]

The chief drainage of the Great Lake region was once carried to the sea by the Chicago outlet. And still later the waters of the upper lakes went through the Mohawk Valley to the Hudson, and later still they went by the Ottawa Valley to the St. Lawrence. Now they go by Port Huron and Niagara. Let us not think that this present arrangement must last forever. We know that in late geological times, even since the close of the glacial period, most of the plain that holds the Lakes has been given an increasing slant toward the southwest. Mr. G. K. Gilbert, following up this suggestion, has shown with an approach to certainty that this tilting is yet going on, with the result that in a few centuries the Lakes would withdraw some of their waters from the Niagara to the Mississippi, and in a few thousand years would leave Niagara dry. The tilting may not, however, go on, and if it

[1] Winsor, "Cartier to Frontenac," p. 4.

does, man can restrain the change of outflow for a long period if he desires.

Vast as the Lakes are, they have seen many revolutions and are still young. They rest in shallow depressions on a widespreading plain, which, so to speak, is so delicately poised that movements within the earth can change the face of things, and might have made quite other than it is, the theater of American history.

It is time for us to tell in a more connected way the story of the Lakes, and to put in their true setting the scattered facts already given. Many questions about their origin cannot now be answered, but the closing events are better known than the early stages of the history. It will be useful, in a preliminary way, to banish false notions about the depth of the lake basins. One thousand feet seems a great depth of water, but Lake Superior is four hundred miles long. The ratio of depth to length is about one to two thousand. With this ratio a lake one mile long would be two and one-half feet deep. If we could drain the basin of Lake Superior, it would present a vast plain, with hardly a variation from the horizontal that the eye could detect. The case would be similar with Michigan, Huron, and Ontario, while Erie is yet more surprising. Her depth is to length nearly as one to seven thousand, and a lake one mile long would be nine or ten inches deep!

We cannot have a fair opinion about the forces that made the basins unless we remember that these basins are mere scratches on the continent, or faint sags, like those that harbor shallow water in a flat

meadow after rain.   We should also put the depth of
the Lakes in relation to sea-level.   All but Lake Erie
reach below this horizon, — Superior about four hundred feet, Ontario nearly five hundred feet, Michigan
nearly three hundred feet, and Huron about 150 feet.
Erie, being so shallow, keeps its bottom 363 feet above
the sea.

Look upon the map of the Laurentian waters and
imagine the Lakes shrinking in width until they become mere sections of a great St. Lawrence River,
rising in Minnesota and on the highlands north of
Lake Superior.   Let it flow somewhere near the
"Soo" and take in a branch from along the axis of
Lake Michigan.   Let it pass the Huron, to the Ontario country, receiving branches from southern
Ontario and northern Ohio, and then go down to the
sea.   If there was such a greater St. Lawrence, this
may not be a true picture of it, but it would probably
do for the essentials.

If we could now imagine great sections of these
river valleys to be deepened, or to be in any manner
shut off from the sea, the surplus rain-waters would
gather in them, and we should see the inland seas of
to-day.

We have taken this way of approaching what is
perhaps the leading theory about the Lakes, that they
lie in blocked river valleys.   Then the query comes,
— what sort of barriers are these, or what could they
be?   The Lake country is now tipping to the southwest; it is not a very disturbing motion, — about
five inches in a distance of one hundred miles in a
century.   But that would be four feet in a thousand

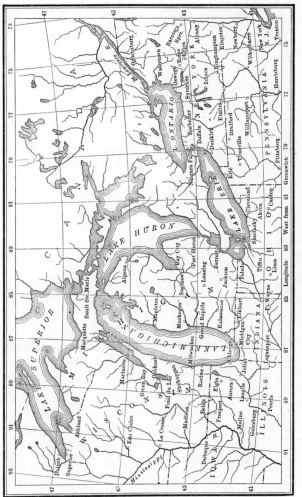

The Great Lake Region

years, and a thousand years in the earth's history is not much. We can see that such tilting would hinder the flow of Ontario's waters past the Thousand Islands and would make the lake deeper. The basins may, therefore, be partly due to uprising of the lands toward the outlets of the rivers.

But the Lakes are doubtless not due to this single cause. Every foot of the Lake country was occupied by glacial ice. Massive beds of drift, in sheets or morainic heaps, were left when the ice melted away. The moraines show themselves in hills, and the sheets are often revealed by deep borings, or by their covering the country so smoothly and so deeply that in certain regions, bed-rock rarely comes to the surface. Ancient valleys were often shut up by bodies of drift, and multitudes of the smaller lakes lie in such pockets in old valleys. There is no reason why great valleys should not in some places have been barred in the same way. Moving glaciers also remove rocks from beneath them. Their weight is great, and they are shod with sand and boulders. But they do not erode equally everywhere. Where the ice is thickest or is hardest pushed, both from its own weight and the onthrust from behind, there it will dig most. Thus some observers believe that the Great Lake basins are more due to glacial erosion than to anything else. There is no reason why all the causes which have been described may not have lent their aid.

There is another word to be added to this bundle of queries. The relations of the rocks here are such that valley-making seems inevitable in the long

preglacial time.   The softer, horizontal strata of
the Northern United States abut against the hard,
ancient core of North America, found in Canada.
Where these flat beds run over the southerly slopes
of the crystalline uplands of the north, they would
suffer most destruction, and by laws known to physiography, valleys would grow, of which the primitive
land forms give no hint.   Some sort of a St. Lawrence River system was to be expected from earliest
times.   Movements of the land, glacial blockades, and
glacial erosion have done the rest.

The later development of the Lakes can be more
clearly told.   When the historian has pieced together
from stray inscriptions and traditions a doubtful
story of early man, he may come down to a point
where records abound, and libraries give him more
material than he can use.   Then, if he have diligence
and judgment, he can move with firm step.   Something like this certainty we have, — when the continental glacier was disappearing, when the lakes were
often larger, — and always of forms different from
those of to-day.   Great bodies of water leave on their
borders inscriptions which centuries may not destroy
or deface.   By records of ancient shore-lines, we
prove that the Lakes were often larger and had
higher levels than they now have.

If the reader would know this history, let him
clearly trace the line of water partings that separate
the St. Lawrence basin from those of the Mississippi
and Susquehanna.   In Minnesota the head waters of
the Mississippi reach close to Lake Superior.   Wisconsin is more evenly divided, where the Fox and

FIG. 23.   Part of Mahoning Iron Ore Pit, Mesaba Range, Minnesota.   See page 137.

Wisconsin rivers head against each other in the central part of the state. In Illinois the parting is hard by Chicago and is overcome by a few feet of digging. It crosses northern Indiana and northern Ohio, and runs close to Lake Erie, as it enters western New York. In New York the divide is south of the Finger Lakes, and we need pursue it no further except to mark on the map the place of Elmira.

When the ice was at its limits it lay far southward over the line of water partings. The ice-sheet was removed by gradual melting on the south. Sometimes it disappeared from great regions and advanced again. When at any point the ice melted north of the divide, a lake would result. Its basin would be formed by the height of land on the south and the glacial ice on the north. Its form would depend on the turns of the line of water parting and the irregularities of the ice front; the water would be supplied by the melting ice; the outlets would be across the divides into head waters of the Mississippi and Susquehanna.

Now we can understand what was happening at the head of the present Lake Michigan. After the ice began to melt northward, out of the Lake Michigan basin, the site of Chicago was flooded. The overflow went along the line of the Drainage Canal into the Illinois River. The longer the ice melted, the greater became the lake, and the more water poured out toward the Mississippi. Exactly similar things were taking place at about the same time, at the head of the Superior basin. Along the slopes about Duluth the old beaches tell the story. The ice filled more or less of the lake basin, holding up the waters so that they poured over into the St. Croix, and thus went to the Gulf. If we go to Indiana and Ohio, the conditions are the same, only now we are at the head of the Lake Erie lobe of the glacier. As before it is melting away, and lake waters rise against the divide and flow over, at Fort Wayne, where the ancient channel, now dry, has been traced and has been shown to be in harmony with old beaches in Indiana and Ohio.

At Elmira in New York, or a little to the north, is the lowest southward pass in the state, east of the Hudson, not quite a thousand feet above the sea. Think of the glacier, still massive, where Lake Ontario now is, and reaching well up into western New York. All the basins of the Finger Lakes then held lakes deeper and greater than now. Southward, these lakes were restrained by the divides. Northward, as before, they laved the ice front. And for a time their northern ends coalesced, and they had a common outlet through Seneca Valley, past Elmira, and down the Chemung to the Susquehanna.

We must remind the reader that these lakes at the head of Superior, Michigan, and Erie, and in western New York, may not have been contemporaneous, but they represent a stage in the retreat of the ice, and were not far apart, as the geologist reckons time. As the ice melted yet more, the lowlands of the Lake region were flooded, larger lakes were formed, and some of the old outlets were abandoned because the passes were too high. One of these vast lakes extended from the Finger Lake region westward, over

much of northern Ohio, southern Ontario, and southern Michigan.   Its outlet crossed the unsubmerged
part of southern Michigan and entered the Michigan
basin, whence the waters passed out by the Chicago
outlet.   This ancient body of water was held to its
place by the great glacier that still blocked the Mohawk and St. Lawrence valleys and the eastern
Ontario region.   The beaches which mark its presence and prove its reality are about 870 feet above
the sea, and it is known as Lake Warren.

By various stages these waters were drawn down, the
channel across Michigan was abandoned, and we find
the outflow taking place by the Mohawk Valley.   The
outline of the Great Lakes has been revolutionized.
Western New York is in great part dry land, but
Lake Ontario washes the base of the Niagara escarpment, flows up the Cayuga Valley, absorbs Oneida
Lake, and sends its waters to the Hudson.   This
drainage makes a great river, for it comes not only
from the greater Ontario but from a vast upper
lake, which, absorbing Superior, Michigan, and Huron, discharges across the Province of Ontario into
Iroquois, for this is the name which we should give to
the ancestral Ontario.   Another great result of the
descent of the Warren waters to the Iroquois level
was the uncovering of the Niagara escarpment, and
the beginning of Niagara River and Niagara cataract.   But it will be observed that it was a small
Niagara, for the upper waters were going more
directly to the sea, by way of the Georgian Bay
region and Lake Iroquois.

Later still we find no ice in the St. Lawrence Valley. Here, then, was a lower outlet for Lake Iroquois, and the Mohawk Valley was abandoned, save by the little stream gathered from the New York uplands. At the same time, the upper lake waters had shifted to a more northern outlet and were reaching the St. Lawrence by way of the Ottawa Valley. The whole St. Lawrence region was now so low that the sea flowed freely in, and the tides were felt far up the Ottawa Valley and to the head of Lake Ontario and in the valley of Lake Champlain. Niagara was still a little river and could boast only of the waters of Lake Erie, and Lake Erie was smaller than it is to-day. And now comes the closing scene in this long drama. The eastern country began to rise and the sea to retire from Lake Ontario and the upper St. Lawrence. By and by the uplift had become too great to permit the upper lake waters to flow east by the Ottawa Valley. They swing back to Port Huron and Niagara, and Niagara became the great river which it is to-day.

This is the upward movement of the land which, as Mr. Gilbert has shown, is probably still going on. In our short story of the Lakes we have been able to see how the ice filled their basins and perhaps deepened them, how small lakes were replaced by greater ones, and how successive outflows of their waters have been directed to the southward, westward, eastward, and northeastward. The lands have changed their levels, and Niagara has been born and grown to be what she is.

At Lewiston, N.Y., on the plain below the Niagara escarpment, is a low ridge of gravel running eastward. It is prolonged through several counties in western New York, and has been used for a line of highway since the days of the earliest settlers. This avenue, leading through rich farming and fruit lands, has always been known as the Ridge Road. It represents in part only the beach of the ancient Lake Iroquois, which has been followed eastward to central New York, and then northward to Watertown. At Lewiston the beach is about 140 feet above Lake Ontario, but at the east end of the lake it is from two hundred to three hundred feet higher than the lake surface. As the old beach must have been horizontal when made, we find here the proof that the region has been given an inclination to the west and southwest. The story of these beaches would be a long one, but when it is read it gives a convincing sense of reality concerning the glacial lakes which we have described. Finding the beaches in Ohio, and girding the slopes of Mackinac Island, or high above the waters of Lake Superior, and surmounted now by the great buildings and busy streets of Duluth, we cannot doubt their meaning. The most skeptical should yield credence, when, correlating with the shore-lines, he finds the outlet channels at Chicago, at Fort Wayne, at Elmira, at Rome, or in the Mattawa Valley leading from Georgian Bay to the Ottawa River.

Where the lands that stretch away from the lake shores are almost flat, the ancient Lakes must have reached far inland. This is true in western New York, northern Ohio, and southern Ontario. And there we find the soils and subsoils consisting of clays and fine silts, that is, of just such material as settles

FIG. 24.   Duluth, Mesaba and Northern Ore Docks.

in the bottom of lakes at some distance from the
shore. The plowman is not annoyed by boulders,
and the farmer finds smooth and level areas, easy
of tillage and rich in production. Transportation is
simple and inexpensive, railways are easily built, and
the land is foreordained to prosperity. Thus have
the Lakes themselves fashioned thousands of square
miles of the lands that lie about them, spreading their
soils upon their rocky foundations, and now bearing
away their harvests to remote cities. Nor are the
Lakes without large influence upon the climate of the
region. There are nearly one hundred thousand
miles of water surface, and the contribution to atmospheric moisture through evaporation is enormous.
More than this, the Lakes are deep, and contain six
thousand cubic miles of water. The heat that is
received into these waters during the warmer parts
of the year is stored and gradually set free during
the autumn and winter, tempering the atmosphere of
surrounding lands. Hence the fields of the Iroquois
plain are garnished with forests of peach trees, and
vineyards cover the Erie shore plains of the Chautauqua region. Soil and climate alike are the gift of the
Lakes. Those who live in the more southern land
rarely think of genial climate in Canada, but the Lake
region of the province of Ontario abounds in orchards
and raises the vine in profusion.

We have approached the Lakes down the long lines
of their physical history only that we may better
know what they have meant in the life of man during the short centuries since America was found
by European people. When the devout missionary

and hardy explorer had ascended the St. Lawrence, the open waters would carry him to the heart of the continent. Or if he pushed up the Ottawa and threaded the rough forests that lay toward the Georgian Bay, he could bid farewell to the bouldery jungle, and paddle his canoe to the Chicago River, Green Bay, or the head of Lake Superior, and thence by easy portages he could find his way into some head water of the great Mississippi. And when the missionary and the trapper were followed by the permanent settler, forts were planted, cabins rose on the prairie and in the forest, towns grew up on bays and in the mouths of rivers, the towns became cities, and the cities sent fleets of vessels up and down these inland seas, bearing the grain of an empire, and at length stores of mineral wealth whose very existence was hidden until our own time.

No other inland navigation in the world compares with that of the Laurentian Lakes, and what it may become in the century just begun it would be rash to foretell. Every lake washes the borders of rich lands, and these lands reach across the prairies and down the Mississippi, over the plains to the far Northwest, and eastward by two great gateways to the Atlantic. Most of the great railways now converge on the Lakes, and it is only sober prophecy to forecast ships of large tonnage sailing from the Lakes to the Hudson and lower St. Lawrence by two or more routes from the Lakes to the Mississippi, and from Superior, by way of Winnipeg, to Hudson Bay. For some of these the surveys are complete, and in at least two instances construction is much more than begun.   Far more wonderful would the present have seemed to those who 225 years ago launched the first sailing vessel on the upper Lakes.

The governments, both of the United States and of Canada, have not been slow to see the meaning of the Lakes.   As early as 1841 the United States Lake Survey was planned, and its work carried on for forty years.   The character of the shores, the nature of the bottoms, and the depths of the water were determined and recorded in maps which are now available to sailors and to all.   The work is similar to that of the United States Coast Survey.   As with the ocean, so on lake borders, conditions change, bars are built, bays are silted up, new shoals are found, and revision of the older work has been found necessary and has been undertaken.

From the head of Lake Michigan, or of Lake Superior, to the lower part of Lake Erie, the shipman finds nearly one thousand miles of continuous sailing. By the locks on St. Marys River, and by dredging parts of the channel between Huron and Erie, vessels drawing twenty feet of water can now make this voyage.   From Buffalo and Cleveland on the east this great highway, forking in upper Lake Huron, finds its western gate in Chicago, Milwaukee, and Duluth.

Down to the present time the lake trade converges eastward upon Buffalo.   Here the products of the West are transferred to railway and canal, excepting those which, in boats of moderate draught, go on their way down the Welland Canal to Lake Ontario and Montreal.   Soon after La Salle had launched the *Griffon* near by, another Frenchman, Baron La

FIG. 25.   Along the Cuyahoga River, Cleveland.

Horiton, saw that the plain at the foot of the lake had meaning for the future, and a fort was built. Nearly a century later the British held the place and called it Fort Erie, and the commerce of the Great Lakes began. The place was not known as Buffalo until 1810, when its first steamboat, *Walk-in-the-Water*, went westward. Its greater development began in 1825, when the Erie Canal was finished.

One hundred and fifty miles up the south shore of Lake Erie is the rival port of the lower Lakes. There seems to be, at first view, no compelling reason why a large city should grow where Cleveland is. It is not at the head or foot of a great lake; it is not so near to extensive mineral deposits as to arouse expectation; it has, indeed, a rich farming land to the south; it is on the lake shore, and a small river, the Cuyahoga, draining a few counties of northern Ohio, enters the lake here. There was a trading post at Pittsburg and another at Detroit. The mouth of the Cuyahoga was nearly on a line between the two, was a convenient halting place, and a trading post was established. In 1796, the Connecticut Land Company sent Moses Cleaveland to survey the ground, and his name, lacking a letter, became attached to it. A real settlement began in 1797, and real prosperity began, when, in 1834, a waterway, the Ohio Canal, joined the place with the Ohio River. No other geographic cause is so compelling in the making of cities as a line of transportation, or, perhaps we ought to say, the convergence of such lines.

Cleveland was, for long, the second city of Ohio, springing to the first place only at the close of the last century, and offering one example among others of the advantages of lake and seaports as compared with river towns. Fifty years ago a trivial consignment of iron ore was here received from Lake Superior. Nobody heard of it, or if it was known, it stirred no thought. But Cleveland was not, after all, so removed from the treasures of the under earth. Coal was mining in the Mahoning Valley, on the east border of the state. It was coming to Cleveland; and later, also, more ore was brought and coal was made to smelt the iron. At length, also, the trail between trading posts had become a railway, and Pittsburg and Cleveland had been made neighbors. There was unlimited coal about Pittsburg, and the ore, coming in vast shiploads through the deepened canal of St. Marys River, was swiftly transferred at Cleveland and sent to the city of furnaces. Meantime oil and gas developed, pipe-lines were run down from the oil fields, and Cleveland became the greatest of petroleum centers. East and west along the lake shore run the transcontinental railways; and so it turns out that the little valley of the Cuyahoga River is at the crossing of two of the greatest highways in America.

Detroit, named from the narrow water passage between Huron and Erie, is, in its name, a lasting memorial of French discovery and early occupation. There were earlier posts on the Lakes above, but Cadillac had the sagacity to see that the fur trade could best be centered and controlled where Detroit now is. He returned to France, convinced the ministry of his wisdom, and gained a grant of land, " wherever on the Detroit (strait) the new fort should be established." The settlement came into English possession in 1762, was held by the British for a time in the War of 1812, and had become by 1818 a populous and lively community. Eight years before, *Walk-in-the-Water* had sailed from Buffalo, and now lake commerce was becoming large, and a more settled and refined life was mingling with the rougher elements of the frontier.

For through commerce on the Lakes Detroit would be but a calling-place, and we must not overlook the essential part which the railway has had in her growth. The great east and west highways must go either north or south of Lake Erie. Those that run north of the lake cross the river at Detroit and, entering Canada, divide in like manner upon Lake Ontario. Here, then, as in Cleveland, we have a crossing of the ways, and here also must converge the more local lines of railway which serve the Southern peninsula and carry its traffic to the South and East.

The greatest of lake ports is not at the head of Lake Michigan, but nearly twenty miles north, on the western shore. Chicago is determined by the same cause that guided Joliet and Marquette, La Salle and Hennepin, when they sojourned in this region, or sought the sources of the Mississippi. Here an insignificant river enters the lake, and its short courses lead to the pass whose history lies in the geological past, and whose importance to man is now beginning to be seen. And yet upon this stream, by dredging and by building docks, forty-one miles of frontage have been made available, and the harborage outside has been extended by breakwater construction, until fleets can anchor here, where two generations ago a small town lay along a straight shore-line and on two sides of a shallow, muddy, and unknown river. It is now ninety-nine years since the first permanent white settlers occupied Chicago, and

FIG. 26. Shipping in the Chicago River. Photograph by Wm. H. Rau, Philadelphia.

the civilian population was barely a hundred in 1830. In the last decade of the nineteenth century Chicago increased her population by fifty-four per cent and has in the beginning of the twentieth century nearly two millions of people. This was due in no measure to local conditions, for her harbor had to be created and the very ground raised from a swamp. The greatness of Chicago is due to its general geographic relations and to the combination, as with Cleveland and Detroit, of railway and water transportation.

From the prairies, the plains, and the passes of the northern Rocky Mountains, the railway lines must round the head of Lake Michigan. All passers between East and West must pay tribute here. Traffic from the Southwest is drawn to the Lakes, and all lines from the farther Northwest must come down to Chicago. Whatever diversions may occur at Duluth or along Canadian lines of railway, they cannot injure the lake metropolis, though they may in some ways check its rate of expansion.

Milwaukee compares in an interesting way with its greater neighbor. Its natural advantages of immediate environment are far greater: a good harbor, fine rising ground for her streets and buildings, and a river for water-power. She is also favored by being the center of interest and the capital of a great commonwealth; but not all of these gains can counterbalance the relations which Chicago holds to the entire country. Like Chicago, Milwaukee bears an Indian name, but like the greater city also the French explorers led the way, and the first white settler upon Milwaukee Bay, in 1817, bore the name of Juneau. But no one thinks of France to-day when he enters, on the shore of Lake Michigan, one of the greatest of German-American cities.

The cold and abundant waters that flow out of Lake Superior encounter a tough sill of ancient rocks, over which, in foaming rapids, they leap down to enter the expanse of Lake Huron. Lake Superior could have little more than local commerce until this

FIG. 27. American Locks at Sault Sainte Marie, — the "Soo."

obstacle was overcome. As she is surrounded, not by prairies yielding grain and fruit, but by rough and rocky lands, bearing forests on their slopes and mineral wealth beneath their scanty soils and bare ledges, exchange becomes imperative, for no region of two or three resources, however rich, can live to itself. The governor of Michigan saw the need as long ago as 1837 and stirred the legislature to its task. Baffled for many years by conservative influences in the national government, necessity won at last, and a canal was finished in 1853. It was twelve feet deep, and its completion made possible a continuous passage from the head of Lake Superior to Buffalo. In a few years enlargement was needed, and the national government took up the work. The deepening of the locks and of the approaching channels to seventeen feet was not enough, and the depth has now been carried to twenty-one feet. Similar works have been completed by the Canadian government within a dozen years, and the tonnage that passes this gateway is stated in figures that baffle comprehension. That of the Suez Canal is light in comparison with it; and where small cargoes fifty years ago were laboriously carried around the rapids, a vessel of eight thousand tons, having on board the product of eleven thousand acres of wheat, or a cargo of iron ore, passes in a few moments. But little of the water of Superior is needed for the locks, and power canals have been built on the American and on the Canadian side of the river. The iron, nickel, and other minerals of the region have been developed, and a railway projected to Hudson Bay to open within a few years the lumber, grain, minerals, and fish of that northern region. Varied manufactures and a route of traffic must here build up one more of the great centers of the Lake region.

Not least of these will be the head of Lake Superior. Historic time in this domain is so short that prophecy swiftly leads one on from the brief records of the past. On the steep slopes rising from the chilling waters of the lake is Duluth, another memorial of early French occupation. We might better say visitation, for Captain Jean DuLuth, in 1760, only built a hut, and it was more than a century later when a city was chartered here. Though not yet one of the greatest cities, it is already one of the greatest ports of the Lakes, and no limit can be placed to its possible unfolding. Here is the focal point for the grain of Minnesota, the Dakotas, and the vast northwest provinces of Canada. When deeper waterways shall have been dug eastward from the Lakes, there will be no breaking of bulk between Duluth and New York, Liverpool, or Hamburg. The head of Lake Superior is five hundred miles nearer to the grain-growing empire of the Northwest than is Chicago, and the result is inevitable. Here, too, within a few score miles are the largest iron-ore beds known in America. And most of the ore lies, not in deeply buried veins, but close to the surface, making it possible to mine it with steam shovels in open pits, into which railway tracks are carried, and from which the loaded cars are run down to the docks at Duluth and in its neighborhood, there to transfer their loads to the lake vessels. It reaches its destination in Cleveland or

Pittsburg at a trivial cost which has made possible the enormous development of iron and steel in recent years. Added to the iron ranges of Minnesota are the great stores of iron and native copper in the northern peninsula of Michigan, and the lumber of Michigan, northern Wisconsin, and the adjacent parts of Canada. We shall not forget that other ports on the Lakes — Ashland, Marquette, Port Huron, Toledo, and many others — are great in commerce, being overshadowed somewhat by their larger rivals.

It has often been said that the great cities are made by railroads. This is the more plausible because shallow waterways, like the Erie Canal, have lost their importance. But the railway can never displace the deep waterway in carrying other than perishable freight. We may, therefore, look forward to enormous extension of traffic of the Great Lakes through the ship canals of the future. One of these will open the way from Lake Erie to New York Harbor. By an act of 1897 the United States government undertook an investigation of routes for waterways between the Lakes and the Atlantic Ocean, and an elaborate report of the engineers was transmitted to Congress in 1900. Should this report lead to action, it is proposed to pass from the Niagara River above the Falls to Lake Ontario, either by a route close to the river, and entering it again at Lewiston, or by a line a few miles to the eastward. From Lake Ontario to the Hudson alternative routes are proposed, one by Oswego and the Mohawk Valley, the other by the St. Lawrence, Lake Champlain, and eastern New York. To accomplish such a plan will

FIG. 28.   Duluth; Railways and Business Section.

go far to perpetuate and increase the commercial superiority of New York City.

Within a few years the Canadian government has completed its great project of cutting a fourteen-foot waterway from Lake Erie to tide-water, by way of the Welland Canal, and by passing around the various impracticable sections of the St. Lawrence River. These channels have a total length of nearly seventy-five miles. Other schemes have been proposed which in the end may mean much to this growing northern empire. A canal from Georgian Bay to the navigable waters of the Ottawa River would give direct passage from Chicago and Duluth to Montreal and Liverpool. If a map be consulted, it will be found that a line from Georgian Bay to Montreal is one side of a triangle, whose remaining sides must be traversed by vessels taking the Port Huron route. This proposed waterway has almost romantic interest because through it passed the waters of the upper Lakes at the close of the glacial period. As railways look back to ancestral trails of savages or wild beasts, so this plan of navigation recalls a yet more distant era.

The Chicago Drainage Canal was not cut across the prairie for a single end. Already it disposes of the sewage and secures greater purity of the lake water-supply, but its twenty-eight miles of channel, cut broad and deep through the drift and solid rock, are to be the first link in a waterway that shall pass through the Illinois River to the Mississippi and join the Great Lakes to the Gulf. This means unhindered communication between the Gulf of St. Lawrence and the Gulf of Mexico. It means more than this; for

when the Isthmian Canal has been built, direct
freight service can be had, for exchange of all the
products of the Northwest, with the Western coast
of America and the entire Orient. Then the dreams
of explorers will be more than fulfilled. They sought
the East by way of the Great Lakes, and their descendants of the twentieth century will have found
the way. No distant future may see Minneapolis
sending its flour in shiploads to Duluth and the East;
for a route .has already been surveyed. From Superior to Lake Winnipeg; from the Mississippi and
Minnesota rivers to the Red River of the North; and
from Lake Winnipeg to Hudson Bay, — these are
among the possible triumphs of the future. Pittsburg and Lake Erie will be joined, Niagara will
merge with Buffalo as the industrial center of North
America, the agricultural riches of the Northwest
and of the arid lands will have been developed, and
the adjustment of human life to its North American
environment will enter upon an advanced stage. It
has been no part of the present plan to give the sta-
tistics of Great Lake commerce, but rather to show
some of the laws and centers· of its growth. If,
however, we remember that the tonnage (not the
value) of Cleveland lake traffic has sometimes surpassed that of Liverpool, and that the Detroit River,
in the seven open months, exceeds the import and
export tonnage of our Atlantic and Pacific ports combined, we shall find that the largest expectations of
the coming half-century are sober and reasonable.

CHAPTER V

THE PRAIRIE COUNTRY

We are beginning to see that geographic provinces cannot be sharply defined. The Appalachian barrier grades down to the coastal plain through the Piedmont Hills, and on the west the Alleghany plateau slopes to the level of the prairies. So when we say prairie country, we mean the great northern central land, whose most characteristic phase is prairie: and yet Ohio and Indiana are but in a small way prairie states. Illinois and Iowa are the typical regions, and we include roughly the lands lying around them: southern Minnesota and Wisconsin, northern Missouri, and the states west of the Missouri River, so far as they are well enough watered to grow crops freely without irrigation. From the uplands of Wisconsin to the mouth of the Ohio, and from the state of Ohio well into Nebraska, lies the land to which we turn. It is the upper Mississippi Valley, shorn, however, of two great regions: one about the head waters of the Ohio, and the other stretching far along the upper Missouri. The former belongs to the Alleghany plateau, and the latter to the Great Plains and the Rocky Mountains. But we cannot draw a line between the prairie and those flat lands that surround the Lakes and once formed part of their bottoms.

Into this great open land civilized man might come by several doorways, and two of them were equally open and inviting. One would have led the explorer up from the Gulf of Mexico. The Spaniard looked in at this door, — indeed, he entered it, and camped just within; but he found no gold, and thus he carried his trails and left the tokens of his language among the mountains and plateaus of the distant Southwest. How blind he was to the seat of empire, we need no special wisdom now to see. He would cede it to his northern neighbor, and it would by and by be sold for a few paltry millions of dollars.

The Frenchman came in at the other open door, along the Laurentian waters. Armed with triple motive, — love of adventure, the gospel of his faith, and zeal for the gains of peltry, — he made the Mississippi Valley for the time his own. If these motives were mingled in some, they burned singly and with pure flame in others. If there were hypocrites among true and suffering heralds of the faith, there were men also mingled with the scoundrels that bartered pelts with the savages and threw off the bonds of decent society in the wilds of the forest. With the mixed motives of common human nature, but always with daring, the prairie country was crossed from north to south and from east to west.

It marked an epoch in the history of the New World when Joliet and Marquette pushed their little craft up the Fox River, toward those head waters from which, by a short portage, they should go over to the Wisconsin. When their canoe was launched again, the Mississippi Valley was won; for they needed but to give themselves to the current, to pass the Missouri, the Ohio, and the Arkansas, and to have sailed out into the Gulf, had not the risks seemed too great, among swarms of hostile natives. Having run by the mouth of the Arkansas, they turned against the current, but entered, as they returned, the Illinois River, found it easy to overcome its sluggish flow, and came back to Green Bay by the portage at the head of Lake Michigan.

Fig. 29.   Bridge across the Mississippi at St. Louis.

It remained for La Salle to assert with larger confidence, and by the warrant of more remote journeyings, the rights of his king in the Mississippi country, a drainage basin which perhaps seems more vast to us who know, than to the explorer who was living in the shadowy realm of the imagination. When La Salle had returned to Paris, he was fully awake to the need of possessing and fortifying the new realm, and said, in almost prophetic language, " Should foreigners anticipate us, they will complete the ruin of New France,

which they already hem in by their establishments of
Virginia, Pennsylvania, New England, and Hudson's
Bay." Several years before, having visited the Illinois country, he drew a picture of the prairies which
may in some points serve as well to-day : " So beautiful and so fertile ; so free from forests, and so full of
meadows, brooks, and rivers ; so abounding in fish,
game, and venison, that one can find there in plenty,
and with little trouble, all that is needful for the
support of flourishing colonies." Indeed the empire
would be built and the meadows would be made populous, but the founders of states would come neither
by the Lakes nor the Gulf, — they would hew their
way across the mountains.

It was in 1682 that La Salle completed the discovery of the lower Mississippi and gave name to the
Louisiana country. By the beginning of the next
century settlements were made. One of the French
centers of population was at Detroit, another was at
Vincennes in the lower Wabash country, on the eastern, or what is now the Indiana, side of the river ; and
the farthest outpost of all was about Kaskaskia, in
the river region between Cairo and St. Louis. Here
and on the Wabash gathered several thousand French
colonists. They were not state builders, as La Salle
might have hoped, but lived in easy fashion, bartering
furs, rearing their half-breed children, and tilling
patches of the soil in their occasional hours of industry. We are not concerned with their story save to
see how they passed, with the fall of Quebec, under
British rule, so to remain until the close of the Revolution. Here, for a short period, **was a** population of

French and of savages, governed by a foreign king, who was alien to both, and bitterly hostile to the growth of his rebellious seaboard colonies, as they pushed into the land north of the Ohio. Against this triangular and unnatural union of vacillating creoles, savage aborigines, and wilful king, were pitted the backwoodsmen of Kentucky.

These hardy souls we have met before, as they colonized the valleys and threaded the passes of the Appalachians. They had not learned to use with slack hand the ax and the rifle. They could travel light, follow a trail like a savage, and shoot sure. They took pride in snuffing a candle or driving a nail with a bullet, and two of them, not the best or noblest of their kind, are said to have amused themselves and shown their confidence in each other's skill, by placing a tin cup full of whiskey on the head, and allowing the other, at a range of seventy yards, to puncture it.

The shadowy claims of Virginia and other colonies to this old Northwest counted for nothing against actual possession by British forts and British commanders, and the land had to be won by successful war. In planting the settlements on the Kentucky and the Cumberland, Boone, Robertson, and the men and women who toiled and fought with them, had opened the way for the prairie realm of the future. They were to win it against all odds, while nations that approached it by other highways were to stand aside, and thus to bring fresh proof that geographic opportunity does not of necessity control.

It is here that we meet the surveyor, frontiersman,

and soldier, George Rogers Clark. There is no finer story of frontier history than his. A Virginian by birth, a Kentuckian by adoption, he saw the problem of the Northwest, and went back to Virginia to arouse the government of his native state. From Patrick Henry, the governor, he received a Godspeed; but there was little more for the exhausted colony to give. Almost with single hand he raised a little force, took it down the Ohio, surprised Kaskaskia, won the French by his kindness and the savages by his union of fairness and defiance; marched through cold floods, often breast deep, to Vincennes, and compelled its English commander with superior force to surrender, — this is, in brief, the dramatic story. Every advance of the Middle West in population, in wealth, and in public achievement should add to the fame of this simple, rough man of illimitable personal force. His work made it easy for the new government to claim and hold, in the final treaties, the country north of the Ohio River and south of the Lakes, where now are Ohio, Indiana, Illinois, Michigan, and Wisconsin. It was, for purposes of conquest and occupancy, a geographical unit; it could not be divided, and the winning of it was essential to the winning also of the Northwest that lay beyond, and of the great Southwest.

Such, in its outlines, had been the history down to the beginning of those decades following the Revolution, when the great rush of the people westward was filling the prairie lands with homes and permanent institutions. Before we follow these throngs along their line of march, or see how they adjusted their life to their new surroundings, we must observe these geographic conditions as carefully as we may, and we will ask the reader to note again the extent and borders of the land.

Ohio on the east is scarcely upland, nor is it lowland, having an average altitude of between eight hundred and nine hundred feet. We may think of it as the Alleghany plateau gently declining to the west, or as the Mississippi plains rising on the east. It has exceedingly smooth lake plains on the north and northwest, and a line of low divides, running north of the middle of the state, turns the streams to Lake Erie and the Ohio River. These streams occupy valleys sunk well down into the low plateau. Ohio is not a prairie state; for she never had more than small areas of open, treeless meadow, to which this name is given. Almost the whole state was originally covered with forests of walnut, beech, maple, buckeye, chestnut, ash, and hickory.

In type of surface Indiana is much like Ohio, with large areas in the east and south, of low plateau, eight hundred to more than one thousand feet in altitude, deeply dissected by valleys leading to the Ohio and the Wabash. In the central and northwestern areas the ground is lower and often a true plain, but, except about one-eighth of the state, is not a prairie, any more than Ohio, and was largely covered in early days with heavy and luxuriant forests, mainly of a hardwood type.

Illinois is prairie, for here La Salle found the open meadows with rank herbage and deep black soil, with shallow valleys and sluggish rivers, which belong to the name. Nor are trees absent, but as a rule they border the rivers, growing upon their flood plains and fringing their banks with sprawling roots and overhanging foliage. If we cross the Mississippi River, Iowa is much like Illinois, for these, more than all others, are the prairie states.

We will not vex ourselves with the unanswered question, whether the forestless condition was due to Indian burnings, or to qualities of soil or climate, for it is more to our purpose to see how the lands were ready for the plow, were suited to rapid occupation, and were overswept by waves of human life in a small fraction of the time required to clear the forests and grub among the boulders of the New England uplands.

FIG. 30. Low Bluffs in Union Township, Iowa. Characteristic Distribution of Native Trees, the South and Southwest Slopes being Bare. Photograph by Professor Samuel Calvin.

When we have crossed the Mississippi River at about five hundred feet above the sea, we begin to rise again, and in central and northwestern Iowa find ourselves more than one thousand feet in altitude. If we cross the Missouri into Nebraska, we rise still more, on the gentle, prolonged incline that will take us up to the base of the Rocky Mountains. As we approach the central portions of Nebraska the rainfall decreases, and the cornfields give way to less luxuriant pasture lands. Here, in a rough way, we may say that the prairies end. There is no change in the forms of the land, but only a change in climatic condition. Thus we see how difficult it is to bound geographic areas; and yet the geographer is right in distinguishing the Alleghany plateau, the prairies, and the Great Plains. But the language made necessary by usage is misleading. Ohio stands less than a thousand feet above the sea, but it is dissected by valleys and joined to higher areas on the east, and we call it plateau. The arid region, beginning in central Nebraska and Kansas, is three thousand feet and upward in altitude, but is little dissected, and is called the Great Plains. We may better follow, however, the newer name, High Plains. If it were not pedantic, we could say the undissected plateau east of the Rocky Mountains. The prairies again are always rather smooth lands, with shallow valleys, but some are lower and some are higher, while the name especially denotes watered and fertile areas in the forestless condition. Thus we have, in outline, an east and west profile of the central Mississippi region.

Missouri, to a line somewhat south of its great
river, is much like the adjoining parts of Iowa.
Using our definition of prairies, as a flat country,
nearly forestless, but well enough watered for agriculture, we may carry the belt through southwestern
Wisconsin, and across southern and western Minnesota and the eastern Dakotas.

Over all this region, from Ohio into Nebraska and
from the Ohio River through Minnesota, the Mississippi River holds sway.   The single exceptions are
the Lake slopes of the Ohio River states, and the
valley of the Red River of the North.   In its drainage, therefore, the region has unity.   It is a surface
also beneath which lie, everywhere, sheets of ancient
sandstone, limestone, and shale, referred by the geologist to ʼthe Paleozoic era.   Rarely are these beds
disturbed, or in any way modified, except by the slow
changes that have consolidated the muds into hard
rocks, and raised them by continental movements a
few hundred feet above the level of the sea.   Long-
continued denudation has stripped away the upper
sheets to an unknown degree, and planed the rocks
down to the strata that remain, and over which the
products of rock decay and the glacial waste have
been deposited.   Thus the character and structure of
the foundation rocks also lend unity to the region.

All New England shows the effects of glaciation.
This is true also of most of the lands with which we
are now concerned, but with this important difference,
that here the glacial sheets accomplished their wear
and spread their waste upon a comparatively even
surface.   Some very smooth lands in Iowa, Illinois,

and in northern Indiana and Ohio, are made so by
the even spreading, under the ice sheet, of a thick
bed of till, or boulder clay, which is the most widespread deposit of a great glacier. Often, too, the ice
front lay along a smooth surface, and the streams
flowing from it were sluggish, and wandered hither
and thither, interlocking with each other, and building up wide-spreading aprons of washed clays and
sands. Frequently, where the ice front lay for a
long time, belts of hills, or terminal moraines, were
formed, and now stand as the most conspicuous reliefs of a flat and often monotonous country.   In
parts of southern Iowa and northern Missouri the
glacial cover is a clayey loam, with a peculiar vertical
cleavage, and known as loess, similar to formations
found in the Rhine Valley and in interior China.   By
the glacial and associated deposits, the till and sands,
the waterlaid clays and the loess, the bed rocks may be
completely mantled over for long distances, giving
the particularly smooth and unrelieved aspect of much
of the prairie region.

But in these spreading mantles of rock waste, we
find the secret of the soils.   They have not lain on
steep slopes of hill or mountain, where their finest
and most available nutritive materials were washed
away into the sea, but all the gains of weathering and
vegetable accumulations have been hoarded through
the thousands or tens of thousands of years of post-
glacial time.   As the surfaces were relatively smooth
before the ice swept in, there was less plucking and
dropping of large stones and boulders, and hence
these do not, as in rougher glacial lands, dissipate the

strength of the plowman and the harvester.   Nor is
energy consumed in tilling steep hillsides.   We
have already had reason to see that the drainage of
the Great Lakes once went down the St. Croix, the
Wisconsin, the Illinois, and the Wabash rivers, and
that the Ohio River is far other than it was before
the ice invasion.   Important changes, too, were
wrought in the upper Mississippi.

A most surprising fact about the ice sheets was
that none of them covered southwestern Wisconsin.
Here is a region, ten thousand miles in area, which is
like the Blue Grass region of Kentucky, or like any
other region outside of the glacial belt, in showing
none of the characteristic proofs of glacial action.
Its soils are not made from the drift, but by the decay
of the underlying rock, while the ice sheets closed
completely around it in Iowa and Illinois.   It is not
proved, however, that the ice was all around it at
the same time.   There may have been successive en-
croachments, now on the east, and now on the west,
of the "driftless area."

It is known that some areas of original prairie have
been reforested in Indiana since occupation by the
white man began.   It appears also that some districts
in Kentucky had been brought to the prairie condition shortly before civilized society took possession of
the ancient hunting-grounds.   So far, these facts are
favorable to the view that the prairies are mainly due
to fires kindled by the native inhabitants of the land.
Certain it is that the horizon is more and more broken
by woodlands, and that the beauty of the luxuriant
ancient meadows will be in some measure restored

in forest and field with the development of an older civilization.

The prairies have their features of climate, and they are as sharp and peculiar as may be found in New England and on the Pacific coast. With little interruption there are lowlands from the Gulf of Mexico to the Arctic Sea. When south winds prevail, the heated air of the tropical belt sweeps unhindered up the Mississippi and Ohio valleys, and the summers are intensely hot in Cincinnati and St. Louis, and they are not cool in Des Moines and St. Paul. For days at a time the thermometer in central Iowa may touch or pass one hundred degrees. And the north winds, in like fashion, take their turn, and bring the extreme winter temperatures of the prairies far below zero. The cyclonic whirls which bring the warm and cold waves sweep from the northwest to the Atlantic coast, following each other throughout the year, and most frequently and fiercely in the winter months. And in these conditions of swift movement of enormous masses of the atmosphere, develops, in the summer months, the dreaded tornado. It is a land of climatic extremes, but the summer heat, with sufficient rainfall and rich soil, brings great harvests, and the tonic of winter's cold is the more efficient because of the drier air that is characteristic of a continental interior. This is more true west of the Mississippi River, where the summer conditions are more favorable than they are in the Ohio River belt.

The prairies display most of their natural riches in the form of soils, a true product of the rocks that lie below. Silver and gold have they none, save as they gain them by exchange for the wealth of their limitless fields. Nor in general have they iron or other metallic stores. But they have one resource of the under-earth that will mean more and more as their industrial life becomes mature, — they possess, in thousands of square miles, beds of soft coal. In large measure the men of the prairies can afford to plow while others turn spindles and build chimneys, but there must also be some place for the town and the mill. Of waterpower nature has been sparing in this land of low levels and little relief, but she has been generous with her stores of fuel, and hence the central West will not be given over to a monotony of cornfields and grain drills, of threshing-machines and elevators. She can have, in some degree, the diversity which will provide for both her wealth and her culture.

If we consider the people that were to work out its destiny, the Northwest Territory was unoccupied at the close of the War of Independence. There was no settled community of white men in what is now the state of Ohio; unless, indeed, the Moravian missionary settlements of 1772 be counted an exception. But this entire region was in the track of the great migrations of the next thirty years, and its soil and its rivers attracted the first and larger share of these early colonists. Extending from the Lake to the Ohio River, Ohio must be the avenue of all who crossed the Appalachian barrier north of the Cumberland Gap. If they came by the Mohawk Valley, they would skirt the southern shore of the Lakes and

enter Ohio on the north.   If they followed the roads
laid out in Maryland and Pennsylvania, they would
touch the Ohio River at Pittsburg or Wheeling, and
enter the region from the south.   The first immigrants followed the latter route, for they went out
under the Ohio Company, and in 1788 took possession

FIG. 31.   River Front at Cincinnati.

of the land where the Muskingum from the north
enters the Ohio River.   Fort Harmer had already
been built on the west side of the smaller river, and
the settlers occupied the east bank and founded Marietta.   As with other communities transplanted from
the East, the traditions of the old home were strong,
and the sons of the pioneers, in 1833, founded the
school which soon became the Marietta College, thus
naturalizing, so far as they could, the spirit of Harvard and Yale on the Ohio River.

Blockhouses were built at Losantiville in 1780, and settlers later came in from New England, New Jersey, and the South. This was far down the Ohio, almost to the mouth of the Miami. This outpost in the western wilderness was soon to be known as Cincinnati; and Moses Cleaveland, a few years later, planted the northern center of the Ohio region at the mouth of the Cuyahoga. By the year 1803 so many people had come in that Ohio was admitted as a state in the Union, and the empire between the Lakes and the Ohio was fairly begun; but it seemed to be thriving at the expense of the East. When foreign trade was active, the people employed, and money plenty, the rush to the West fell off. But when stagnation ruled on the seaboard, the farmers, mechanics, and laborers sold their homes, gathered up what they could, took their children and their goods, in wagons, in carts, and on their backs, and began their weary march from Maine, Massachusetts, Connecticut, and the central Atlantic country to the land of promise beyond the mountains. There fields could be had for little more than the clearing and tilling, there the soil had unheard-of richness, there they would not be put in prison for debt, and there they and their children could start life afresh.

McMaster has gathered from many sources the records and incidents of this early rush across New York and Pennsylvania.[1] From a little Pennsylvania village on the road to Pittsburg, it was reported that a month in 1811 saw the passage of two hundred and thirty-six wagons, with nearly two thousand per-

[1] " History of the People of the United States," IV, Ch. XXXIII.

sons, toward Ohio. Similar stories were told from Auburn and elsewhere in New York. Mount Pleasant in Ohio, from a trivial beginning in 1810, had five hundred people five years later. One hundred and twenty people, from one town in Maine, passed Haverhill, Mass., in a single day, and the westward movement not only stirred the East with fear, but took such proportions in Great Britain as there also to arouse alarm.

In the clearing of the forest, in the rude log-cabin, in the poverty of food and clothing, and in all the hardships of the frontier, the early days of Ohio compare with New York or Massachusetts. It was not a prairie state which could be overrun with a plow in a decade.[1]

Almost the same story is to be told of Indiana, but it came a little later. She already had a populous settlement on the Wabash, but its interest was in the past rather than the future. In her present territory there were twenty-five hundred settlers in 1800; but there were twenty-four thousand in 1810, and seventy thousand in 1816, when she came to statehood. The state had been entered along the three great lines of movement, controlled by geographic features, and now become familiar to us. The first was along the Mohawk Valley and the Lakes, and the stream was soon to become a flood, with the finishing of the Erie Canal. The second approach was by the new National Road, crossing the Ohio River at Wheeling, marked along its course in Ohio by Zanesville, Colum-

---

[1] The story is well told by King, "Ohio," in "American Commonwealths," Ch. XI.

bus, and Springfield, and entering Indiana at Richmond. The third entrance was from the Kentucky and Cumberland settlements, crossing the Ohio River and coming in on the south.

Illinois had about the same white population in 1800 as her eastern neighbor, and was but two years behind in her admission to the Union, since this took place before the close of 1818. It was but a step to cross the Mississippi. There had long been on its western banks a mongrel population of Spaniard, French, Indians, and negroes, and St. Louis had been a fur-trading post since 1764. But the great inrush followed upon the Louisiana Purchase of 1803, the year in which Lewis and Clark set out from St. Louis on their western exploration. But here, as north of the Ohio, the permanent settlers came from the East. That East, however, was not all on the Atlantic slope, for the sons of the Kentucky backwoodsmen were moving on. More than that, and as if typical of the march westward, Boone himself crossed the Mississippi, lived many years, and in 1820 died on the borders of the Missouri River.

In 1819 Jacob Astor made St. Louis the center of his western fur trade, and in 1821, after stormy times, Missouri became a member of the Union.

At length the stream of population crossed the Mississippi farther to the north and laid the foundations of Iowa. Once a part of Louisiana, later under the wing of Michigan and then of Wisconsin, she was herself to surrender Minnesota and the Dakotas, and in 1846, ten years before a railway crossed the Mississippi, join the sisterhood of states. Iowa has been called Mesopotamia, and another river crossing set the home seekers over the Missouri, and sent them on the long up-stream trails, by the Platte and the Missouri, that have peopled Nebraska and the Dakotas, and carried the dominion of man to the foot of the western mountains. We may call it about an even century from the time when Boone struck into the Ohio Valley to the day when populous states filled the basin of the Mississippi.

In the eighteenth century the long struggle for the Northwest lay between the East and the Northeast. From the latter realm on the St. Lawrence it had been ruled first by the French and then by the British, with the always uncertain savage now in one balance and then in another. George Rogers Clark, at Kaskaskia and Vincennes, drove the wedge that split the Northwest from the Northeast, and the settlers that poured through the gateways of the Appalachians cemented it to the young nation on the east.

It has been left for the nineteenth century to see whether the prairie country would be tied by the closer bonds to the East or the South, and the answer is not yet given. On the whole, geography favors the South, and there are signs that she may win, or at least divide the spoils of commerce. In those older days, when the frontier was on the western slopes of the Alleghany plateau, both the East and the West shared in the fight for freedom. In the East the more disciplined armies of the thirteen colonies fought the armies of Great Britain. In the West the fiercer fighters of the backwoods won the lowlands of the Mississippi in the critical inch of time that saved the interior for the Republic. There was enough to do; there was a common foe, and no time for jealousy. But when the war was over, the problems of statehood and of commerce presented themselves, and the Appalachian barrier and the trend of Mississippi waters asserted their power. The conservative East felt that the seaboard had won the struggle, and that her wisdom and her sound judgment were not to be sacrificed to the rough instincts and growing vote of the untutored men across the mountains.

It was not easy to persuade Virginia, in the first years of peace, that she should voluntarily release her subjects, as she regarded them, across the mountains. Nor was it a light task in the face of Indian outbreaks, and the real or supposed neglect of the mother state, to check the self-reliant, and, in some cases, turbulent men, that were for breaking away and setting up an empire in Kentucky. All the motives were hammered to white heat by the talk of cutting off the navigation of the Mississippi. The cleared patches and prairie glades of the Ohio country were beginning to produce more than the hominy needed to feed the pioneer. The trails across the mountains might do as a toilsome road to come in by, but they were no highway to a market. New England and the East had no care about boating down the Mississippi. They would be content to preserve the favor of the king of Spain; but not so the Kentucky pioneer, who knew that the water flowed freely to the Gulf, who had timber for flatboats, and produce that he could market in New Orleans, but for a foreign king and a selfish New England. Nor was he

brought to calmness of spirit when one of his bold
fellows had taken a flatboat of flour and utensils
down the river, had seen it confiscated by Spanish
officers at Natchez, had toiled home by land, and had
spread over all the transmontane country the story of
his wrongs.   Such in brief were the conditions, and
they were chiefly geographic, that almost carried the
West and Southwest to Spanish intrigue and to sepa-
ration from the states that adopted the Constitution.

But in 1796 a treaty with Spain opened the trade
of the Mississippi River, and in 1803 this source of
possible disunion was removed by the purchase of
Louisiana.   But federal writers in the East rung
the changes on the folly and iniquity of this vast
expansion into remote and alien regions.   In particular was the extravagance of the purchase denounced;
fifteen millions of dollars for the South and the far
West!

When the wheels of statehood and of expansion
had been set upon their course, the problems of commerce still arose between the East and West, and
they still grew out of the physiography.   Water ran
downhill, and it was hard to make roads and drag
food and clothing and other things across mountains.
Hence arose those disturbed cries of Washington and
other statesmen of the East, for landways and waterways across the barrier, and thus followed that generation of way-making which has already engaged our
attention.   When steam had fully established itself
on the Ohio and the Mississippi, and the railroads
had not come, it would seem that the domain of New
Orleans and the South should be complete, and the

prairies become linked to the Gulf of Mexico. But there were at least two causes which threatened, and indeed almost destroyed, the growing and natural union of the north and south Mississippi country. One of these causes lay in the interests which led up by a long road to the Civil War, severing the two sections by loss of sympathy and by several years of actual hostility. The other was the construction of through lines of railway, along easy grades, with swift service, between the prairies and the seaboard. To this of course was added the growth of Lake commerce in connection with railways and canals, and the fact which counts for something, that the Atlantic ports are nearer Europe than are those of the Gulf. With these great unfoldings in the North has gone a relative decline in Mississippi River commerce, and of St. Louis, as compared with Chicago.

But will not the pendulum swing and carry the central states to their natural fellowship with their southern neighbors, giving to geographic conditions their proper control again? Not alone for men is the Mississippi Valley an open road. Professor Shaler has made reference to the resemblances of the animals and the plants for long distances north and south in that country, and to the alternate dominion of tropic heat and arctic cold. The harvesters follow ripening wheat fields from south to north, and the valley is marked out for unity and interchange. Not long hence the prairies may supply the Orient through an isthmian canal; and even a half-dozen years ago we were bidden to look upon the new commercial alliance of the West and the

South, along railways that will carry the surplus products of Nebraska, Kansas, and Oklahoma to Galveston or some other Gulf city by a haul five hundred
miles shorter than lies between any of these states
and the Atlantic. These projects will be immensely
favored as the South develops its manufactures and
can provide thus for a haul both ways, making railway traffic profitable, and so much cheaper South
than East, that the extra carriage by ship across the
Gulf need not be considered. This " probably means
decreased revenues for the eastern traffic lines and
the related industries, but unless the judgment of the
West is at fault, it means better times for the plains.
The East may as well realize that its child has come
to the years of maturity and is acting for itself." [1]
Galveston is nearer by more than two hundred miles
to central Iowa than is New York, and there are not
wanting signs that here also the north and south
lines of movement will in the end be lines of control.
Whatever the adjustment be, it will be achieved in
another generation, but the prophet may well be
cautious, in view of the unforeseen and unforeseeable
expansion of artificial waterways.

Passing by the hundred years of fugitive French
and British occupation, we may say that the whole
West is a product of four generations: it has grown
since the War of Independence, and the oldest state
north of the Ohio River, reaches this year its hundredth birthday. There is no history here, in the
ordinary sense of the term; we have no perspective
when we look back, for we are yet in the midst of

[1] Charles Moreau Harger, *No. Amer. Rev.*, CLXV, 383, 1897.

things; and difficult as it always is to separate geographic from other causes, here our perplexities are multiplied, for there has not been time to work out the problems, or, if we may say it, such has been the stirring, that the waters have had no time to clear and let us look to the bottom.

It has been lately said that the East is not the parent of the West, that New England and New York need not boast of so lusty a child, for the South is the real mother. But this is rhetoric, no doubt pleasant to the writer, and as full of fallacy as rhetoric often is. The door was opened by the South, if it was the South that lived on the Holston, the Kentucky, and the Cumberland, and sent forth Boone, Robertson, Sevier, and George Rogers Clark. But we have followed the streams of western migration with little attention, and have read the story of the Mississippi Valley to little purpose, if we do not see that the later fabric, warp and filling, was woven from the East. It was New England and New York that were transplanted to Ohio, Illinois, and Iowa. But Ohio and Iowa did not become a second New England. The stress of a thousand miles of change will strain the most rigid institutions and mold custom and thought into new shapes, even though the material is much the same. Some things were unconsciously lost in the journey along the Seneca Turnpike or the Erie Canal, and other things were as unwittingly taken on from the soil and free air of the prairies. There were no hills to confine the view, and by a very old law, if newly recognized, a change of environment was modifying ancient organs and unfolding new ones. The East is the parent of the West, but children are different from their parents, and not seldom outgrow them. "Blue laws" could hardly flourish in Illinois, where an exhaustless soil bloomed with glorious color in native meadows, only waiting for the plow to yield a more substantial harvest. Nor were there veins of gold or silver, to lure thousands of daring adventurers and herd them in mushroom cities, where restraint would be abandoned and the worst passions would thrive unhindered. Rather, from the crowded nursery, with its thin soil and doubtful climate, there was a great transplanting, and the prairies gave depth and room and sunlight.

We may take Iowa as a typical prairie commonwealth. Down to 1840 her place in the census is a blank: then she records a little more than forty thousand people; by 1860 she had gained a population of nearly seven hundred thousand, and at the close of the century was the tenth state in the Union, with more than two millions. With this throng of inhabitants, she has one city that passes the limit of sixty thousand. But three others exceed thirty thousand: Iowa is a rural state. A recent writer has perhaps done full justice to the virtues and to the limitations of Iowa:[1] "She is a huge overflow meeting, thronged with the second generation of middle-westerners." So uniform and rich are her soils that scarce an acre in the whole domain need run to waste. Tillage was easy, and the only serious trials in the early days were the prairie fires and the difficult transportation. The latter was solved, as it

[1] "The Iowans," R. L. Hartt, *Atlantic Monthly*, 1900.

seemed, by the railways; but when the short hauls became more costly than the long ones, Iowa "went to grass," saved her soils from running out, and so concentrated her grains into beef and butter that she suffered less at the hands of the railways, and had still before her, as we have seen, an open way to the

FIG. 32. Shade on the Prairies. Cottonwoods in Iowa.

ports on the Gulf. Our writer brings to us another's epitome of Scotland, — "Scott, Burns, heather, whisky, and religion," — and then gives us his own for Iowa, "corn, cow, and hog." But we will not let him be misunderstood. He does not charge this great commonwealth with dirt and materialism. She may have no history and not yet any material for fiction, but "industry, morality, intelligence, and loyalty," these are hers; and "when your soul is bent upon finding a

happy augury for your country's future, what better
can you seek?"

Such traits we may ascribe in part to the type of
men and women that would be attracted to such a
land to found a home, and in part to steady fellowship with the soil and sky, remote from cities, and
set apart to simple and single interests. But the
growth of railways did not merely bring an outlet for
surplus hoards of grain; it brought inevitable contact
with the outside world, and the prairies have not been
behind in their crop of social and political ideas. No
state in the last generation has been more prolific
of public men than Iowa. Prevalent agriculture and
the absence of mountains do not mean sordid purpose
or narrow vision. The prairies have their own ex-
pansiveness and may lure the eye to the horizon
when older countries are looking at their own garden
patch. A cluster of great universities has grown in
the states of the old Northwest. Nowhere has the
state fostered the higher education with so steady
and so generous a hand. And the small colleges,
often too small and too many, have expressed and
met the needs of the time, and the fittest will survive.
A score of others might be named where we choose
one, once a small college, now grown large, — Ober-
lin, a type of the western school, preserving the in-
tegrity and faith of New England, and truly western
in its free, modern organization of courses of education.

In political ideas, also, the prairies have not seldom
shown the freedom and erratic energy of the frontier,
but have invariably swung toward the poise and
secure verdicts that are at once as sound and safe as

those of the East, and yet have in them the promise of the future and the courage of action. At first the westerner belonged to the debtor class, and if conditions pressed, he was restless and radical, and impatient with the lenders of the East. It is the land of summer heat and winter cold, with a tornado now and then thrown in, prairie breaths of populism and fiat money, but in the end a nursery of ideas, sound and progressive, outgrowing the vagaries of an infant state, but free from the satisfied conceit and sullen cocksureness of older communities. The man of the prairie is ready for action at home or abroad, balanced by a reasonable culture and poised by an experience whose lessons he does not leave to be learned by his grandsons. Mr. Frederick J. Turner in an excellent discussion of "The Problem of the West,"[1] quotes the assertion of Mr. Bryce, "the West is the most American part of America," and admits that there is force in the claim that if there is a sectionalism in this country, it is eastern; for "the old West, united to the new South, would produce, not a new sectionalism, but a new Americanism."

If we could follow the details of history in these central states, the illustrations of physiographic control would perhaps be as common as they are in New England or New York, unless for this reason, that along the railroads of the prairies towns have been laid out with reference to convenient intervals and sometimes in the complete absence of determining local features. No town was ever so fortunate in a change of name as Cincinnati, whose early appella-

[1] *Atlantic Monthly*, September, 1896.

tion was the unhappy invention of a schoolmaster, L(icking)os-antiville, a thrice mongrel compound, meaning the town opposite the mouth of the Licking.

Like every town by the water, it has come to be the center of many railways, and will retain its greatness though it must now divide its honors with the city by the Lakes. Columbus has no conspicuous geographic causes lying behind its prosperity. It is indeed on the Scioto, it is in the midst of a rich region, but most of all, it is in the center of a rich state and is its capital. It is in part, therefore, due to political causes, and may be briefly dismissed by the geographer. The state has twenty-eight towns of more than ten thousand people, and is thus full of such local centers of trade as must always develop in a great agricultural state. The same is true of Indiana and every upper Mississippi commonwealth. Indianapolis, indeed, is much smaller than the twin cities of Ohio, but added more than sixty thousand to her numbers in the last decade. Like Columbus, she is on a small river, the geographical and political center of a great state, and sends her railways in every direction. Louisville had its beginning in a ledge of limestone in the bed of a river, and in the need of portage, at low water, around the rather high-sounding "Falls of the Ohio." It is a river town, therefore, as well as the metropolis of a state.

St. Louis cannot run in the race with the city by Lake Michigan, yet may hope for great and permanent development as a river town. She is on the Mississippi; is almost at the mouth of the Missouri;

is on the future highway between the prairies and the Gulf, and is in the line of traffic moving between the far Northeast and the far Southwest, and she is at the same time the chief city of a state. Save for Chicago, Illinois is a state of local communities of modest size, and Wisconsin has no interior town of thirty thousand people. These conditions are altogether favorable

FIG. 33. Library and Campus of the University of Nebraska.

for the growth of a strong and clean civilization, saved from the dearth of rural life by the school, the free delivery of mails, and every other means of constant and swift communication. Minnesota has no population centers that compare with Minneapolis and St. Paul, though Duluth, with her fifty thousand people, is a rival in the volume of her business. Aside from these three, Minnesota has but two towns of more than ten thousand people, and is distinctly a rural commonwealth.

Across the river from Iowa is Nebraska, and Omaha its metropolis. It represents the second tier of states beyond the Mississippi, prairie on the east and arid on the west. It is like its eastern neighbor in its soils, — fine, deep, level, and easily tilled, — and in its dominant agriculture, for its factories are yet to be built. Like Iowa, Nebraska has learned to pasture some of its lands, but here the division is a geographic or climatic one. She found to her sorrow that corn could not regularly be grown west of the middle of the state, and hence adjusted herself to environment, by pasturing the west and plowing the east ; and like Iowa, also, she is learning the routes that lead southward, and the bulk of her corn goes to New Orleans. Typical of the progress of this young and physically monotonous state, her state University gathers at Lincoln two thousand of her sons and daughters, and takes no place inferior to cattle or corn in the hearts of the citizen of the plains.

CHAPTER VI

COTTON, RICE, AND CANE

IF any reader is disposed to think a blunder has been made in choosing a head-line, no offense will be taken and no defense made. Grain, lumber, and iron would do just as well, and perhaps better, and both together would be better still, for they tell us at the beginning of the old South and the new. Never until now has nature rightly had her way in the Gulf country, but she is fast winning her hold, and that process of adjustment of man to the earth, which takes place in all lands, is here coming about in a day.

The Atlantic plains of tide-water Virginia continue through the Carolinas and merge with like plains about the Gulf. They seem to be separate from each other because the long peninsula of Florida runs so far down into the half-tropical seas, making an outside and an inside realm. But, in a general way, a description of Virginia or South Carolina would answer for Alabama or Texas; for all have outer lowlands and inner uplands. The uplands differ greatly in height and character. South Carolina has little mountain land like Virginia, and no great plateaus like Texas, but they all have the coastal plain, and to the geologist the coastal plain is young, wherever found. Its beds are undisturbed, its surfaces are low and flat, its rocks are soft, and its rivers often entered by the tides.

The characteristic South of the old days has grown upon this lowland belt, bordering the sea. South Carolina would be as good an example as we could find, for her rivers cross the Piedmont plateau, and, on a dividing line about five hundred feet above the sea, enter the plain belt, and reach the open sea through tidal inlets. The coastal plain makes two-thirds of the state and is more than twice as large as Massachusetts.

In many ways the local life and industries have long been fitted to the land. Sea-island cotton, rice, and truck farming find their place on the marshy plains and low islands of the coast. Between the plain and the plateau is a belt of sandy country, twenty miles wide or more, and the "sand-hillers" live in ignorance and share the poverty of the soil. The "black belt" is along the seaboard plain, for here the cotton, rice, and indigo were grown which made slave labor profitable, often a toil in swamps which the white man was unwilling or unable to endure. Here the blacks vastly outnumber the whites, while in the colder northwest corner of the state, with its poorer soil, its cooler climate, and its absence of rice and cotton, the whites are threefold more numerous than the colored people.

As in the North Carolina lowlands, the railways often run straight toward their destination, as unhindered by physiographic barriers as on the plains of Nebraska. The shore-line of South Carolina, broken like that of Virginia, drew the colonists and gave dis-

Fig. 34.   Avenue of Live Oaks, Savannah, Georgia.

tinction to its early history.   Even if Florida had not
been under Spanish rule, she was farther away, and
her eastern coast-line was less inviting to emigrants
from the more northern peoples of Europe.   Georgia
was a kind of afterthought to South Carolina, as population extended across the Savannah River westward.

North Carolina is as rich in the gifts of her plains
and mountains as her neighbors on the north and
south.   She has fields, forests, and genial climate,
but these counted for little at first, for the land does
not present the right front to the sea.   The long
sand reef, that culminates in Hatteras, and the fitful
seas outside cut off easy approach to the mainland.
North Carolina, before the colony passed from the
proprietary to the royal authority in 1729, was for
the most part a resort for the poorer and less intelligent colonists who came to the greater northern
neighbor.   She was, as Fiske has described her, a
kind of backwoods appendage to Virginia.   Even at
this early time, however, "more substantial stuff,"
as Lodge [1] says, was joining the emigrants.   They
were in part Presbyterian, from Jamestown, settling
on the Chowan.   And after 1729, the best kind of
emigrants, mainly liberty-loving Dissenters, came in
from the northern neighbors and from across the sea.
But during the proprietary period, ignorance, thrift-
lessness, and disorder mainly reigned, and it took the
colony years to recover from the unhappy conditions
of its early days.

Florida is altogether a part of the coastal plain,
with its low-lying lands and its thousand miles of sea-

[1] H. C. Lodge, "Short History of the English Colonies."

coast.   Nowhere is there a surface more than a few
hundred feet above the level of the sea, and all of its
rocks belong to late periods of geological time.   From
the geologist's point of view, one does not go far back
to find the Atlantic shore sweeping around by the
Fall Line through South Carolina and Georgia into
Alabama, leaving vast tracts of open ocean, where
Florida now lies.   The old sea bottom has been
raised, by the broadest and lowest sort of an arch
that can be imagined, to form the wide, flat peninsula
that now divides the Gulf of Mexico from the Atlantic
waters.   Physically so youthful, it is also by far the
youngest of the Atlantic states in the growth of civilization, even though the oldest civilized settlement
in the United States is on its eastern shore.   But this
backwardness has no physiographic origin, unless in
the rather roundabout reason that the seas brought
the Spaniard here for a long and repressive rule.
Great Britain held Florida for a few years before and
after the war of the Revolution, and in spite of her
awkward handling of her American colonies is cred-
ited with more advance for Florida than the Spaniard
made in two hundred years.   No doubt many who
have looked with keen feeling upon American doings
in Cuba have forgotten, or never knew, that Spain
ceded Florida to the United States as late as the year
1821.   Great towns have always been few in the
South, and Florida is in this more southern than most
of her neighbors, for she has but four communities of
more than five thousand people.   Tampa, Pensacola,
and Key West range from fifteen thousand to eighteen thousand, and the metropolis is Jacksonville, with

a little less than thirty thousand, but known far beyond most northern towns of its own size.

That the town will give way to the country in Florida for a long time, and perhaps for all time, may well be believed. She has little water-power, few mineral deposits, and no coal. The only doubtful element would seem to be in her commercial opportunities, which may be very great in the changes that are coming in and about the American Mediterranean. The geographer meets a full share of exceptions to his rules, and one of these comes to light in the flat stretches of this peninsula. He is likely to say that thousands of lakes betoken the recent invasion of ice. But no ice invasion has touched Florida, — nothing colder than killing frosts, — and yet the lakes, in thousands, are here, due, it seems, to the solvent action of water upon the soft limestones of the upraised sea-floor.

And when one goes along the sluggish rivers and lagoons that lie back of the low barriers of the shore, or tries to pierce the thickets of the Everglade swamps, or sees the mangroves dropping their pendent branches to root in the shallow water, or counts the coral keys that link Key West to the mainland, he knows that he is seeing a continent in the making, he has caught the weaver at his work, and about him lies a new fabric, with an unfamiliar stitch and a fresh pattern.

And after all, Florida is not so much unlike the other commonwealths of the South. She is a little more tropical, but is not singular in the fields of cotton, cane, and corn, or in the enormous forests of live

FIG. 35.   Orange Grove, Florida.   Photograph by Wm. H. Rau, Philadelphia.

oak and pine that afford about half of the annual product of the region. Oranges and pineapples are a little more her own. Florida is something more than a sanitarium for Northern victims of consumption and nervous prostration. The North regards Florida as a comfortable refuge from the blizzards and cold fogs of what is often called spring in those higher latitudes, but when the overcoat has been thrown off, the tourist among the live oaks and drooping mosses may not detect the thrill of business and of new thought that has reached this Land's End. Alligators and even orange orchards are not likely to monopolize a state which has a thousand miles of indented shore-line and thirty-five hundred miles of railroad, with warm skies, rich soil, and plentiful rainfall.

Geologists are familiar with an ancient outline of our southern shore, which comes to mind when mention is made of the Mississippi embayment. This means that sea-waters covered the regions of the lower Mississippi as far north as the mouth of the Ohio River, while a great peninsula of older Appalachian land came down as far as middle Alabama and Georgia. On the west, too, older lands reached into Arkansas. The southern half of all the Gulf states, and all of Florida, had not yet come into being, and the broad, deep gulf of the Mississippi included parts of Tennessee, Kentucky, and Arkansas. Two great lobes of ancient land flanked the embayment. This gulf has filled up, the whole shore-line has moved southward by half the width of the southern tier of states, and Florida is a new land thrown in. And all this young land is coastal plain, continuous around to

New Jersey.   There is one exception worth mention, and that is the lowland bordering the Mississippi River.   In the old days of the embayment the delta of the Mississippi lay below the site of Cairo ; and it has been moving a little farther south ever since that time.   The older sea muds of the delta region have been covered up by the muds that came from the prairies and the Rocky Mountains, so that if we dig or bore in the delta we should be apt to find wood and seeds and bones from the land, while if we dig farther west or east we shall find marine shells and other organic growths of the sea.

The Appalachian uplands are even now like a peninsula, — they are a mass of mountain and plateau, reaching out into a plain.   In the peninsula the rocks are either folded, or at least much uplifted and hard.   In the plain the beds are flat and low and soft.   The typical South is this never ending stretch of coastal plain ; the opportunity of the South is in its closeness to the useful things on and in the earth within the upland.

In the old days the Arkansas River had its own opening into the sea, and so also did the Red, and whatever represented the Tennessee.   But as the gulf filled up, and the edge of the sea was pushed southward, these rivers were joined to the main trunk, so that the Mississippi was growing, roughly speaking, like a tree, at its roots, at its outmost boughs, and by the grafting on of full-grown branches.

Every great river in its lower course spreads down much of the waste that it has gathered in its upland flow.   Some of the mud sinks, regardless of the slack current, far within the banks, and the rest goes out to sea. Every overflow carries the waste widely out on the bottom-lands and builds them up, — the flood plains of the river. The Mississippi has its thousands of miles of these bottom-lands, sloping off from the edge of the river, which drops more waste close by than it does farther away, and, by silting its bed, comes at length to flow on a broad, low ridge of its own making. So we can understand how a break in a levee sends the waters rushing over vast fields of the lower lands.

Of the ten Southern states that border the sea, three, Louisiana, Mississippi, and Florida, belong almost wholly to the coastal plain, and they are throughout low, flat, and young, while all the rest share in the older uplands that lie behind. The average elevation of Louisiana is seventy-five feet, and no point within the state is five hundred feet above the sea. There are twenty thousand miles of river lands, and coast swamps and shallow lakes abound, either lagoons shut off from the Gulf by low barriers, or cut-off lakes left by the wide migrations of the fitful river upon its flood plain and delta. As we might expect in such a land, Florida has but one mineral of importance, — the phosphates; and Louisiana likewise has one, — rock-salt.

The lower Mississippi was to see many changes before it should come to its final place as the southern gateway of a modern and united nation. The Spaniard would come to it first, and, yielding it more than once to the French, would release his final claim almost three hundred years later. Twice after it became, in 1803, a part of the American Union it would be the scene of bloody strife, and only now, as the twentieth century is coming in, is the Louisiana country entering upon the heritage which nature has always held in trust for it. Thus far the accidents of foreign intrigue and the bonds of a social system have laid their restraints upon the land. But now the Gulf plains will be joined to the prairies, the adjoining seas are held in friendly and progressive keeping, the isthmus is to be opened, and New Orleans should become a southern rival of the ports of the East.

The French stamp now borne by the region was given to it in 1700, when Iberville came from the North and planted his colony. La Salle had tried to do what his later countryman did, and in the attempt had come to his tragic end. In the North and in the South, from Minnesota to the Gulf, this race has left the marks of its enterprise and daring, but nowhere has the impress been so deep and so lasting as in New Orleans. Thirty-eight years of Spain, from 1762 to 1800, made little difference, and then Louisiana came back by secret treaty to France, only to be transferred by Napoleon to the new power in the West in 1803.

The Exposition at St. Louis will commemorate this sale, and will, perhaps, recall to some that the Louisiana of that bargain was a narrow strip as now on the Gulf, but widened on the Red River, leaped westward again along the Arkansas, and then took in everything between the Mississippi River and the Rocky Mountains up to the British boundary.

The backwoodsmen of the Appalachians had won Kentucky and then the prairies, and now had faced the issue which led to the acquirement of the west bank of the Mississippi and the Great Plains. If we had not bought this great land, we must in the end have fought for it, for a river is no natural boundary between peoples. It may be difficult to cross it in face of an enemy, and national pride may sigh for such a border, as France for the Rhine, but rivers join more than they divide, and tend to concentrate the life that resides upon their opposing slopes. When, therefore, Jefferson bought Louisiana first, and patched up the Constitution afterward, and, in the same year, sent Lewis and Clark to spy out the new estate and go to the Pacific, he was following the law of reason and of nature.

The river affects the life of the people in very direct ways, and, leaving out the phenomena of the atmosphere, is less easily subdued by man than any other natural feature of our domain. Many years ago Captain Eads devised and planted jetties at one of the mouths of the Mississippi, thus narrowing the channel, making the flow more rapid, and turning the waters into a kind of broom for the maintenance of navigation. Levees are built which restrain the flood, save in exceptional years, and the forewarning of the Weather Bureau adds another element of security to those who live below the level of the river waters. But we may well doubt whether man can ever harness the river with a sure hand. The Mississippi often flows beneath the bluffs that rise from her waters on the east. She has made these bluffs

Fig. 36. River Front, New Orleans.

by encroachment and undermining. Because bluff and stream adjoin each other at certain places, cities have grown at these eastern bends, — Memphis, Natchez, and Vicksburg. But the river is quite capable of forsaking her children by swinging widely to the westward, and it is at least an open question whether man could prevent, or afterward reverse, such a change. It is the willful behavior of the lower river, indeed, which brings in the only grave query as to the future water commerce of the Lake regions and the Gulf. About boats drawing a few feet of water there need be no fear, for skillful pilots from Mark Twain's day until now can "learn the river." Nor does New Orleans as a seaport depend upon the meanders of the stream, save as the produce of the north might in some measure be diverted along lines of rail to other Gulf centers.

Mr. Robert T. Hill, who, more than anyone else, has been the geographer of Texas, has drawn in a few strong lines a picture of her greatness. She is as large as France; or she is equal to the Eastern and Middle states, with Maryland, Kentucky, and Ohio thrown in. She has one-third of the Gulf coast of the United States, and to cross her territory from east to west by rail would accomplish one-third of the distance from Cape Hatteras to Cape Mendocino, or take one from New York to Savannah, Chicago, or Labrador.

In her broad stretch of coastal plain Texas is like other Gulf states. As the plains lead away into the interior they often are interspersed with belts rich in timber. And then the plains rise to vast plateaus, lofty and arid, bringing the state into relation with the high plains of Kansas and the north.   Still farther west Texas embraces an area three-fourths as large as New York, belonging to the southeastern Cordilleras, and culminating in mountains from ten thousand to thirteen thousand feet in height. Texas is therefore a southern and western state, ranging from sandy shore to lofty mountains, with almost every sort of soil, climate, and surface relief.

This vast land illustrates in its own way the progress of empire in America; colonized as a Mexican province by Austin with his emigrants from the north; won to national independence by Houston and his handful of frontiersmen, routing the Mexican army and capturing Santa Anna in a sharp battle lasting eighteen minutes; and coming nine years later, in 1845, freely into the American Union. This is within the remembrance of many who yet live, and marks the movement of our story into a region whose history lies in the future, and in whose bounds man is as yet far from his ultimate adjustment to nature.

The tilling of the soil made Southern history what it was down to the Civil War, and the growth of crops is a matter of soil and climate; it belongs, in other words, to geography.   But here also we must be careful not to charge too much to environment. The soils of the South do not shut one up to tobacco, cotton, sugar, and rice; and it was the conjunction of these with the holding of slaves that built up the social system that ruled so long under Southern skies. It was tobacco, which, in the plantations on the Rap-

pahannock and the James, first showed that Africans
could be imported with profit; and then followed the
cotton, rice, and cane, in those long belts of semi-
tropical lowland which came one after another
under the dominion of the colonists.   And the better
and worse phases of slavery seem also to have followed from geographic diversity; for in the planta-

FIG. 37.   Residences on the River Front, Charleston.

tions of Virginia the master lived on the plantation
where the slaves wrought, but among the rice and
often among the cotton fields of the black belt of
South Carolina and the Gulf the master was a non-
resident, the toil was severer, and irresponsible over-
seers were too often left to their own will.

In 1760 North Carolina had two hundred thousand
people, of whom one-fourth were slaves.   In South
Carolina conditions of freedom and servitude were re-

versed, — of one hundred and fifty thousand inhabitants, three-fourths were slaves.   The soil of the more
southern state was favorable to slave labor.

A chief outcome of this system of things was the
great plantation and the great plantation owner.   In
the cotton belt there could be few small holdings of
land, for only the large proprietor could keep a retinue
of slaves and grow cotton on a profitable scale.   The
planter was much like the feudal lord of older days
across the seas ; he was lord of hundreds or thousands of acres and of the human population dwelling
on them.   He commanded their service, and he gave
them protection, but whether the relation was kindly
or otherwise, it was still master and slave.   And inci-
dental to this plantation system there had to be another class, — the poor white.   He could not acquire
land, unless it were a plot of the poorer soil, or back
in the mountains ; and he could not rise in trade or
in mechanical industry, for trade was looked down
upon, and manufacture was either primitive and simple, and done on the plantation, or it was elaborate
and skilled, and its product brought from England or
New England, in return for consignments of cotton.

The Southern gentleman, generous, hospitable,
given to public affairs, often imperious and passion-
ate, brought the Old World pattern of society down to
the last generation in America.   Yet it would not be
true to say that the cavalier shaped the entire South.
No Southern state is more typical than South Carolina, and the early settlers of South Carolina were in
large measure Puritan, and "the economic circum-
stance which chiefly determined the complexion in

South Carolina was the cultivation of rice and indigo." [1]   The same writer asserts that a single slave
could in a year produce more value in rice or indigo
than it took to buy him.   Remembering human nature, and taking account of the times, the propulsion
toward slavery was strong.   But taking the South as
a whole, we must see that the ancestry of its colonists, the adaptation of its soil, and what we may call
the accidental beginnings of slavery, united in ways
that defy analysis to produce the old South.

The Southern system promoted the mastery and
strength of the few, and produced some towering
figures in the early and middle decades of the last
century.   The family was safeguarded and made permanent, as the sons of the fathers lived on the old
plantations and accumulated the ancestral advantages
of education, wealth, and social refinement.   " In the
placid air of their enlightened mediævalism lingered
the brave ideals of courage and beauty and gracious
dignity . . . and there arose an assertive, sensitive,
sincere, dauntless race of men, esteeming life less
than honor, and loyalty more than gold, who wrought
with a sad, Titanic sincerity for their doomed cause." [2]
This triangular social system could not develop the
riches of the South, for no measure of culture or personal power for the few could atone for the lack of a
sinewy, forehanded, and intelligent middle class, and
a great army of free, well-paid toilers in field, factory,
and mine, whose children might aspire to better things
than their fathers could achieve.

[1] Fiske, " Old Virginia and her Neighbors," II, 325.
[2] Edwin A. Alderman, *Educational Review*, II, 30.

The prevalence and independence of the great plantation, and the absence of an industrial class, caused in the old South a dearth of towns and town life. The men of wealth lived in the country, and for the poor the town had nothing to offer. No general statements can do justice to this condition of the

FIG. 38.   Cotton Levee, New Orleans.

South, and we shall have to deal a little in figures. Remembering that the towns have had their great growth since 1865, we will take the nine seaboard states from Virginia to Texas.

There is but one city that compares in size with Cleveland, Buffalo, Pittsburg, or Milwaukee; and New Orleans, with her present population of 287,000, has

gathered more than one-third of her people since
1870. With this exception there is no town of 100,-
000 people in the nine states, Richmond and Atlanta
coming nearest, with 85,000 and 90,000. In 1870 Atlanta had but 22,000, and before the opening of the
war she had less than 10,000 people. In this entire
chain of states there are 49 towns of more than 10,000
inhabitants, while Massachusetts has 47 such towns.
If we seek the totals in both cases of people residing
in such communities, the figures stand at 1,525,564
for the nine Southern states, and 2,050,862 for Massachusetts. If we now compare the paltry 8,000 square
miles of the New England commonwealth with the
637,000 miles of the nine, the result is little less than
astounding. There was vast elbow-room in the early
South, and there is still in the new, and a hundred
millions of people could live within the valleys and
on the wide plains of the old Confederacy.

As the holdings and the tillage of the land were at
the heart of the Southern social system, so the first
and greatest revolution came in this field at the close
of the Civil War. The freeing of the slaves greatly
reduced the property of all the plantation owners,
and through debts and enforced neglect of their
properties for four years, they afterward lost what
emancipation might otherwise have left them. They
thus could neither own, nor, in the absence of service,
till if they did own, great estates, and the lands were
in large measure sold and broken up into small
holdings, and the building of a new life upon an industrial as well as an agricultural foundation was
begun. The mill and the forge and coarse loom of

the plantation must now give way to the factory
and the furnace, and such towns must grow as meet
the traveler's eye in Connecticut or Pennsylvania.
Hence such cities as Atlanta, Columbia, Chattanooga, Knoxville, and Birmingham have sprung into
strength, feeling the thrill of new life that followed
upon the trying years of first adjustment to the new
conditions.

The isolation of the old South has departed with
the alien institution of slavery, and with it is passing
the conservative spirit that held the states of the
Gulf from onward movements of thought. Fiske
does not hesitate to say that more Puritanism lingers
in the South to-day than is left in New England, but
the young South is modern and will be so, as she develops the school, the mill, the farm, and the mine
with equal hand. Geographical causes have wrought
with power during the last generation to bring the
North and the South to common ways of thinking
and doing, and perhaps no fair and intelligent person
on either side of Mason and Dixon's Line would fail
to agree with a son of the South, the Honorable
Hoke Smith, Secretary of the Interior in Cleveland's
second administration, when he says, "Had it not
been for the institution of slavery, checking white
immigration and hindering development, the South,
with natural resources in its favor in 1860, would
have been the greatest manufacturing and mining, as
well as agricultural, section of the Union."

Nothing speaks more clearly of the new South
than the growth of cotton manufacture. As cotton
was first in the ancient system, so it may become in

the years of the future.   The mill owners of New
England do not fear what may be done in Manchester, or anywhere else across the Atlantic, but
they must take steady account of what is doing in
the Carolinas, Georgia, and Alabama.   Before the
nineteenth century closed, Massachusetts had sent a
commission to inquire into the cotton mills of South

FIG. 39.   Cotton Wharf from the Battery, Charleston.

Carolina.   The president of a Southern cotton mill
rings out no uncertain call to build up the business
of the home land: "Every bale of cotton produced
in Georgia should be spun in Georgia.   There is no
such thing as too many mills in the South so long as
a single bale of cotton is shipped to New England
or across the water."   Then he tells the Southern
farmer of his losses, when he sells cotton at $25 per
bale, and later brings it back in fabrics or garments

for three times the price, enriching the rich or feeding the distant poor, at the expense of those at home.

All that is lacking at the South is the skilled superintendents and operatives, and these are already available in large degree. The streams of the southern Appalachians will furnish perennial water-power, if indeed, as now seems likely, their forests are rescued and preserved. If water be lacking, coal is plentiful, and in many parts is near at hand. Labor will be abundant, when the colored population have had another decade of industrial training. In one of the new mill towns of the South, visited by a Northern writer, coal was bought at $1.50 per ton, while competitors in Massachusetts were paying three times that price and more. The saving in freights was $2 per bale; and while these figures are not the average, they point to enormous savings and untold economic gains for the Southern states, by following the simplest laws of geography, and using their superb facilities for working up the raw materials of the field, forest, and mine.

Cotton did not begin to take its place in Southern industry until 1880. In 1881 the exposition at Atlanta set the ball rolling. On one of the mornings of that summer, cotton was picked from the plant in sight of the fair grounds, spun, woven, and made into a suit, which appeared later in the day on the person of the governor of Georgia. Single establishments in Massachusetts now pay more in wages than did all the cotton mills of the South combined in 1880. But in 1900 there were more establishments in the South than in New England, 400 to 332.

This does not mean that the South is now first, for the concerns are smaller, but she grew from 610,000 spindles in 1880 to 4,298,000 in 1900. In the latter year her capital was $124,000,000, as against New England's $272,000,000; but her percentage of increase in the previous ten years was 131, and that of the older home of the industry was 12. The southern cotton crop of the early eighties was about doubled in the last years of the nineties.

But cotton is not king, though it may long be among the great single interests in the South. There is no larger factor in the present unfolding of the South than the diversification of her crops. The wasteful days, when cotton and tobacco wore out the soils, and these were abandoned for fresh fields, are over, and rotation and variety have come in to save the soils, fill up the wastes, give rich and poor a place, and develop the riches of the land to their utmost. There is as much variety of soil and air as in the North, and almost everything that can be raised north of the Ohio can be raised south of it, with a wealth of characteristic fibers, grains, fruits, and timbers thrown in. "Locations can be found in which wheat, corn, cotton, and fruit can be raised in the same field." [1]

It is the day of grain elevators in Galveston, wheat conventions in Georgia, and roller mills in South Carolina.

Thus the newer products are putting some of the older interests far in the rear, as sugar, which in Louisiana holds its place, and may always remain a landmark of the past, even while the product of the

[1] Hoke Smith, *North American Review*, 1894, Vol. CLIX, p. 134.

beet with strides is overtaking it. But another ancient crop still grows, in rice fields of increasing size,
cutting in half the importations of the grain, and rolling up to vast values in Louisiana and Texas. Here,
too, the South has felt the enlivening touch of modern
industry and practical science, for she has learned the
uses of irrigation and has largely made her gains
through the importation of a new variety of rice from
Japan, under the care of the Department of Agriculture. It would be rash to say that the South will
not grow her own and her neighbor's tea, and she is
releasing herself from the grip of the herders and
packers of the plains and prairies.

What more does the South need to warrant the
largest prophecy for her future? If it is lumber, she
has perhaps the largest reserves yet available in the
United States. If it is iron, she has it in veins of unlimited extent. If it is coal, she can supply it through
the long future from every Appalachian state. If it
is fertilizer, she has the phosphates of Florida and
South Carolina ; and she has building stones, clays,
asphalt, petroleum, salt, and gold. Her Appalachian
uplands, with water-power, timber, iron, and coal are
sandwiched between her lowlands with cotton, rice,
corn, and fruit. And she is fringed by the sea,
whose warm, moist breath gives her blossom and
fruit without stint, and anchors in quiet waters at
Charleston, at Key West, at Mobile and New Orleans
and Galveston the growing fleets of her commerce.
Already it has been projected to build for a hundred
miles or more, across the coral islets and their shallow straits, a railway from the mainland to Key West,

where, with the new prosperity of the Antilles and the new isthmian canal and the new South at the gateway of the Gulf of Mexico, one of the greatest American cities may in a few generations rise. The southern man cares little for the issues of the past, for the golden chances of to-day and the beckonings of a future too big for his imagining are before him.

Fig. 40.   Mississippi Steamer at Levee, Mobile.

It is easy and safe to predict an era not far away when the Appalachians and their Piedmont fringes shall be as full of wheels as New England, sending their products as widely; when northern Alabama and Birmingham shall be another western Pennsylvania and Pittsburg; when the commerce of Galveston will compare with that of Boston, and New Orleans become a rival of Chicago. No region of the United States is like the South in variety; she has the water-power and spindles of New England, the lumber of the far Northwest, the soils of the prairies, the coal of Pennsylvania, the iron of Minnesota. In every one of these she is a first, or a good second, and in the total outrivals all. Her incubus is gone, the carpetbagger is gone or has left his sons to honest citizenship, and the negro is her greatest problem; but this will be solved by industry and the training of the hand, with growing intelligence and the building of self-respecting character. Not many years will pass before sectionalism, already dissolving, will be lost in the industrial, agricultural, and commercial unity of what for convenience we shall always call one of the great "sections" of our country.

CHAPTER VII

THE CIVIL WAR

AFTER the Civil War had closed, a citizen of the South said to Horatio Seymour: "The North would never have beaten us if it had not been for our rivers. They ran from the north into the heart of our country, and we could not get away from you." This must not be taken to mean too much; but it raises many questions and may set us upon thought. The Mississippi does flow from north to south, and joins the prairies and plains to the lowlands of the Gulf. Hence, that man of the Northwest was right who prophesied that the Mississippi Valley must belong to one nation. But the invading armies went down rather than up, because in no other way could the North force the South to stay in the Union. So far as natural highways are concerned, Tennessee could overrun Illinois as easily as Illinois could hurry her battalions into Tennessee.

There is no boundary of much military significance between the North and the South, and indeed the great physiographic belts cross the line and lie partly in one section and partly in the other. New Jersey and Maryland are in no important ways different from Virginia and South Carolina, for all belong to the Atlantic coastal plain. The valleys and mountains of the Appalachians are found in Pennsylvania, and they are found in Tennessee. And the lowlands of the Mississippi continue from the Lakes to the Gulf of Mexico, while farther west the uplands of Missouri and Kansas are separated by no barrier from those of Arkansas and Texas. East of the Rocky Mountains the natural land units were divided between the opposing groups of states.

We may indeed trace a line of rivers and count it for what it is worth as a boundary. The Potomac made such a limit with Maryland and the District of Columbia on the one side and Virginia on the other, but the Potomac did not keep Lee from Gettysburg or Grant from Richmond. Maryland was in sentiment almost as much a Confederate as it was a Union state, and West Virginia was sliced off and joined the North. By any nice theory of river barriers, the Ohio should have marked the line; but Kentucky on her south bank clung to the Union as a commonwealth, while thousands of her men entered the southern army. On the other hand, many in southern Illinois and Indiana were in close sympathy with the Confederacy. Similar things might be written about the Missouri River and the halves of the great state which are made by it. These streams had no large importance for the war, therefore, because they ran through states checkered with opposing ideas, and because the Northerner in accomplishing his aim had to go where the Southerner was, and fight his battles there.

But there were rivers of the utmost importance in the strife on both sides of the Appalachians. In

Virginia the Potomac, the Rappahannock, the York, the James, and the Appomattox all flow southeastward through the lowlands to their mouths in sea or river. Washington is on the Potomac, Richmond is on the James, and every movement of the armies of Virginia between the hostile capitals had to take account of these streams of the coastal plain. And to the west was the Shenandoah River and its valley, a road which neither the Confederate nor the Union commander was ever at liberty to forget.

No less a critical factor in the long struggle was the Mississippi River from Cairo to the Gulf. In the War of 1812 Andrew Jackson had made his name and paved his way to the presidency by crushing a British army with his hardy Westerners at New Orleans. But from 1861 to the summer of 1863 the great river was to yield its points of advantage to this side and to that, after fierce land attacks, bitter naval encounters, and prolonged sieges. If we leave out the Atlantic coastal plain, the rest of the Confederacy was about cut in halves by the Mississippi. Its possession was, therefore, of the utmost importance to both sides. To the Confederates it was necessary, because to hold it was to have free communication for their armies and for supplies between the east and the three great states that lay west of the river. It was correspondingly the object of the Federals to cut this line, and thus isolate from each other the two groups of the Southern states.

The situation was much like that of the thirteen colonies in relation to the Hudson in the Revolution. In both cases we have a chain of states crossed by a

FIG. 41. Tennessee River and Lookout Mountain. Photograph by W. H. Stokes, Chattanooga.

navigable river, and the important points on one, New York and Albany, may well be compared to New Orleans and Vicksburg or Memphis. And if Grant had failed in his attempt in 1863 as Howe and Burgoyne failed in theirs in 1777, the South might have maintained its independence, at least for a time, as the colonies had done.

A little to the east, in Kentucky and Tennessee, are two other rivers which figure constantly in the first years of the Civil War, and often in close relation to the Mississippi. One of these is the Tennessee, born in the mountains of North Carolina and Tennessee, pursuing its way down the Appalachian Valley, turning aside at Chattanooga to cut through the plateau and cross northern Alabama, where it changes its course and flows almost directly north across Tennessee and Kentucky to the Ohio. Another stream, the Cumberland, rising in the plateau of eastern Kentucky, makes a bend much like that of its southern neighbor, southward by Nashville, and then, turning north, runs closely parallel to the Tennessee, and enters the Ohio but a few miles above it.

The Tennessee was to see stirring times at Chattanooga and Knoxville. Both rivers could be navigated by gunboats a long way above the Ohio, and both were to be guarded and stubbornly fought for in the early days of the conflict.

If there had been no Appalachians, the northern people would have had a very different problem to study and solve. But for these, cotton and tobacco would have been spread where now are bold mountains, forested slopes, and a temperate climate. Cotton and tobacco would have brought slavery and the plantation with them, and the South would have been " solid " in a sense that has never belonged to that word. Instead of scores of thousands of Federal soldiers from the uplands and forests, there would have been a vast increase of the Confederate armies, and what might have been the issue of such a contest we can never know. Virginia was divided against itself, and the mountains went to the Union, and the plains joined hands with the South. Even in Tennessee were many Union citizens, and it was at one time a prime object of the administration at Washington to bring an army into eastern Tennessee, to co-operate with the great body of sympathizers with the North that was to be found in the mountain valleys and on the Cumberland plateau.

If there could have been any doubt before, the great conflict seems to have proved that our land, from east to west, is cut out for one people. The Appalachians were a great barrier in colonial days, but we cannot think of them as a national boundary, now that the forests are so largely cut away and the highways of traffic run everywhere. If this were not enough, there are open gateways betokening unity along the St. Lawrence and the Mohawk, and the wide Gulf plains wrap completely around the southern end of the mountains, joining the plains of the Atlantic with the prairies of the Mississippi. The Rocky Mountains alone, within our domain, might conceivably divide nations, and now, almost forty years after 1865, we can look with a bird's eye upon the physical features of the United States and say that final union was inevitable.   The only other possible thing would be a group of changing and quarreling powers, for two compact, stable republics could not arbitrarily cross all lines of geographic control and live side by side in peace.

FIG. 42. Vicksburg from the West.   Photograph by A. L. Blanks, Vicksburg.

Professor Shaler, in his history of his native commonwealth, Kentucky, has described what he well calls the "geological distribution of politics" in that state. The Blue Grass region, rich in its limestone soils, was hospitable to large holdings of land, the slave system was dominant, and here were the strong southern majorities. The poorer sandstone soils, on the other hand, especially in the large and wilder tracts of eastern Kentucky, supported a poorer population which was commonly hostile to slavery, and furnished many hard fighters for the Union armies.

Thus the rivers, the soils, and the reliefs of the land are all to be counted in if we would appreciate the causes that led to the war, or would understand its campaigns and its battles. Before we study some of the more special problems we must recall one very general condition that had a profound bearing on the fortunes of the South, namely, their almost exclusive agriculture. They did not have the mills and the shops to make what they needed for peace or for war; and when northern gunboats at last made the blockade of southern ports effective, the pressure on the South was severe, for she could neither send out the cotton which would give her money to buy, nor could she count on bringing in, after she had bought them, the munitions of war or the necessaries of life.

Not trying to follow, in this short sketch, the strict lines of division into military departments, we can see in a general way how the centers or lines of action located themselves. For the South to hold independence, or for the North to enforce union, there must be a struggle between the Appalachians and the sea; and because the two capitals lay, one in Virginia and the other on its edge, barely more than one hundred miles apart, the first and last great operations of the war were between the Potomac and the Appomattox. And because the South had an extended shore-line and many harbors, and foreign commerce was vital to her success, swiftly improvised navies on both sides made the ocean border the theater of some of the hottest and bloodiest fighting of the war.   West of the Appalachians lay the Mississippi Valley and a river whose final holding was vital to success on either side.   Here lines many hundred miles long had to be maintained; here rivers were fortified, railways were few but important; here the great generals of the war were taught, and here some of the most brilliant battles of the war were fought.   It was not until this great campaign ground was in full possession of northern arms that there could be sufficient concentration in Virginia to bring hostilities to a close.

The first line of outposts established by the southern forces lay in Tennessee and Kentucky, well down toward the Ohio River.   If this could be held, there could be no effective or lasting invasion of the lower Mississippi country — unless it came from the sea.   And such a line would serve as a base from which to win the Ohio and harass or overrun the states lying to the north.   The main artery to be held was the Mississippi River itself.

Cairo, at the junction of the Ohio with the Mississippi, was held by the newly commissioned General Grant.   About a dozen miles down the river, upon a high bluff on the Kentucky side, was Columbus, which the Confederates had strongly fortified, planting there 120 guns.   This was the Confederate left, and is a good sample of those fortified points mainly on the east side of the Mississippi, well suited by nature for military defense, because the river offered a natural moat on the west, and the batteries could hurl a plunging fire upon vessels going up or down.

Sixty miles or a little more to the east, the Ten-

nessee and Cumberland rivers in parallel courses flow
north across the southern boundary of Kentucky.
Just south of the line, in Tennessee, Fort Henry had
been erected on the east bank of the Tennessee, and
Fort Donelson on the west bank of the Cumberland.
These two points of defense were scarcely a dozen
miles apart, and so long as they were held, Tennessee
could not be invaded from the north along the valleys.   This was especially important, because Nashville lay on the banks of the Cumberland, and it was
appropriate, therefore, that Donelson should be the
stronger of the two forts.

About eighty miles northeastward from Fort Donelson was Bowling Green, at the point where the railway from Louisville forked toward Nashville and
Memphis.   Here was the Confederate right, and the
line, like a crescent, swung down into Tennessee,
across the twin rivers, and back into Kentucky, to
Columbus, on the Mississippi.   It was the object of
the South to hold this line, and any proposals to push
it toward the Ohio or invade the North were dismissed.
But the North had no alternative but to try to break
the line.   A step in this direction had been taken
when Grant sent a force up the Ohio and occupied
Paducah, at the mouth of the Tennessee.

It was possible to make a direct effort to open the
Mississippi, and this at first was planned, but this involved great difficulties.   Columbus was likened to
Gibraltar : ships alone could not destroy this secure
perch on lofty bluffs.   A land force could not take
it, so long as connection along the river was open.
To have attempted the post would have involved a

siege, and might have anticipated much that happened about Vicksburg more than a year later.

General Halleck decided upon a different plan, which was carried out by Grant and Admiral Foote. The center of the line was to be broken by a land and water attack upon Fort Henry and Fort Donelson. If these could be carried, the two rivers would be open, Nashville would be exposed, and the whole southern line would be pushed southward. And so it turned out: Fort Henry was taken, and as soon as Fort Donelson was invested, Bowling Green was abandoned; and as soon as it fell, Nashville was given up also; and on the west, Polk withdrew his stores and forces to Island No. 10 and New Madrid, thirty miles or more down the river. The stream there makes a great double bend, and the town, although ten miles northwest of the island, is still down stream from it. But the possession of the Tennessee and Cumberland rendered this position and outpost too exposed to be long held, and the next withdrawal was to Fort Pillow, fifty miles down the river in Tennessee. It was much like Columbus, being on a high bluff east of the river; but the flanking movement on the east had carried the Federal forces still farther south, and the great battle of Shiloh was fought, inflicting vast losses upon both sides, but leaving the Federals in possession of the Memphis and Charleston Railroad, and jeopardizing such positions as Fort Pillow and Memphis on the Mississippi. The issue of the naval combats at both these points was favorable to the North, and the positions were yielded without siege or land operations of any kind.

Our object must not be lost from view, which is not the story of marches, attacks, or capitulations, but to see how the large lines of movement were made ready by nature, and seized upon by men versed in military strategy. It was seen by Halleck that fugitive operations west of the Mississippi could have no great relations, although they had been important to the North, since, in the first months of strife, Missouri had been restrained from going out of the Union. But now the river and the states to the east must be held by the side that would win. Everything west of the Appalachians belonged to the combatant who could hold the Mississippi, the Tennessee, and the Cumberland. If the North could do this, it would cut off Texas, Louisiana, and Arkansas from the Eastern states of the Confederacy, and center the conflict on the Potomac and the James. Halleck saw this without question, though it required his greater subordinate officer and two years of tenacious struggle to bring it to pass.

The campaigns around Vicksburg illustrate both the local and the general problems of the Mississippi in those days of war. Most of the river above that point had been opened by Federal gunboats, while Farragut from below had taken New Orleans and Baton Rouge, leaving only Vicksburg and closely associated fortresses in the hands of the Confederates. Farragut had run under the Vicksburg guns, and said it could be done again; but this would not do for regular transmission of men and supplies. So long as this single point could be maintained, therefore, the South could keep her enemy from using the river, and the enemy could not keep her from such communication as she might wish between the Eastern and Western Gulf states. So strong was the position that the repeated efforts of such commanders as Sherman and Grant were foiled, and one plan after another was given up.

Vicksburg is one of those river towns which have been determined by a bluff, at the base of which flows the stream. Upon any good map of the region there is evidence enough that the river does not always keep the same track; but here for the present is the bend, and on the slopes to the east is the town, stretching up to the low plateau above. It is a rule of meandering streams also to cut a deeper channel on the outer curve of the bend, and thus we can see two reasons for the growth of a town, for there was a commanding site high and dry above the swamps and bayous on the west, and there was approach for the largest vessels to the wharves at the base of the bluffs.

Both above and below Vicksburg there is a considerable tract of the low bottom land lying between the Mississippi and the base of the bluff. North of Vicksburg, the Yazoo River follows the foot of the escarpment, and then, through a maze of lakes and swamps, bears to the west and enters the Mississippi. Vicksburg is on the steep slope that separates the bottoms from the upland. West of the city a great meander doubles the river on itself, as it flows first to the northeast, and then abruptly southwest, under the city. Above is the Yazoo, sending its several mouths into the `Mississippi as the greater

FIG. 43. Vicksburg from the North, showing the Great Bend of the Mississippi. Photograph by A. L. Blanks.

river sends her distributaries into the Gulf. One of these is Chickasaw Bayou, under the Walnut Hills. From the river opposite Vicksburg runs the railway to Shreveport, and north and south of this road is a tortuous network of bayous and swamps.

A fleet could not capture the town, perched upon its heights. And when Grant at last was free to make the trial, he proposed to come at his goal by a combined attack, sending Sherman down the river to the mouth of the Yazoo, and coming himself from the northeast. The cowardly surrender of Holly Springs by an unworthy subordinate, and the loss of vast supplies stored there, compelled Grant to abandon his plan until a new base could be established. But meantime Sherman had gone down the river, only to find himself among the marshes of the lower Yazoo, exposed to the sharpshooters and batteries of the towering wall on the east, and without the support that was planned. He failed completely and withdrew, to share the fortunes of Grant when later it was decided to make the river the great line of approach from the north.

Grant's problem was to get a foothold on the plateau back of Vicksburg and at the same time keep an open line of communication from the north. His attempt to come directly to his goal had failed, and he will now try it from the lowlands and the river, moving down in conjunction with Porter's fleet. He does not attempt the bluffs north of Vicksburg and east of the Yazoo, for the obstacles were too great and Sherman's failure there had made them known. He does try to complete what had the year before

FIG. 44. Shirly House and Federal Encampment, Vicksburg. From a View taken at the Close of the War.

been begun, — to turn the Mississippi across the narrow tongue of land within the bend, at a point four miles below the city. If this could have been done, there would have been no need to capture Vicksburg; for, isolated from the river, it would have been no more important than any similar town. But Grant failed in this, and again nature gave her favor to the Confederates. Indeed, such was their confidence in the difficulties of the ground, that the lowlands were practically unoccupied, the batteries commanding the river being thought sufficient. Unsuccessful efforts also were made to find or cut navigable channels among the bayous on the west, between Milliken's bend on the north and New Carthage on the south.

What Grant did was to take his army swiftly across the watery lowlands, — while Porter ran his boats under Vicksburg loaded with supplies, — cross the Mississippi thirty miles below the city, cut loose from his supplies, seize Jackson and the region east and south of Vicksburg, fight several battles upon the provisions carried in knapsacks, keep reënforcements from coming to Pemberton, drive him into Vicksburg, and open communication with the Mississippi north of the city. The difficulties interposed by physiographic conditions were so great that a much larger army must have been required by a commander of less judgment, promptness, and daring.

The underground formation in and about the town to which siege was now laid was such as to give distinct shape to the events of the hour. The great mass in which the Mississippi has carved the high bluffs consists largely of tough clay, so coherent that

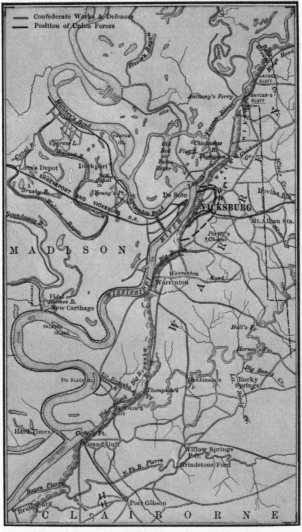

VICKSBURG AND SURROUNDING COUNTRY
Scale about 8 miles to one inch.

vertical walls of it will stand for many years. Thus we can see how easy it was, when the bursting of shells went on week after week, until scarcely a dwelling was unscathed, to burrow in the earth, and live, as thousands did, in subterranean rooms. The same conditions made it easy to open tunnels, in which mines could be sprung. The plateau also is furrowed by short ravines which have been made by the streams that drain the heights toward the river. They could only be short; for a dozen miles east of the city the Big Black River runs parallel with the Yazoo and Mississippi toward its union with the latter stream. These ravines alternate with narrow table-topped spurs, which could be easily fortified so as to command every point in the ravines with cross-fire. Hence it was that the siege line could not be drawn too closely around the beleaguered city, but had a length of eight miles from bluff to bluff on the north and south.

It should not be thought that Vicksburg ended the war in the southwest, while the Federal army had still a daring and persistent foe in the fertile region west of the Mississippi. The bayou country was still to embarrass the invader with conditions of war that could not be found in the north. Early in 1864, following the capitulation of Vicksburg, an expedition was planned for the west, which resulted in entire failure. A force was to go up the Red River, take Shreveport near the Texas border, disperse the Confederate forces in those places, and make accessible the cotton and other supplies of Texas. There was to be a fleet on the river, but land communications must also be

kept up, for the river is subject to changes that would
hinder the passage of boats. Indeed, a map of the
river belt shows a kind of geography that is rarely
seen — many tributaries swollen into lakes, making the
whole river above Alexandria look like a ragged cluster of grapes. A sluggish stream grafted upon the
Mississippi, setting back with the silting of the bottom of the trunk river, builds up its own bed in turn,
and thus ponds the water in its own branches, forming the lakes already mentioned.

Thus the country was difficult, the expedition was
blunderingly handled, the Confederates moved rapidly
and fought fiercely, thousands of men and many guns
were lost, and the Federals were fortunate in bringing
off a remnant of their invading force. The national
campaign had, in the words of Draper, "but one re-
deeming feature — the engineering operations of Col-
onel Bailey." Porter's fleet was caught at Alexandria
by the falling of the waters, making its abandonment
and destruction probable. The Yankee engineer, in
the face of much ridicule, built a dam at the falls,
deepening the water and allowing the vessels to pass.
The retreat was thus at last successful, but the expedition was a defeat, and a disgrace as well, to the
Federal arms.

If there is a point in the South which for the uses
of strategy compares with the lower Mississippi, that
point is the southern gateway of the Appalachian
Valley, the country around Chattanooga. This region
is sharply defined in all its geographic features.
On the east are the wild forest slopes of the Unakas ;
on the west is the frowning Cumberland escarpment

FIG. 45. Chattanooga and Missionary Ridge; looking East from Cameron Hill. The Small Hill, X, on this Side of the Ridge is Orchard Knob, Grant's Headquarters during the Battle. Photograph by W. H. Stokes.

and the Cumberland plateau.   Down this great valley to the southwest runs the Tennessee River, already majestic with the tribute gathered from the mountains and valleys of Virginia and North Carolina.   But instead of passing out at the wide-open southern door, it suddenly swings off to the right, and follows a deep gorge through the plateau into Alabama.

Just where the river leaves the spacious Appalachian Valley and enters the plateau is Chattanooga, on the east bank.   Northward the railway runs, eighty miles, to Knoxville, on the river also, and then on into Virginia to Richmond and Norfolk, or down the Shenandoah to Harpers Ferry.   Westward, through the gorge, is a railway which branches in the northeastern corner of Alabama, and leads to Memphis and Nashville.   Southeastward, another line connected with Atlanta and Savannah.   Chattanooga, therefore, by nature, and by man's use of nature, is a key to all military movements in the southern Appalachians, especially as it controlled at that time the only direct line of communication between the southwest and the Confederate capital.

A little below Chattanooga a small stream, called Lookout Creek, enters the Tennessee from the southwest.   It flows in a narrow valley which it has cut in the Cumberland tableland.   East of it runs a long, flat-topped hill, about fifteen hundred feet above the valley. It is like a wedge, narrowing at the north and ending at the bank of the Tennessee where the river turns west at this point, forming Moccasin Bend.   This hill is a spur of the plateau, and is the historic Lookout Mountain.   Standing upon its northern end, one may look

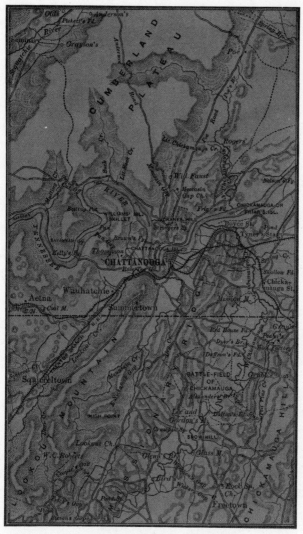

CHATTANOOGA AND VICINITY
Scale about 7 miles to one inch.

northward upon Chattanooga and the river, eastward over the wide lowland, and westward across the gorge of Lookout Creek upon the parent plateau, from which the observer's perch has been separated.

Between Chattanooga and the river is Cameron Hill, nearly two hundred feet in height. We may stand on this, as upon the stage of an amphitheater, and see all the features that controlled the lines of battle. Lookout Mountain, with its steep slope, crowned by a sandstone cliff, is south, on the right. The river is at the left and in the rear. The city is directly in front, and three miles to the east runs a hill extending from north to south for several miles, and three hundred feet high. This is Missionary Ridge; it is a small example of the innumerable worn mountain ridges that run up and down the Appalachian Valley from Alabama to Pennsylvania. It is the upturned edge of a mass of the Knox dolomite, the common rock on the floor of the great valley in this region. It has not only been turned partially on edge, but has been pushed, in ancient days, from the eastward somewhat over the rocks that form the base of the ridge. The geologist would say that the structure shows a fold and a thrust fault.

Now we have the conditions of battle, but we must go a few miles south from Chattanooga to follow the line of events. In September, 1863, a little more than two months after the capture of Vicksburg, the Federal army entered Chattanooga, under Rosecrans. The Confederates under Bragg were believed to be in retreat southward, but were in reality preparing for aggression. Rosecrans moved out and was met at

Chickamauga, twelve miles southeast of Chattanooga. Here is another longitudinal stream, Chickamauga Creek, parallel to Lookout Creek, the Lookout Mountain Ridge, and the Chattanooga Creek; its Indian meaning is the River of Death. The bloody battle on the banks of this stream was a defeat for Rosecrans, and would have been a rout but for Thomas, the " rock of Chickamauga." The *rocks* of Chickamauga are not so well known, those gently slanting beds of limestone whose outcropping edges furnished a natural fortification to many riflemen in the two days of battle.

Rosecrans took refuge in Chattanooga, and his foes well thought that he was in a trap. But he was relieved from duty, and Thomas was in command, until Grant, now free, could be brought, from the west.

Our story of the great battle can be told in a moment, for our only purpose is to see how the movements of war followed the forms of the land. The Confederates held Lookout Mountain and Missionary Ridge. Grant observed the great battle from Orchard Knob. He deployed his army in three divisions,— sending Hooker to dislodge Bragg's left from Lookout Mountain, Sherman to push back the enemy's right, and Thomas to storm the Confederate center on Missionary Ridge. That this was perhaps the most spectacular battle of the war was due primarily to the geographic conditions, but also to the unerring skill and certainty with which the plan of battle was carried out by the three great subordinates of the commanding general.

FIG. 46. Moccasin Bend, Tennessee River, from Point Lookout. Photograph by W. H. Stokes.

It would require a separate chapter even to sketch the geographic conditions which controlled the movements of the great armies in Virginia from 1861 to 1865. We have more than once in this volume had occasion to look upon this part of the Atlantic coastal plain, backed by the mountains and crossed by tidal rivers flowing to the southeast. Roads were few and in part because the rivers were many. ·The ground was often flat, swampy, and covered with forest, while the maps were too commonly poor and inadequate. The direct line of attack or retreat between Richmond and Washington lay across the rivers and these tangled lowlands. A dilatory, not to say timid, commander kept the Federal forces from striking a blow, and allowed Lee to organize the Southern army, and maintain an ascendency that was never shaken until Grant came from Chattanooga to Virginia.

McClellan had made himself a slave of geographic conditions when he had organized his costly and useless Peninsular campaign, by which he intended to come up between the York and James rivers and enter Richmond. But commanders who win are not only organizers and strategists and students of the map — they are fighters, a consideration never to be overlooked in the study of campaigns.

The Shenandoah Valley, lying behind the Blue Ridge, offers, in connection with the Virginia lowlands, perhaps the best illustration of our theme in all the South. The relations of this "Valley of Virginia" were briefly given in Chapter III. We there traced it northward beyond Harrisburg and southward to Chattanooga. All its northern portion in Virginia

Fig. 47. Shenandoah Valley, Luray.

drains through the Shenandoah into the Potomac at Harpers Ferry. West of the immediate valley of the Shenandoah are other parallel valleys and ridges until we come, farther west, to the Alleghany escarpment. Snugly protected by mountains, well watered by many streams, rich in soils derived from ancient beds of limestone, filled with fertile farms and comfortable homes, it afforded a scene of rural beauty and human prosperity, until in the four years of war it was found to be a great highway for armies. Running transverse to the rivers of the plain, and cut off from them by the Blue Ridge, either army could use it to flank the other, although it was the Confederates who used it most.

At the very beginning of disunion the shops and arsenal at Harpers Ferry were seized, and war did not desert the valley for the next four years. In 1862 Stonewall Jackson was sent beyond the Blue Ridge to make a diversion that might destroy the effectiveness of McClellan's campaign in the Peninsula, especially by threatening Washington. Jackson enacted along the Shenandoah one of the most brilliant chapters in the history of the Confederate arms.

It was expected by McClellan that he would take to the Peninsula one hundred and fifty thousand men, but in this he was disappointed. Jackson being in the valley, the President held back thirty-five thousand men under McDowell to defend Washington. Banks was sent from Manassas to Winchester, and McDowell was ordered to Manassas. Jackson thus had McDowell on his right, Banks in front of him in the valley, and Fremont in the mountains on his left. His object was to

Fig. 48.   Shenandoah River.

crush them one by one before they could unite.   He
drove Banks on a breathless retreat down the valley,
until the Federal soldiers had crossed the Potomac to
avoid destruction.   He then sought and scattered the
force under Fremont, and was ready to give fierce
battle to Shields who had come across the Blue Ridge
from McDowell.   Having already diverted McDowell's
great corps from McClellan, he now himself hurried
to join Lee.   "Thus in thirty-five days Jackson's
army had marched two hundred and forty-five miles,
had fought three important battles, besides two
minor ones, winning them all, and had practically
destroyed three Union armies." [1]   The next important
movement in the valley led up to the greatest and
most critical battle of the entire war.   It was in 1863
when Lee determined to execute the vast flank movement that should carry him down the Shenandoah,
across the Potomac, through Maryland, into Pennsylvania.   Nature had planned a spacious highway and
walled it in.   Through this avenue Lee would go,
and transfer the seat of war from southern to northern soil.   Once across the Pennsylvania line Lee
turned to the right, entered the passes of the South
Mountain, thus leaving the valley to the west, and
met the Union army at Gettysburg.   After the battle
Lee withdrew across the Potomac, as he had come.
Failing to reap all its advantages, the North had
won a great victory, and at a most dramatic moment,
— on the day when the future commander of the Potomac was receiving the capitulation of Vicksburg.

In 1864 Grant was before Petersburg and Lee

[1] "History of the United States," Adams and Trent, p. 391.

sent Early to make in the valley the same kind of diversion that Jackson had made. Early was a fighter, but he was not Jackson; and it was not McClellan now, but Grant, who stayed stubbornly where he was and sent Sheridan to take care of the Shenandoah. Early had even appeared before Washington, but was soon driven out of the valley by his foe, and the brilliant Irish soldier under Grant's orders proceeded to burn everything that could subsist an army. The Shenandoah Valley was a smoking ruin, and it was thereafter to know the pursuits of peace.

CHAPTER VIII

WHERE LITTLE RAIN FALLS

New England, or the Great Lakes, or the South, offers us a single continuous region, but when we study the pattern of the West, it is a patchwork, made up of mountains and plateaus, and the latter are often so smooth and so girt about with mountains that we call them plains. And these plains are so dry that they have long been put in a bundle and called the arid lands. Their dry climate is the feature which more than all others affects the lives and doings of men, and therefore we place under a common title lands as remote from each other as the plains of western Kansas and the great valley of California.

The westerly winds strike the edge of the continent, heavily freighted with vapor from the warm Pacific Ocean. When these seas of moist air roll up the cooling slopes of the Pacific mountains, condensation is rapid, and abundant rains and snows support the forests and feed the glaciers of these lofty lands. East of the mountain belt, which includes western Washington, Oregon, and much of California, the arid lands begin, and they include nearly all the territory eastward to about the hundredth meridian. This line runs through the Dakotas, central Ne-

230

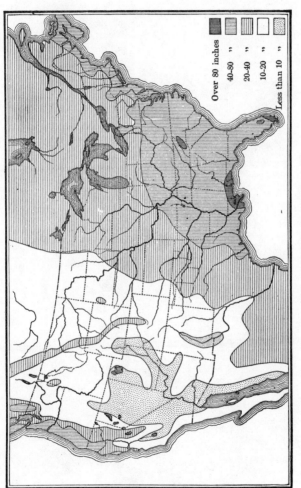

Over 80 inches
40-80 "
20-40 "
10-20 "
Less than 10 "

RAINFALL MAP OF THE UNITED STATES

braska, and western Kansas. It is not the exact climatic boundary, but is nearest it, and it is easy to remember that eastward more than twenty inches of rain fall in a year, crops are raised without artificial watering, and we call the lands prairies. West of the line there is no sudden change either of climate or topography, but on the average the rainfall is less than twenty inches, and irrigation is needed, except in unusual seasons, or for crops that require but little water.

From western Kansas to the Sierras is a solid arid country, save patches of mountain land which are cold enough to condense and comb out of the atmosphere the water that yet remains after it has swept over the Pacific ranges. This area of dry land in the United States is enormous, and in much of Utah and Nevada the rainfall is less than ten inches, and in parts of Nevada and southwestern Arizona it is less than five. That an empire of a dozen states and territories should sometime lie in this arid country would not have been dreamed by the early explorers, who thought themselves lucky if they eluded the savage, and got water enough for man and beast. They wrote the region down upon the maps, at least so much of it as lay east of the Rocky Mountains, as the Great American Desert, and made it seem to the childish geographer behind his atlas at school as inhospitable as the Desert of Gobi or the Sahara. Indeed, in such mistaught minds, a desert was a place where nothing could live or grow, for the world had not begun to learn its wealth of life, or to discover those changes of heredity and environment by which lowly populations are fitted to the dryest and wettest, the hottest and coldest, the steadiest and the most shifting conditions.

There was no dearth of life on the Great Plains before the prairie schooner crossed them, or the swift train sped without hindrance from Omaha to Denver; the savage knew the highways of the plains, the buffalo and prairie dog made them populous, and the desert grasses thrived and kept the sands from nakedness. The green slopes of New England would be missed and might be sighed for, but the skies were always bright, the gray landscape had its own spell, and it was the land of the imagination, with vastness like the sea.

When we cross the hundredth meridian, going west, we begin to be three thousand feet or more above the sea, and when we have reached the eastern base of the Rocky Mountains, in Wyoming or Colorado, our altitude is five or six thousand feet. We have crossed a plateau which has a gentle slant to the east. The rivers flow out of the mountains and down this upland floor toward the Mississippi. Such are the Missouri, the Platte, and the Arkansas. In many places in Kansas the Arkansas River and its branches flow almost on the surface of the country, or have cut shallow valleys, barely one or two hundred feet below the plains. There is good reason for this in the long, gentle slope over which the rivers must run, and in the soft and destructible strata in which they often work. The streams cannot have much velocity, hence their working power is small. And the land waste is so abundant that it clogs the streams, and

FIG. 49.   Pike's Peak from Pike's Peak Avenue, Colorado Springs.   The Growth of the Cottonwoods is made possible by Irrigation.

they become, as the geographer says, "overloaded," and tend to struggle over a waste floor of their own making, frequently dividing into strands which reunite, making a "braided" river, such as the Platte often is. This tells why the French discoverers saw a torrent of muddy water when they passed the mouth of the Missouri — waters described by a modern witness as "too thick for a beverage, too thin for food."

Yet we must not let ourselves think that the country is as smooth as it might appear to a tourist on the Union Pacific or Burlington Railway. The rocks are not all soft, but they are nearly always horizontal, and the weathering of the softer strata leaves the edges of the harder often outstanding in escarpments, or walls, that relieve the monotony. And in many parts of western Nebraska, and elsewhere, the fitful streams of this country and the perpetual weathering have cut the strata into a maze of scarps and slopes, which remain utterly naked and barren, through failure of herb and tree, and make what the early French voyageurs called *mauvaises terres*, bad lands — bad to them because they were hard to travel over, as bad they must always remain, save for weird scenery and their great harvests of fossil remains, which have kept many scholars to their tasks and filled many museums.

In some parts, too, the winds have shifted the waste and done what they could to give variety to the land surface. This has especially happened along the rivers, which have made the earth and sand available for wind action. The contoured maps of the plains will often show, by the crowd-

ing of small circles and ellipses, great patches of
such dunes on the leeward side of the Platte, the
Arkansas, and lesser streams.

The land is not, then, absolutely smooth, for rivers
and winds and weathering have diversified it much,
but reliefs of a few hundred feet count for little
when the eye sweeps vast areas, reaching from
Dakota to Texas.

There is a central belt of the Great Plains which
is smoother than the rest.   It runs through Nebraska
and Kansas and into Texas, and has been distinguished as the High Plains.   We can better understand them if we go back to the origin of the Great
Plains as a whole.   Under these lies a vast floor of
older beds of marine origin.   After this sea floor was
uplifted it was overswept for long by river torrents
from the young and high mountains on the west.
These torrents wandered this way and that, and laid
down the materials that now form the surface parts
of the plains.   Thus there is a veneer of younger
waste, often five hundred feet thick, carpeting a
floor of harder and more ancient rocks.

In this central area there is rain enough to allow
the forming of a sod, which is firm enough to check
erosion by rain and by small streams.   Hence, the
old débris plain is almost perfect in its preservation.
West of it, however, as in eastern Colorado, there is
less rain, no real turf can form, and yet the streams
from the mountains are more forceful than farther
east, because nearer the rain belt of the Rockies.
Hence, though it seems a contradiction, the semi-
arid, middle belt is smoother, and has suffered less

erosion than the arid belt west of it or the well-watered prairies east of it. The character of this singular land, with its horizon like that of the ocean, can be read in a recent report of the United States Geological Survey.[1]

As distinguished from the still drier plains on the west, the High Plains became known as the "rain belt," and there followed on this several years of the most disastrous experiment in agriculture ever tried in the United States. Every one knew of the fertility of the prairies, and the prairies lapped well over into central Kansas and Nebraska. So the inrushing settlers, from 1885 to 1895, failed to mark that vague but stern boundary which separated the regions of ample and deficient rainfall.

As if fate were in league with their ignorance, there were in this period several seasons of increased rainfall; and it was bravely asserted that the climate was changing, and some thought the plow was doing it, and that any region once plowed and set with patches of trees would woo the rains.

In earlier days, when the westward extension of slavery was pending, Kansas had seen storms that rivaled her tornadoes. But she never perhaps saw so much suffering or enacted so large a social and geographical experiment as when excited emigrants from the East, or men who found no place in Illinois or Iowa, rushed across the one hundredth meridian and began to take up quarter sections, lay out cities by the square mile, build county seats and court-

[1] "The High Plains and their Utilization," by Willard D. Johnson, Part IV, Twenty-first Annual Report U. S. Geological Survey.

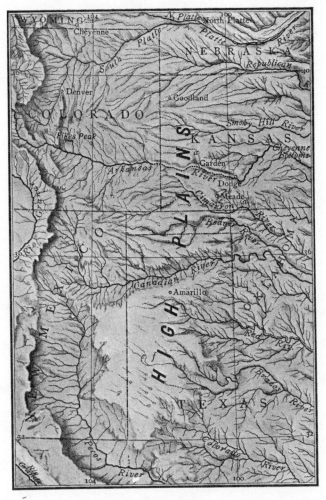

THE HIGH PLAINS

houses and palatial schoolhouses, and boom the country. One might expect such conditions at Virginia City a generation ago, or at Cripple Creek in later years, but hardly on the dull, endless acres of western Kansas.

The men who worked the boom did not bring their money in their pockets or draw their checks on eastern bank accounts. The checks were drawn in the East, but by men and women who, with equal haste, accepted mortgages upon lands they never saw, lands which, with square miles enough, would raise cattle, but would not raise wheat. When the bubble collapsed, many men had learned many things. One dry season after another taught them that the climate had not changed. The boom towns did not fill up ; the farmers had no money with which to pay interest, to say nothing of principal. Banks and loan companies failed, the eastern lender and western borrower had hard feelings toward each other, and the one became wisely conservative about western investments, and the other learned economy in a hard school, either by sticking to the ground, or after his prairie schooner had carried him back to Illinois or over into Oklahoma.

A people pressed for ready money is a people ready to hold and preach extraordinary doctrines, and thus we are able to see how the populistic wave of antagonism to eastern financial ideas swept the plains, and how a large political and social movement grew out of the failure of a frontier population to adjust itself properly to geographic conditions.

We can see how this adjustment has now come, and

that these commonwealths may now look safely forward to an era of unbroken progress.   Kansas increased her population between 1870 and 1888 by much more than a million.   Her numbers were quadrupled in that period.   She now knows that there is a limit to the people she can support, especially in her western counties.   She has found that only here and there can these lands be watered.   They are too far from the sources of supply in the Rocky Mountains. Too much water has been evaporated, or has soaked away, or has been drawn into Colorado ditches, or it flows, as in Arkansas, too low to be run out on the uplands.   The artesian supply will be small and confined to special places.   Smaller population, more grazing, and forage crops that will thrive in a dry climate — such are the secrets of adjustment which have now been learned.   The Kaffir corn product alone is now worth millions of dollars every year, and here, as in Nebraska on the north, the cow is known as a "mortgage lifter."

The Llano Estacado of Texas is the southern continuation of the High Plains of Kansas; but its true nature as a plateau is more visible because, on the east and south, it fronts the seaboard lowlands by a steep wall formed as the streams have gnawed back into the upland, and on the west the Pecos Valley separates it from the mountains.   The region is hot and almost too dry even for pasturage.   And yet as much rain falls here as upon the wheat lands of Dakota, but the difference is in the spasmodic character of the rains, the greater evaporation, and low relative humidity.   The amount of rainfall does not assure paying tillage of the soil, for many things must be counted in. A region may seem to have water enough, but it may fall at the wrong season of the year, when it can do crops no good. Thus storage is added to the great bundle of irrigation problems.

Irrigation, indeed, is of universal interest west of the one hundredth meridian, and has become in many

FIG. 50. Desert Vegetation. Foothills of the House Range, Western Utah.

ways of national importance. And yet few saw this until within the last two or three years. National recognition came with the opening of a new century, and long before its close fifty millions of people may be dependent on this phase of agriculture, and the society of the West will be profoundly molded by it. Seven and one-half millions of acres are now made productive by artificial watering within the United

States, and the work is only in its beginnings.   Before
1900 a proposition to give federal direction to irrigation was met by a united protest from the press of the
East that this was a scheme to take money from the
eastern farmer to give it to his brother in the West.
It is now seen that more than one-third of the United
States must depend on irrigation.   It is not merely
the value that lies in the soils that is in question, but
the profitable development of every natural resource
of the West, for food cannot permanently be brought
across half a continent to provide for a vast and stable
society.

We know now, also, that only a fraction (about one-
tenth) of all the dry land can be irrigated, because
there is water enough for this and no more.   It becomes, therefore, a question of wisdom in the use of
water, of the right choice of lands, of the proper
crops, of skillful handling, and of a conserving use for
grazing of lands that cannot be brought " under the
ditch."   Irrigation means, also, intensive agriculture,
for economy requires the use of the shortest canals,
the fewest weirs, the least machinery, and the largest
cropping of small fields.   And this means small holdings, a compact rural society approaching the conditions of the town, with convenient churches and
schools, the best roads, telephones, free delivery of
mails, and constant social life, divesting the farm of
its ancient narrowness and loneliness.   Such is the
attractive picture presented in a recent writing,[1] —
whether too sanguine or not we will not affirm, — but
suggesting that at length the germs of discontent and

[1] Guy E. Mitchell, in *Forestry and Irrigation*, January, 1903.

anarchy in the cities may be made harmless by bringing out of the slums the men and the women that would with opportunity respond to the call of a better life.

Irrigation is national in other ways, for millions of people, frugal and wealth-producing, would thus be added to our population, ready to spend vast sums for articles manufactured in the East; while the growth of cities in the East, and the diffusion of money there, would enrich the farmer of the older states as well. Within a few years, also, bulletin after bulletin has appeared from the presses of the United States Department of Agriculture, dealing with irrigation experiments and results in humid regions. Every farmer knows that he loses half or far more than half of some crops because of the failure of rains at the critical time. More and more out of the principles established in western experience will the eastern farmer profit. Especially will this be true of crops which, like fruit, are especially dependent on water, and are grown on compact areas. Gradually the skinning processes, so well known in American agriculture, will disappear, and their place will be taken by intensive tillage, small farms, special crops adapted to locality, closely settled lands which are indeed communities; and the unhappy line which makes the city a slum and the country a wilderness may be at least relieved, though it be a large hope that it should disappear.

Those who frown on federal supervision have not considered the inherent difficulties of irrigation policy and law. The early settler takes up a claim, cuts a ditch, and uses the water. He has a prior right, but

others come and water rights become involved. Long
and big ditches and storage reservoirs are needed,
and the corporation replaces the individual and the
difficulties thicken.   Finally a great river like the
Missouri or Arkansas crosses the boundaries of
states, and even state governments become helpless
to protect their citizens.   It would not be fair for
Colorado to stop all the water of the Arkansas, leaving but a dry river bed in Kansas.   Only federal
authority can adjudicate such claims as this, or provide for the fair and continuous economic progress
of this great western domain.   In March, 1902, the
United States Senate performed its part in enacting
the new irrigation law, without a dissenting vote and
without so much as a roll-call, and it seems at last to
be recognized that the arid lands and the forests of
America are as proper subjects of legislative attention as our manufacturing or our shipping.

In President Roosevelt's first message to Congress
he said, "The forest and water problems are perhaps the most vital internal questions of the United
States."   He rightly puts these questions on their
highest ground.   They do not belong to the mere
technique of agriculture; they pertain to the making
of homes, to the right use of our greatest resources;
they are social and economic problems that effect our
whole national life.

In a recent report President Wheeler of the University of California included a department of irrigation among the immediate needs of the school, and
such a department was almost at once established.
More or less instruction in this field is given in all

the agricultural colleges and higher schools of the
arid region. Somewhat over seven million acres, as
we have seen, are now watered in the arid states and
territories, which are eleven in number. California
and Colorado are at the top of the list with more than
one million acres each. But in the western United
States there is believed to be water enough to irrigate
sixty million acres. This means that but one-eighth
of the work has yet been done, and a map showing
the watered areas of the West is barely specked with
the black patches used to represent them. Professor
Elwood Mead compares the Missouri with the Nile.
The African river supports five million people with
its fertilizing waters, while our own great river and
its branches can be made to water three times as
much land as is now cultivated along the Nile. There
are now fifty thousand miles of irrigating ditches in
this country. The cost of them has been enormous,
and yet upon authority we are told that "the total
cost of all the irrigation works in use in the country
is only three-fourths of the value of the crops produced each year on irrigated lands."

In Colorado the latest figures give more than
1,600,000 acres under the ditch. The state has
thus outstripped California in its extent of watered
land, though not in the value of the products, for
some valuable fruits of the Pacific state will not
grow in the colder climate of the Rocky Mountains. The agriculture of Colorado has often produced more annual value than its mining; but both
go together, for the miner gets subsistence and the
farmer gains a market, so that, with cities, farms,

railways, and mines, Colorado has fast risen to the
complete possessions of a civilized and advanced
community, and few richer or finer regions can be
found than that which stretches along the eastern
foot of the Front Range past Boulder and Greeley.
If the one is known for its university, the other has

FIG. 51.   Dust Whirl in the Desert, Western Utah.

its potatoes and alfalfa, and is not without its normal
school, and both together typify the vigorous, untir-
ing life which has grown out of a desert by right use
of soil, sunlight, and mountain streams. The value
of crops grown by irrigation in 1899 in Colorado
was more than $15,000,000. The settlers at Greeley
in 1870 were second only to the Mormons of Utah
in the early beginnings in the reclamation of dry
soils; but now the watered lands of the state border

the Rocky Mountain front, stretch down the South
Platte River into Nebraska, and form great patches
on the Rio Grande, and also on the Gunnison, and
the Grand, beyond the Continental Divide.

West of the Wasatch Mountains and east of the
Sierras is a land which we know as the Great Basin.
We call it so because it has no drainage to the sea.
The mountain slopes that border it are well

FIG. 52.   Great Salt Lake.

watered, and some rain falls everywhere upon its
surface; but not enough to fill up its central lowlands
and pour across the bounding divides upon the slopes
that lead to the Pacific. The western half of Utah
and the whole state of Nevada occupy the greater
part of this basin. Many swift streams rush through
the gorges of the Wasatch; but their goal is not the
sea, for the remnant of water that is not dissipated in
soil and air mingles with the shallow brines of Great
Salt Lake. With more than temperate heat, and with
little rainfall, the air is like a dry sponge, and absorbs

so much of the scanty moisture that the lakes cannot fill up and run to the sea. Hence the minerals dissolved from the surrounding lands and brought into Great Salt Lake cannot escape, and they completely saturate its waters.

Within the basin itself are many mountains, though they do not rival in breadth or height the bordering ranges. They run parallel to each other and from north to south, and are separated from each other by smooth areas that make up the general floor of the basin. This floor is especially flat and wide around Great Salt Lake, and southward.

If we look out over the fields and gardens that blossom at the base of the Wasatch, and would know the meaning of the soils, we must lift our eyes to the lower slopes of the mountains. It will take no skill to see horizontal platforms cut as strong lines on the mountain sides, and some of them are formed as high as one thousand feet above the lake and the railways. They are not such forms as streams and rain wash make on a mountain. Instead of ravines and buttressed ridges, we find what might be railway grades.

They could only be made by the waves of a body of water, and they mark the days when the Great Salt Lake was 1050 feet deep (it is now less than fifty); when it was not salt at all, but found a northward outlet into the Snake River, the Columbia, and the sea, and when the climate was therefore far more cool and moist than it is to-day. The reader has already been asked to imagine the wide flats that would greet his eye if Lake Erie or Lake Michigan could be drained. Here is a similar case: the ancient lake in Utah was as large as Lake Huron and deeper; into its waters floated the waste of the uplands, and sinking it formed the mud plains which have been uncovered by the drying away of the lake. If we ask when all this happened, we can only answer that this era of cool and wet climate seems to have been contemporaneous with the glaciers and great glacial lakes of the East.

We need not look for any finer instance of geographic control of the forms of land and water and of the ultimate doings of men. The earth's crust had to be wrinkled and broken to raise the mountains that bound the basin and run along its floor. Their wasting was made swift by the abundant waters that not only formed an inland sea, but brought the ruins of the land to rest in it; and a change of climate, as yet unexplained, dried away the waters, until but a salty patch is left, leaving the wide plains dry and barren, and compelling man to guide out of their natural channels and use with economy the streams that remain. This the Mormon colonist began, more than fifty years ago, to do. It was the only way in which a community could then live in so distant a wilderness, and it continues to be the only way in which a commonwealth can prosper even in the days of great railways and swift communication.

As on the Great Plains so in the Great Basin it is an economic fact of greatest meaning that the water supply avails for but a fraction of the land. We shall never see a thousand miles of wheat and corn, as one might see on the Mississippi prairies. But here is little land of absolute dearth; grasses grow, and their nutritious qualities outlast the process of drying, and keep alive the roving herds even when snows cover the mountains of the horizon. Millions of sheep belong to the wealth of Utah, and cattle not a few.

The Colorado colony at Greeley and the settlers of Utah were the pioneers in irrigation, and have demonstrated that states can be built and can thrive upon this mode of tilling the soil. Hereafter it is only a question of using the experience of the past, with the necessary capital, to achieve like gains in New Mexico, Arizona, and other parts of the West.

Centuries ago aboriginal peoples made ditches and watered their crops in what is now Arizona, and the later Indian inhabitants were doing the same when the white man came. Nature has one unvarying command when man insists on dwelling in that dry and heated country. He must use the water with economy, and use as much of it as he can.

Northern Arizona will never be made into farms, for it belongs to that high plateau, cool and rocky, through which the Colorado has worn its great canyon. It has a fair rainfall, however, and will have its quota of prosperity through its pasturage. The southern and western districts are much lower, and they are hotter and drier as well; for at Phœnix, and westward, the rainfall is not above five inches in a year, and the average temperature is that of New Orleans.

The Gila River rises on the eastern border of the territory, and crosses it to the west and south, entering the Colorado at Yuma, and it is in the low and tropical basin of this river that man is finding a home. The irrigated lands of the Gila River are already worth millions of dollars, and without such use of water

FIG. 52 *a*. Orchard Irrigation, Riverside, California

there could never be anything here but tropical deserts and desolate uplands, crossed by the railways and visited by the tourist and explorer. Here it is proposed to make one of the beginnings in federal aid and supervision by building on the Gila River what is known as the San Carlos dam. By erecting a dam somewhat more than two hundred feet from the bed rock, enough water can be held in reserve to water two hundred and fifty thousand acres of land. If this can be done, the million dollars which the reservoir will cost will be a trivial outlay for so large a return, and would be far more than earned in any single year after the land is fairly under cultivation.

Similar to the Arizona lowlands is the Colorado desert of southeastern California, and this whole Colorado region may gather an importance all its own through the cultivation of tropical fruits. The Department of Agriculture at Washington is now coöperating with the University of Arizona in supporting at Tempe, near Phœnix, an experimental garden for date palms. These trees need plenty of water for the roots, a hot, dry atmosphere for the foliage, and winters not too severe. The tree will flourish in Florida, but the southern summer is neither hot nor dry enough to mature the fruit. It is at home in the Sahara, and at a single point in southeastern Spain. In 1900 the Department brought from Algeria shoots of the best varieties, and experiments are now in progress in Arizona and California. The fruit will not ripen unless the mean temperature exceeds 80° for a month in the summer, with a mean of 70° from May to October. The soils, however, must be moist, and will not injure the plant if they are alkaline, as is often the case in arid regions. Earlier experiments have been tried here, and a single tree, eight years from the seed, bore four hundred pounds of fruit in a season. The Colorado Desert in California is thought to be the best date region in the New World. It would be deeply interesting if this land of perpetual heat and cloudless skies could be so watered as to grow rich with this Old World fruit.

Little attempt has been made to use the water of the Colorado River. For much of its course the deep canyons prevent all diversion to the adjoining lands, but there is no good reason why considerable patches of the hot desert farther south should not be reclaimed. Some of this land in southern California lies three hundred feet below the sea level, being isolated from the Gulf of California by the delta of the river. Exceptional floods now and then break across the river banks and form a lake in this depressed area, a lake which is at length destroyed by soakage and evaporation. If nature can do this, man might make canals serve a like purpose. His greatest obstacle would be the silting of the ditches by the waste with which the river is heavily loaded.

Along with a new reservoir on the Gila River, it is proposed to control the waters of St. Mary River in Montana, keep them from running their natural course into Canada, and turn them into the head waters of the Missouri, and make them the means of reclaiming, on their way, several hundred thousand acres of land. Whether such diversion of waters might become a still wider question is a problem for

FIG. 52 *b*. Sunnyside Irrigation Canal, Washington

Irrigation by Flooding

those familiar with international law. It would not be difficult at least to raise the question of equity on our southern border, if erelong the progress of agriculture in Colorado and New Mexico should dry up the Rio Grande and destroy the value of lands that lie across the Mexican boundary and have been for generations refreshed by the waters of the river.

America is surely not a good field for showing what, in the long run, geographic environment can do with a people. History is here too short, and the tree is but a sapling, not bearing its mature fruits. And our people have scarcely recovered from the shock of migration, and we do not know to what account our changes should be charged. And we are a mixture of races, forming something as yet new and unknown, and who can tell how much is due to country and how much to amalgamation? No result may fairly be called final, and no type has been perfected. We can only study beginnings.

We know well what the desert type of society has always been, — nomadic and tribal, without cities, without settled interests, and almost without tillage of the soil. Flocks and herds were appropriate to the wastes of the Orient, familiar to us in many annals of the Old Testament, and in the tales of many a traveler. The heat of the plains, the keenness of the sun, the coolness of shadow, the preciousness of springs, — these are the earmarks of desert literature. Houses must be tents, or something easily renewed, in a migrating society, and the garb must protect from heat by day and the chill air by night. Or, if life is more settled, the primitive man or the pioneer must build his hut as he can; if he is in the "short grass" country, that is, on the high plains, he uses sod, and in the arid belt, or "bunch grass" country, he must have recourse to "adobe," or sun-dried mud.

An environment so pronounced could not be without its distinct power over thought and spirit. Nowhere

FIG. 53. Desert Valley at the Base of the House Range, Utah. The skeleton is that of a horse. The lower part of the valley is un-drained, holds a shallow lake after a storm, and is covered with a fine earth, "adobe," containing gypsum and salt.

is this more finely seen than in the literature of the Bible, perhaps superlatively in the Psalms. In the desert the very insects seem to catch the spirit of the place and make themselves over into a protective oneness with its gray and neutral tones. And the dweller in verdant lands, entering the desert wastes with a recoil from their dryness and silence and soli-tariness, finds himself after a time bound by their spell. He has never breathed air so pure and so purged from all odors, he has never looked into such measureless depths of stars, he never knew or dreamed that the desert could be so full of life, that its trails and water pockets, its grasses and its sage-brush, its coyotes and jack-rabbits, its rocks and its bordering mountains, all conspire to make a world in the wilderness. " The absence of dark green is soon not noticed, for the grays, reds, browns, and yellows are so quiet, so soothing, so varying in their intensity, and so thoroughly mingled that their quality cannot but be constantly in mind. To see the grand colors of a deep brown cliff brought out in a clear moonlight is to see one of the most wonderful effects. In the desert tints, as in the green of the humid country, the value of shadows in bringing out the quality and the contrast is not to be overlooked. In fact, after we become accustomed to the desert range of colors, the green of an oasis comes with a shock, like a misplaced touch in a beautiful picture." [1]

Arid America will not be, in just this way, the land of the imagination, when the American of to-day has tried his hand upon it. If there were water enough, he would moisten it all, and make it as populous as Massachusetts; but nature will have her way with much of it, and man will cross it with his railways and range over it with his herds, but he may only settle it here and there. But where man does conquer a dry wilderness, the change is absolute and profound. Instead of a nomad, we shall find dense and deep-rooted

[1] " Life Amid Desert Conditions," R. E. Dodge, Bulletin American Geographical Society, Vol. XXXIV, p. 416, 1902.

communities, like jewels in wide settings of gray desert. In a large settlement the single farmer cannot make his own ditch from the river, but there must be communal or government action. This, with small farms, intensive tillage, and close contacts everywhere, compels an approach to socialistic conditions that may never be reached on the watered prairies or among the Appalachians, where in some larger measure each man can be a law to himself.

Indeed, most of the embarrassment and embittering litigation of the arid country has arisen from an unconscious attempt to apply the old English law, made for a moist country, that allows a man to control the water that flows past or across his land. It has been well said that in an arid country water is like sunshine and air, and to monopolize it is infamous.

The young state of Wyoming has led the way in brushing aside the injustice of ancient customs, and the burden of unfit statute, and placing under just public regulation all the waters within her boundaries. She is fast being followed by older states, and we may look with amazement upon a flourishing commonwealth, less than thirteen years a member of the Union, rising in population, strong in agriculture and in mining interests, with a well-developed educational system and an enlightened government, where a generation ago there appeared a high and barren plateau beset with rugged mountains.

CHAPTER IX

MOUNTAIN, MINE, AND FOREST

THE East has its mountain ranges and they are covered with forests; but the mountains are low and in no important degree do they hold deposits of gold, silver, copper, or lead, and they are set in the midst of a moist rather than an arid land. The mountain ranges of the West are far from the older home of civilization on this continent, and the conditions of human life are as different as well could be from those of the East.

Colorado is in many ways the typical western state. Its mountains are broad and high; it supplies some of the sources of every great river in the West except the Columbia; it has unequaled mineral resources; irrigates more land than any other state; and has, in addition to its mountains, an area of the Great Plains on the one hand and a part of the Colorado plateaus on the other. Pike entered this land in 1807, Long in 1819, and Frémont in 1843. Gold was found in the Platte Valley in 1858, a territory was organized in 1861, and it became a state in the Union in the centennial year of American independence. It has a composite people, with all the qualities of the West, and has come in fifty years to an advanced civilization.

In 1893 a historical and descriptive pamphlet was prepared to accompany the state's exhibit at the Columbian Exposition. Upon its cover were placed the seal of the commonwealth, a mine gang at work, a view of irrigated fields in the Poudre Valley, a potato,

FIG. 54. A Mountain Highway, Ute Pass, near Manitou.

and the state Capitol building done in native granite. If a university had been included and a mountain railway, the representation would have been complete. The world has few such products to show for a half century of development.

Colorado is a quadrangle more than twice as large as the Empire State. North and south across the central parts of the state lie the Rocky Mountains, a name that ought not to be used of mountains farther west. We may, however, carry the name northward into Wyoming and Montana, and southward into New Mexico. This means that the eastern ranges of the Cordilleran system are properly the Rocky Mountains.

East of the mountains, more than one-third of Colorado belongs to the Great Plains, looking toward Kansas and the Mississippi River. West of the Rockies is a region high, often rocky and barren, which continues into Utah and Arizona, and is a part of the plateau drained by the Colorado River. Its surface is much more broken than that of the Great Plains; for it is beset with lofty and pinnacled mountains, like the San Juan in the southwest, and the rugged and tangled Elk Mountains farther north; and it is carved by deep gorges like the Black Canyon of the Gunnison, and the canyon of the Grand River.

Nor is the Rocky Mountain Range simple and single; for it is made up of several north and south belts of mountains, separated from each other by broad and almost treeless valleys, which by a perversity of language are known as parks. Thus as one comes from the eastern plains he sees the Front Range looming on the horizon back of Denver, or south of the Arkansas it is the Wet Mountain Range or the Sangre de Cristo. Back of these mountains is a chain of parks, — North, Middle, South, Huerfano, and San Luis. These are smooth floors sloping gently up to the base of the mountains all around, and from six to seven thousand feet

above the sea. Their strata are young and loosely
put together, having been washed in by mountain
streams from every side. North of the Arkansas
River the parks are too cold for grain and fruit, but
yield pasturage. To the south, as in San Luis
Valley, along the upper Rio Grande, thousands of
acres are under the ditch. West of North and Middle parks is the Park Range, a part of the Continental Divide. West of South Park is the Mosquito
Range and the Sawatch, the latter separating the
Atlantic and Pacific waters; and between the Mosquito and the Sawatch is the open, longitudinal valley
of the upper Arkansas River, which turns at Salida
and passes, by the Royal Gorge, through the mountains to the plains. West of San Luis Park are the
heights of the San Juan.

Perhaps best by a study of the drainage does
one learn and remember the physiognomy of a new
country. On the east the South Platte and Arkansas extend many slender fingers up the slopes
and gather the abundant moisture of the mountains.
The Platte reaches into South Park, and the Arkansas into the heart of the mountains around Leadville.
The North Park drains by the North Platte out into
Wyoming; while to the south into New Mexico
flows the Rio Grande. On the west the Grand flows
from Middle Park, the Gunnison from Marshall Pass,
the Animas from the southwest, and the White and
Yampa from the northwest. Colorado has not glaciers to feed its streams, but it does scatter its waters
in every direction, like the Po, the Rhone, the Danube, and the Rhine, coming from Alpine sources.

We shall have a suitable idea of Colorado if
we think of it as an upland whose general surface
is from 4000 to 7000 feet above the sea, with' long
and strong ranges of mountains resting on it, and
rearing many peaks to heights of a little more than
14,000 feet. If the land mass of Florida were so
graded as to be everywhere of equal height above the
level of the ocean, this average altitude would be 100
feet. The average altitude of New York is about 900
feet, that of Oregon is 3300 feet, and of Colorado, the highest of all the states, 6800 feet. Thus
a rarefied atmosphere is to be added to our catalogue
of conditions that here make up the environment of
man.

Nearly as many kinds of natural causes for the
growth of towns can be found in Colorado as would
reward inquiry in any other state. These causes
sometimes lie close at hand, and often in the more
general conditions. Denver belongs to the latter class.
It might, so far as the stream is concerned, have been
at any other point on the South Platte River. But it
is on the plains, where it was accessible to all lines of
railway. On the east 'is the long approach from the
Mississippi River. From Wyoming on the north and
New Mexico on the south the lines of traffic follow
the eastern base of the mountains. And twelve miles
to the west the Clear Creek passes from the mountains
to the plains. In the deep narrow valleys of this
stream and its branches are the older mining camps,
which developed forty years ago and ran the output
of gold and silver far into the millions. For the sale
of ores and the entrance of supplies Denver was the

center, and such it has remained, as remoter and richer masses of ore have been brought to light in later years throughout the state. It is the business and financial headquarters of the Rocky Mountains and the metropolis of the region between Kansas City or Omaha and San Francisco. It has a relative importance which no town of its size could have in the East.

FIG. 55.   Product of a Leadville Smelter.   The " Pigs " contain Silver, Gold, Lead, and Copper.

A village added to Toledo would bring it up to Denver with its 134,000 people. Rochester has 28,000 more people than Denver, while Newark equals Colorado's four largest towns combined and has 50,000 to spare. But Denver is the focus of larger interests than belong to any of these eastern cities, and we are not to forget that Denver dates from 1858, that she had but 35,000 people in 1880, and that she trebled her population in the next ten years.

The resident of Colorado Springs makes light and cheerful reference to the population of "lungers," of which perchance he is one, and tells you that the place is "a very good Siberia." But as a land of exile he does not seriously regard it, nor should he. The town was founded through the force of an unusual motive, for in the summer of 1871 its site was deliberately chosen for a health resort. The dry air, the towering Pike's Peak and lovely Cheyenne Mountain, the springs of Manitou, and the weird monuments of the Garden of the Gods, with natural routes of travel along the plains and through the passes of the Front Range, — these make the geographic foundation; while thirty-five years ago it could not have been foreseen that the richest mining district now open in the state, at Cripple Creek, would be largely tributary to Colorado Springs.

Pueblo was a village of less than a thousand in 1870, and is now the second town in Colorado. Several conditions combine to rear a city. It is on the highway leading south from Denver; it is on the Arkansas River at the gateway of the Rocky Mountains; it is within easy hauling distance of ores, coal, and flux, and draws tribute from the agricultural belt along the Arkansas River above and below.

Thus the three largest towns of Colorado occupy similar sites at the eastern foot of the mountains; none of them are surrounded by mineral deposits, but the three owe much of their wealth to the stores so long hidden in the mountains on the west.

Of the mining towns are Aspen in the west; Creede in the south; Ouray, Silverton, and Rico in the San

Juan; Cripple Creek in the east; — we pass them and
take Leadville, in the center of Colorado, two miles
above sea level, in the heart of the mountains. It
does not require long in America for gold, or silver,
or gas, or oil, to make a town. The mining that made
Leadville was not the first in the neighborhood. California Gulch cuts the Mosquito Range east of the
upper Arkansas. Here Tabor, later a senator of the
United States, and his partner washed the placer
gravels and cleaned up $75,000 in sixty days. They
and others were always annoyed by masses of heavy
iron-stained rock that clogged the sluices; but these
alien pieces of mineral proved to belong to the silver-
bearing carbonates that would yield untold millions.
From a mine salted by one "Chicken Bill," and
refused by Denver buyers who found out the trick,
Tabor afterward took $1,500,000, and then sold it
for an equal sum. A mine sold in the morning for
$50,000 was bought back by the same parties in the
evening for $225,000. Where in 1877 there was a
post-office with 200 people, there was in 1879 the
second city of Colorado, with a population of 15,000.
A year later there were almost thirty miles of streets,
gas, water, thirteen schools, and five churches.

Unlike some boom towns its life continues, though
more quietly. The count of 1900 showed 12,000
people and more; and you may enter Leadville by
rail from the east, south, and west, and regulating
your steps with moderation needful to a "tender-
foot" at an altitude of two miles, may wander
among the dump heaps of Carbonate Hill, descend
the shafts, visit the smelters, or look off upon the

rocky crests and snowy gorges of the Continental Divide.

The mining interests of Colorado have been about equally distributed on the two sides of the Continental Divide. West of the mountains is Aspen, which for several years was one of the first mining camps in the West. Here is the Mollie Gibson Mine from which $60,000 in value were once taken in eight hours. One car of ore weighing twenty-four tons was worth $76,500. One hardly need say that such cars were protected, en route to the smelters, by armed guards.

We have seen how the need of irrigation forces a recasting of the laws concerning water. Thus mining has its code, one point of which is that the lode or vein, which often is not far from vertical, can be followed to the depths by the owner of its outcrop, even though it runs beneath his neighbor's claim. But at Aspen and Leadville "blanket lodes" were found, which in geological phrase means that the ore-bearing mass is not a vein, but a bed. Now a bed is often horizontal, and it would be clearly unjust to allow it to be followed indefinitely. Both veins and blanket lodes run so indefinitely, that in a rich region the courts are full of claims, representing a fierce underground war for the treasures of the mountains.

Another great cluster of mining communities has grown up in the rugged San Juan corner of Colorado, so that the excitements and fascinations of the claim, the tunnel and the shaft, often overshadow the more sober but equally rich agricultural interests of the Centennial State. Yet here, as everywhere in the

western country, the crude life and unsystematic
methods of prospecting, mining, and ore reduction
have largely given way to systematic, scientific operations, with abundant capital and sober business
management.

Many things must be remembered if we would understand the human type which is unfolding in these
mountains. The cowboy does not typify the life of
the plains and Rocky Mountain plateaus, though we
could not know its beginnings or fully understand its
quality without studying him. Nor does the miner,
to whom we are introduced in Bret Harte's tales, re-
flect all, or the most, that is to be found in the Rockies and the Sierras; yet he does most truly enter into
it, and we could not know the West if we left him
out.

He is the hardy spirit who in 1849 or the decades that
followed found eastern life too cramped to suit him,
or had seen ill fortune on the Atlantic seaboard, or
had found prairie farming too slow, or perchance
had not been a welcome member of settled society.
Whatever his conditions, he found himself in a land
of realities and of dreams, and there were no greater
dreams than some of the realities; he was apart
from the restraints of society, and was often the
more careless and violent, but more honest rather
than less, for there is something in the western air,
belonging perhaps to any frontier, which keeps
being and seeming close together, and marks hypoc-
risy as the most loathsome of vices. Unduly careless
it may be of conventionality, a new country frees
itself from many self-imposed thralls of older com-

munities.   As the frontiersman is free from the restraints, so he is bereft of the protection, of civilized
society, and he becomes his own sheriff, court, and
executioner; and the past generation in California or
Arizona has in this regard brought back the conditions of a hundred and twenty-five years ago on the
Holston and the Cumberland.

FIG. 56.   Panning Gold at Cripple Creek in Earlier Days.

The very names given to the mines are full of the
flavor of the frontier, and draw, in a bold line or two,
pictures of men that must decide instantly, stake all
on a venture, and follow failure with another trial,
untrammeled by ordinary standards of conduct, and
undismayed even by fate.   Some personal history
of success or failure is often hinted, — Lost Contact,

Last Dollar, Puzzler, Pay Rock, Last Chance.   The fair sex are generously remembered, — Yankee Girl, Henrietta, Minnie, Della, Edith, Little Annie, and Maid of Erin.   And some shall remain unclassified, — Smuggler, Modoc, Argonaut, Big Indian, Muldoon, Whale, Holy Moses, and Morning Glim.   Even the saloons are not to be outdone in invention, — First Chance (at the fringe of the camp), Chamber of Commerce, Board of Trade, Early Morning, and Magnet.

Shall we say that the young, the hardy, and the daring went West?   And when they reached the mountains they dropped the shell of custom, took up their great tasks, grew strong with achievement, made fortunes for themselves or others, and hewed out states.   He looks on the surface, who sees only profanity and light regard of human life, and does not see the bursting of a seed in new soil, and its upward growth in air free from the vapors of the lowland and the fogs of the sea border, where the sun ever shines, the pulse beats sturdily, and all the physical conditions tend to maintain, into more settled days, the energy and pace of the frontier period.

It is hardly safe to discount a pair of overalls anywhere, much less among the Rocky Mountains. There are universities now among the heights, and if there were not, under the coarse garb is apt to be a son of Harvard, Yale, Columbia, or Michigan.   With enterprise go cordiality and helpfulness, and neither projects nor men are scrutinized with long and suspicious gaze before confidence is extended.   And there is more moderation than the East gives the West credit for having.   In the depressing months of 1893, among the mines, one heard no recriminations, and more often a pleasantry, as upon the "inconvenience of having a poor father-in-law."   And there was no disloyalty to the western home.   "You'll dream about this country," said an old-timer from Aspen, coming through South Park.   And a mulatto woman in a town on the Rio Grande and Western voiced beyond doubt the feeling of every citizen of Colorado, —"Well, I'm *heah*, and I guess unless there's a mighty upheaval, I'll *stay* heah!"

If we follow the Rocky Mountains southward, they will carry us into New Mexico, and when we have reached Sante Fe or Las Vegas, the ranges have melted away into the plateau, lofty and dry, of which the territory is mainly composed.   Southward, in western Texas, distinctive ranges reappear, and connect, across the Rio Grande, with the mountains of Mexico.   Eastern New Mexico continues the high plains of Texas, and must mainly serve as a land of pasturage, except where irrigation is possible.   This limits tillage to the borders of the Canadian and Pecos rivers.   Western New Mexico is much of it too arid even for herds, except along the San Juan River in the northwest, which gains thus a store of water from the mountains of Colorado.   The chief stream is the Rio Grande, which divides the territory from north to south.   But here comes in a vexatious interstate problem, for there are canals enough on the upper river in Colorado to take all the water in the dry months, and no water now reaches the southern end of the territory during the irrigation season.   The only solution apparently lies in the construction of reservoirs.

Northward the Rocky Mountains lead us into Wyoming. It is a state similar in size, shape, and climate to Colorado. Like its neighbor, it is made up of mountain and plateau, but the differences are important. Colorado has a continuous backbone of high mountains. In Wyoming the ranges break down, leaving an easy passage from east to west through its central parts. This easy way has been found and followed by the Union Pacific Railway in its course from Nebraska to Utah. The Park Range from Colorado fades out in southern Wyoming; but the mountains reappear in rugged grandeur in central and northwestern Wyoming, in the Wind River Range, with its gorges and glaciers, and with few peaks ever scaled by man. Out of the northwestern corner of the state is carved the Yellowstone National Park.

Wyoming is in its drainage almost as inclusive as Colorado. From the North Park in the latter state it receives the North Platte head waters, which take a wide curve in the heart of the region. Northward it sends the North Cheyenne, the Powder, and the Big Horn to the Missouri. Over against the sources of the Big Horn River the Wind River Mountains send rolling to the south a great portion of the waters that have worn the canyons of the Colorado, while in the west the Snake River gathers its contribution for the Columbia. Without violating strong state pride one may yet aver, that having told the story of one Rocky Mountain state, it has been, in essentials, told for all. Each has its mountains and dry uplands, each has its

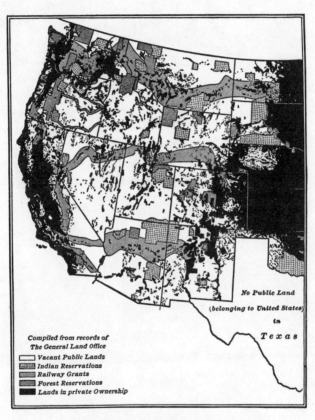

Compiled from records of
The General Land Office

☐ Vacant Public Lands
▒ Indian Reservations
▦ Railway Grants
▨ Forest Reservations
■ Lands in private Ownership

No Public Land

(belonging to United States)

in

Texas

LAND MAP OF THE WESTERN UNITED STATES

Compare with the rainfall map in Chapter VIII

waters of which it saves as much as it can, each sends its herds over wide ranges for the sparse but nutritious grasses of the desert, and each has its share of mineral wealth.   More than six hundred thousand acres are under the ditch in Wyoming, and nearly all of this land is devoted to forage crops, for agriculture here belongs almost entirely to the herd.

The ranges of the northern Rockies are in Montana and Idaho, and their direction is northwest and southeast.   They are rugged, but not so lofty as the mountains of Colorado; and being farther north they harbor most of the small glaciers yet remaining in the Rocky Mountain region.   Here are the northern sources of the Missouri and the southern sources of the Columbia River.   Montana is a vast state, with a broad western hem of mountains, and a wide stretch of plateau watered and drained by the Missouri and its branches.   Being in the far northwest, it has been occupied until recent years by those who were willing to live in isolation and care for cattle and sheep, or by those who, with more adventure or more capital, sought mineral treasure among the mountains about Butte and Bozeman.   But with a climate not too severe and wide areas of arable soil, agriculture has risen to enormous proportions, and the ranch shares the state with closely settled groups of farmers. Almost a million acres are now subject to irrigation, as much as in Colorado or California a few years ago. The climate is more moist than in the states to the south, and being cooler there is less evaporation, so that much more is possible without irrigation than in most plateau and mountain states.   Two transcontinental lines of railway serve for exchange with the East and the Pacific coast.

Like Montana, Idaho consists of mountain and plateau, but the latter is of another origin. The plateau of Montana is but a westward extension of the Great Plains, and in its northeast has an area of dissected strata forming bad lands, which are wholly as bad as any in Nebraska or Dakota. The plateau in Idaho lies broadly along the Snake River, which, rising in the Wind River Mountains of Wyoming, crosses southern Idaho by a wide curve from east to west. Here are the beginnings of the lava plains of the Northwest, and they occupy many thousand square miles, stretching broadly across southern Idaho and far over the eastern parts of Oregon and Washington, along the Snake and Columbia rivers. These lavas have been poured out of many vents or fissures now concealed and unknown, and are in some places three or four thousand feet in thickness. Often they have exceedingly smooth surfaces, and elsewhere they are diversified by volcanic cones and necks, by dislocations and by deep-cut channels of streams, such as the canyons of the Snake River. The prevailing species of vegetation is sage-brush, which gives its hue to the landscape; but hundreds of other plants occur, and the grasses furnish pasturage, and the soils when brought under the ditch are productive. And in the more northerly parts of Idaho, and near the base of the mountains, are lands better watered and raising the hardier grains and fruits freely. Few states show more variety of surface than Utah. In most of its eastern half are the

FIG. 57. Marshall Pass, Colorado. Sheds at the Summit Level.

Colorado or High Plateaus, regions of horizontal strata whose capping beds are six to eight thousand feet above the sea, broken into blocks by profound fissures, and dissected by streams, forming canyons only inferior in greatness to the Grand Canyon of Arizona. On the borders of the Colorado are the Henry Mountains, formed by subterranean intrusions of lava which domed up the overlying strata. The present mountain form has been reached through the removal by surface erosion of the upper parts of the domes, down into the lava itself.

In the north are high mountains of another sort. Contrary to Cordilleran custom, the range of the Uinta Mountains runs east and west — a broad up-arching of the strata, making a range eleven thousand feet in height. It stands like a rampart against the border of Wyoming, and through it the Green River has cut a sinuous gorge.

On the west the plateaus are bordered by the Wasatch Mountains, which present a less imposing front to the higher land on the east, but rise lofty and magnificent from the Great Basin. The basin we have entered already, to observe its ancient shore lines, its lake-bottom soils, its narrow ranges of mountains, and its clusters of human habitations clinging to the streams of the Wasatch. Four groups of mountain heights, all showing important differences of origin and structure, and two sets of plateaus, one lofty and broken, the other low and smooth, fresh waters, salt waters, deserts, forests and farms, gardens and mines — such are the contrasts of this central commonwealth of the Cordilleras.

THE GREAT BASIN AND ITS ANCIENT LAKES

No state has more curious interest than Nevada, whose conditions as a whole are more discouraging, not to say hostile, to human life than in any other field of the western United States.   With western Utah it is a part, and by far the greater part, of the Great Basin.   It is shut in by the Wasatch on the east and the towering Sierras on the west.   It sends no stream to the sea, and the rivers which its meager waters keep in flow lose themselves in lakes which often become alkaline flats in the dry season.   Like Utah, Nevada bears the records of a vast prehistoric lake, not so large nor so compact as its eastern neighbor, the Lake Lahontan of the geologists.   The land is about five thousand feet above the ocean at the north, and declines below the level of the sea in the extreme south of the basin.   The Basin Ranges interrupt the plains and save them from the monotony and dryness of absolute desert.

Nevada could scarcely have been admitted to the Union but for political necessity, and now has a population of 43,335, less than that of Akron, O. ; Dallas, Tex. ; Holyoke, Mass. ; Norfolk, Va. ; or Saginaw, Mich.   Rhode Island has 428,000 people, or 407 for each square mile.   The big western state, more than twice as large as New York, has four-tenths of a person for each square mile.   Arid Wyoming has nearly a hundred thousand, and Oklahoma, not yet admitted to statehood, has almost four hundred thousand people.

The future population of Nevada is absolutely limited by her scant supplies of water ; and yet, with all possible storage, some hundreds of thousands of men

and women can find homes within her borders.
And when this day comes there will be stable prosperity, in no way like the fitful boom that built
Virginia City and worked the Comstock Lode until
the scalding waters of the lower levels could be
endured no longer, and Nevada ceased to herald its
bonanzas.

The state has three incorporated towns, and not
one with a census roll of five thousand. Virginia
City declined in the last decade from 8511 to 2695.
But this is of small import when we look at the irrigation map and see black patches representing more
than a half million of acres of watered lands, whose
annual product is worth nearly six million dollars.
For whatever of human comfort and prosperity is
possible, the way is open, even in Nevada, and, as in
southern California, intensive work with careful adaptation of valuable crops to small watered areas may
achieve results beyond expectation.

The sparseness of populations of the West appears
in another way. Twelve cities in the eleven divisions of the Cordilleran belt had, in 1900, twenty-five
thousand people or more. Eight of these are in
the three states of the Pacific coast, leaving but four
to the eight vast states and territories that remain.
Those four are Denver, Pueblo, Butte, and Salt Lake
City. No Cordilleran state or territory has as many
as ten people to a square mile, though California
almost reaches it, and for more than half these states
the average population of a square mile is less than
two persons. Even under the limitations of the
water supply the field for expansion is enormous.

In 1803 Louisiana was purchased, bringing an empire to the United States, but it was the Great Unknown. The fur trade had its headquarters at St. Louis, and the trappers brought their pelts and their stores from the plains beyond; but no map had been made, little was known of the wild and mysterious tribes of the upper Missouri, and no white man had seen the northern Rocky Mountains or gone from the Mississippi River to the Pacific Ocean. Jefferson selected Captains Lewis and Clark to find out what lay beyond the horizon, and with a small party of laborers and soldiers they left St. Louis in 1803. They went up the Missouri River and were lost in the wilderness, whence they emerged in 1806, having completed the most daring, important, and famous exploration ever undertaken within the United States. Their route could be traced by the chain of names which they gave to river and mountain between the mouth of the Missouri and the mouth of the Columbia rivers. On the Missouri in Nebraska they made peace with the Indians of the plains, and of this the city of Council Bluffs, across the river in Iowa, is a memorial. They saw the dark coniferous forests of the Black Hills, passed the mouth of the Yellowstone, carried their boats around the Great Falls of the Missouri, climbed the Rocky Mountains, named the sources of the Missouri, went down into the basin of the Columbia, appeased their hunger upon its salmon, saw the glistening Rainier, and camped upon the desolate shores of the Pacific Ocean. They conciliated where they could, fought where they must, waded the snows, kept their note-books, traced

their maps, finished what they were sent to do, and
came back to civilization.

In 1807 Lieutenant Z. M. Pike, having previously
sought the sources of the Mississippi, turned his

FIG. 58.   The Old Way.   Pike's Peak Trail at Minnehaha Falls.

steps westward toward the waters of the upper Arkansas, and fastened his name upon the best-known
though not the highest peak of the Rocky Mountains.   Major S. H. Long went from Pittsburg to
the Rocky Mountains in 1819–20, and likewise left
his name upon one of the lofty peaks of the Colorado.   Three years later, in going to the upper

Mississippi country, he passed Lake Michigan and found at Chicago "a few miserable huts inhabited by a miserable race of men."

The explorations of Captain B. L. E. Bonneville have more than geographic interest, because his jour-

FIG. 59.   The New Way.   Cog Railway at Minnehaha Falls.

nals afterward came under the editorial hand of Washington Irving, who gave them literary form and sent them out in the series of his works.   Bonneville was a soldier, who asked leave from the United States Army to carry out, with such funds and men as he could himself secure, a search into the distant West. His work was done in the years 1832–36 and was primarily in the interest of the fur trade, a business which lies at the foundation of much primitive history in the United States. Later authorities have ascribed to Bonneville the first correct account of the drainage of the region west of the Rocky Mountains, the region now known as the Great Basin. He it was that showed the interior character of this drainage, fixed the sources of the Willamette, San Joaquin, and Sacramento, and brushed away some of the geographic myths of Spanish writers. His search extended to the sources of the Yellowstone, of which he made a map.

The explorations of Captain J. C. Frémont followed by a dozen years and more. His work suggests the persistency of an error which was natural enough at the time, the belief, based on his reports, that the Great Basin is walled in by lofty mountains, making a continuous rim. This is suggested by the Wasatch and the Sierras on the east and west, but is not true to the north or south. Indeed, the long descent of the floor of the basin southward makes it perfectly possible, so far as land form is concerned, for an ordinary drainage system to develop, to drain all the shallow lakes of the basin and join the lower Colorado. The dryness of the climate is the only obstacle.

The roll of explorers for the middle decades of the nineteenth century is a long one, and bears the names of many soldiers, engineers, and men of science, and their scattered tours and investigations led down to that comprehensive system of surveys for opening routes of travel to the Pacific Ocean which was in operation in the fifties under the authority of the War Department, of which Jefferson Davis was secretary. Profiles, climate, magnetism, geology, botany, zoölogy,

and native tribes were all made objects of study, and
a half-dozen routes were followed, in the north, in the
south, and across the Rockies of Colorado.   In this
region Gunnison sought a line by the Sangre de Cristo
Range and the Coochetopa Pass of the Sawatch.
This was pronounced impossible, and Lieutenant
Beckwith, who took command after Gunnison's death,
said, " No other line exists in the immediate vicinity
of this worthy of any attention in connection with the
construction of a railroad from the Mississippi River
to the Great Basin."   This reads oddly in the presence
of the Denver and Rio Grande, threading the Royal
Gorge and the Marshall and Tennessee passes, or the
Colorado Midland, sending its trains by Ute Pass and
the South Park, past Leadville, and over the Continental Divide.

In these early explorations the naturalists who
accompanied the engineers got their knowledge as
they could, often only in fragments because of haste.
But there followed upon the close of the Civil War
the formal geographic and geological study of many
areas, by various bodies known as the Hayden,
Wheeler, King, and Powell surveys, and finally by
the United States Geological Survey.   The union of
theoretical knowledge with the lessons of experience
has never had a finer illustration than in the development of the mountains and plateaus of the West.

Will man in the West or in the East be friendly to
the forests?   There is no greater economic question
than this, and there can be in the end but one
answer, for experience has taught hard lessons in
some parts of our domain.   The forests are on the

mountains of the Cordilleran province, and they
shield the lowlands of the Pacific coast. They
belong in the most vital way to the problem of irrigation, for they store and dole out the waters which
otherwise would rush unhindered to the sea, carrying
the soils of the slopes, and destroying the bottom
lands with floods. Hence the life of millions of
people depends on the saving of the forests. It is a
worthy sentiment that would save from fire and ax
the noble Sequoia that has been growing for two
thousand years, but there is more than sentiment in
it. The earth's machinery is full of mutually dependent parts, to injure one of which is to destroy all.

In the Cascade and Ashland Forest reserves of
Oregon but 25,000 out of 3,000,000 acres of forest
have escaped the havoc made by fires. Some of the
fires belong to the period of Indian occupancy, but
by far the greater fires and in greater number have
occurred since the white man came. But fires are
less common in recent years. Little game is left,
hunting-parties are few, there is much private ownership and more precaution, and the humus layer, once
destroyed, no longer harbors and spreads the blaze.
The Indian's reasons for firing were: that grass
might grow near his camps, or that he might have
clear hunting-grounds. The white man fired the
woods to attract game, to open roadways, to promote
the growth of grass, or through careless leaving of
camp-fires. In one case where a fire was set to
allure game, a half-dozen deer were obtained and
fifteen to twenty million feet of timber were destroyed, the fire raging until put out by the fall

FIG. 60. Valley Lands, ruined by Recent Floods and abandoned; Southern Appalachians. Photograph by U.S. Bureau of Forestry.

rains. One fire was set to remove a windfall log from the road, and three thousand acres of forest were burned. In some cases the soil, almost purely vegetable in constitution, is completely burned away, leaving the bare rock. Many hundred years would be required to renew the soil and replace the forest. In the Cascade Reserve the fire loss during the past forty years amounted to seven thousand million feet of mill timber.

The shake maker has wasted untold amounts of timber. For these long coarse shingles he seeks the straight, well-splitting trunks, especially of the sugar pine, leaving enormous tops to rot, or to feed forest fires.

Sheep pasturing is more ruinous than cattle grazing, and there is a conspicuous dearth of seedlings where herds and flocks have filled the forest. The sheep herders start many fires, and while the forest ranger warns the trespasser to leave the ground, he is likely to get the answer that " bullets alone will be obeyed." Shake makers chip the trunks to test the grain. The resin runs out and down the tree, and the fires follow the line of fuel up the trunk and enlarge the scars made from year to year.

The Sequoias are not as near extinction as is supposed. There are many thousands of them in the reserves of California, but these noble patriarchs must be guarded from destroying selfishness.

There is but one course for the national government, and this has been entered upon with vigor and reward. The Cascade and Sierra ranges show an almost continuous belt of reserves. Others are found

Fig. 61. Appalachian Mountain Field ruined by Erosion. Photograph by U.S. Bureau of Forestry.

in every Cordilleran state, scores of thousands of acres, to be kept for the common weal, to be policed, and saved — their perennial springs, their straight trunks, their ample shade, their rich soil, their refreshing silences, rescued from the wickedness of the few, for the good of all.

The national government has a like problem and a similar duty in the East. The President, the Secretary of Agriculture, the geologist, and other men of science have pressed the need home upon Congress, and within a few days of this time adjournment has been had without action upon a forest reserve in the southern Appalachians. Here are the finest hardwood forests in America. Here is one of the heaviest rainfalls in the United States, with enormous capacity for destructive floods. As in the West, so in the East, the spongy soil cover once lost is lost forever, so far as present generations are concerned. Centuries do not work as much ruin under the forest cover as is done in a single storm after the lands have been made bare. Every southeastern state is involved, either bearing the forest slopes or receiving the waters upon its lowlands. Every water power in the hilly south is put to risk, and every acre of rich soil upon the river bottom. To save the forests for their timber, their beauty, and their health-giving shades, to save them for the farms and factories, and to save them at once, is the duty of the nation.

More than $10,000,000 was the sum of flood losses in the Appalachian states during the year 1901. With the abundant rains, wherever a slope of any steepness is cleared, it is cropped but for a few years, the soil is washed into the streams, tillage is given up, and the field is abandoned to ever deepening, gullies. Meantime the rich bottom lands below are either excavated and removed bodily by the torrents, or they are deluged with five, eight, or ten feet of stony waste, and become as useless as a gravelly river bed. Ten years of delay would be fatal. The single states cannot do the work. North Carolina owns much of the forest, but the advantage is more for Tennessee. One state cannot be expected to legislate, and tax itself for the benefit of its neighbor. As with irrigation, so here is a federal question.

These are the fresh problems of the twentieth century. We must control the mountains streams, to turn wheels, to avert floods, to make the soils fruitful; we must save the forests for themselves, for the soils, and for the fruitfulness of the lowlands. We must find, the world over, the grains and fruits that will grow with most water and least, in the hot south or cool north; we must adjust ourselves to mountain, plateau, and plain, to river and sea; and future generations better than ourselves will be able to see how geographic influences gave permanent molding to the national life.

CHAPTER X

FROM THE GOLDEN GATE TO PUGET SOUND

NATURE rarely accomplishes her ends all at once. When she would set a bulwark in eastern America in front of the Atlantic, she makes the beginnings of a mountain system, and perhaps what we count beginnings were not such at all. Then she rears the Green Mountains and wrinkles thick strata into Appalachian folds, and even then her work is not done. So there were Rocky Mountains and a Wasatch Range and Sierras and Coast Ranges and Basin Ranges, in the plan of the West, made in different periods, and the same range often due to long-separated epochs of disturbance and upheaval. The sudden possession by man, of these lands that took such a bewildering while in the making, is fitted to stir the wonder of many, and to set the few to philosophizing.

Our story has taken a westward course, and we might be deceived into the impression that California and Oregon waited upon Colorado and Utah to know the beginnings of civilized life, but this would have reversed the laws of geography by planting the interior and leaving the sea border a waste — and such a seaboard as fringes the western United States! Hither navigators had been coming, who during centuries of modern sea wandering had strayed into the Pacific Ocean. And after the last century came in, Spanish civilization, such as it was, moved up from Mexico, of which the California coast was then a part, and lived its easy life and founded its missions, and left its long roll of musical names on the shores and among the mountains.

The unfolding of the United States was given its order and rule from Europe. Because the progressive peoples and the discoverers and colonizers came from Europe, New England and Virginia became the front door of America. If the Chinese had been the expansionists of the sixteenth and later centuries, the Pacific shore would have been the front door of the continent, and something like New York, Philadelphia, and Baltimore would now be covering the heights around San Francisco Bay and Puget Sound, or fringing the shores of the Columbia and Willamette rivers. Indeed, something like these great cities can now be found there, inferior, indeed, in population, but not behind in energy, in self-appreciation, and perhaps with no inferior possibilities.

A pair of mountain ranges, the lesser fronting the sea, the greater overlooking the dry interior and the wide valleys lying between the two— such is the shortest account of the geography of California, Oregon, and Washington. For several hundred miles the Sierras make an eastern rampart for California, bearing summits which are sometimes more than fourteen thousand feet above the sea. Some of them commemorate the names of famous men of science,— Dana, Lyell, Tyndall, and, loftiest of all, Whitney, perpetuating the name of a student who did much to set in order the geology of California.

This great range is the backbone of the country through Oregon and Washington. In those states the dry plateaus of the Snake and Columbia lie on the east, as, with California, the arid lands of the Great Basin lie on the side of the rising sun. And from northern California to the Canadian boundary the great mountains, known in the more northerly states as the Cascades, are crowned with lofty peaks, volcanic cones, speaking of the more convulsive energies which in no distant past have helped to shape the Pacific lands. Shasta, St. Helens, Hood, and Rainier are set like jeweled crowns, gleaming white with snow and glaciers, upon the dark green forests of the wide uplands of the mountain range.

Close by the sea and parallel to the Sierras is another range of mountains, known by various names, but really one, from southern California to Puget Sound. In California it is the Coast Range; going northward into Oregon, it becomes the Klamath Mountains; and in Washington, stretching northward between the sea and the southern arm of Puget Sound, it is the Olympic Range.

Between these great belts of mountain, the higher on the east and the lower on the west, is a spacious valley, not indeed continuous, but the same in its general relations. In California it is the Great Valley, reaching far up and down the state, including most of the orchards, vineyards, and fields of wheat. In Oregon it is the Willamette Valley, and is likewise the center both of country and town life. And in Washington it is the Puget Sound Basin, which is described by the geologist of the state as " a broad

THE VALLEY OF CALIFORNIA

Showing the Sierras with their broader western slope, and the Coast Range,
broken by the Golden Gate and San Francisco Bay

trough, its large central area being less than a hundred feet above sea level, while its eastern and western sides rise gradually until they coalesce with the mountains."

About California we may say what sounds like bold contradiction, — it is the land of absolute contrasts, and yet it has, in a very special degree, geographic unity. Its mountains are of every height, from hills to Alpine summits, and there are wide vistas of low plains. It includes the torrid wastes of Death Valley, and the glaciers and ice-cold lakes of the upper Sierras. It is dry here and wet there; the plains are drenched in winter, and it never rains on them in summer; one may hide himself in remote valleys, in inaccessible mountains, and he may stand in open gateways on the sea, where he is neighborly to all the world.

And yet there is unity; for the Sierran wall rising unbroken for nearly five hundred miles on the east, and the Coast Range on the west, are knotted together at the north, and again far in the south, closing in around the long basin in which the people of California live. From the north flows the Sacramento River, and from the south the San Joaquin, still recalling Spain, and these streams unite and pour their waters through a chain of bays, and then through the Golden Gate into the sea. The Golden Gate is the portal of the one great gap in California leading through the Coast Range. There are other harbors in California, but none like these spacious, perfectly shielded waters. Here is the focus of movement and trade for the great valley and the interior slopes of the mountains. Human intercourse flows with the rivers to the Golden Gate. This interior basin, with its magnificent outlet, is not all of California, but it far outweighs the coast region of the south, the deserts of the lower Colorado, and the arid belt running east of the Sierras along the border of Nevada.

We shall still better appreciate the valley of California if we study the form of the Sierras. The range has a broad base of about eighty miles, but its crest is not along the middle line. Rather is it near the eastern border, which means that the eastern front rises bold and steep against the Great Basin, a real mountain wall, while the western slope is gentle, stretching down toward the axis of the valley, and the foothills melting imperceptibly into the plains on the west. Thus we see how it is that short rivers of little volume reach the lakes and alkaline flats of Nevada, while ranks upon ranks of living rivers flow down into the Sacramento and San Joaquin.

And we can understand the origin of the canyons, of which Yosemite is the most famous and perhaps the most wonderful. Older mountains stood where the Sierras are. These ancient heights were worn away by the ever working means which destroy the lands, and then the region was upheaved again, not equally everywhere, but most on the east. The earth's crust was profoundly fissured at the east base of the Sierras, and the vast block, several hundred miles long and nearly a hundred miles wide, was raised and tilted to the west, turning the old worn-down land into the west slope of the Sierras, and bringing up their eastern wall out of the depths.

Since the uplift, powerful glaciers have wrought on

FIG. 62. The Golden Gate and the Campus of the University of California, from the Berkeley Hills.

the high slopes and in the upper valleys, and a few patches of glacial ice remain as memorials of the cold epoch. Meantime the streams, rejuvenated by the uplift, have channeled the western slopes, and some of them have dug canyons with walls almost vertical and three or four thousand feet in height. It is a land great in heights as it is great in its extent, and the sober truth often sounds like exaggeration when repeated under the somber skies and in the heavier atmosphere of the East. There are waterfalls in the Yosemite, writes one appreciative of the Pacific country, that would be the objects of pilgrimage in Europe; yet they are overlooked by the traveler in the presence of greater and grander things.

But there are other stories which the streams on the west slopes of the Sierras have to tell. The rocks beneath them have been subjected, in the ages, to no common disturbance. Besides other changes they have been cracked and the fissures filled in with veins, those most common sources of precious metals. In the veins of the Sierras was gold. The veins were wasted by the frosts and worn by the streams, and the gold, along with the quartz that held it, was washed down the mountains. If the gold was in pieces of some size, the miner pocketed the nuggets. If it was dust, it lay in the gravels of the streams, often at the bottom, because it is heavy and would settle first. Then the miner would "wash" the gravels in a "pan," or a "cradle," or in an immense "sluice," and separate the dust, bags of which, like currency, he gambled away, or sent to San Francisco to pay for his supplies. By and by his washings took such proportions along the branches of the Sacramento that he was deluging the plow lands on the rivers below with worthless sheets of gravel, and the law had to step in with special enactments to restrain the gold finder in favor of the farmer. But this did not hinder the miners and the companies who sought and worked the parent veins, set up stamp mills, and did their work and reached fortune or failure without disturbing their agricultural neighbors. It is, over and over again, the adjustment of human life to the conditions of the earth in a new land, and this, it may be added, is the very essence of geography.

In some places the ditches once used in hydraulic mining are now filled with irrigating waters. No longer laden with superfluous gravels, their mission is beneficent, and California, whose mountains are still full of gold, is the land of garden, orchard, and field.

The valley of California has seen many changes. We cannot pretend to describe them — indeed, not all of them are known. But it is perfectly safe to picture a time when the region was open sea and the Coast Range was not built, but there were Sierras of some sort on the east. And there has been a valley, between the mountains and occupied by the sea, something like Puget Sound, only the interior waters were vaster. Two things could turn such a gulf into land, — uplift of the continental border, and filling in by waste from the mountains. No doubt both means have wrought, but it is the latter whose effects we can best see to-day.

One should turn to a map of California and see the streams that join the Sacramento and the San Joaquin. Nearly all of them and all the longer ones flow from the Sierras. As they flow down, their track inclines more and more gently, and they drop little by little

FIG. 63.   Grove of Big Trees, California.   Photograph by Wm. H. Rau.

their load of waste. A stream descending along a steep floor and abruptly entering a flat valley bottom will drop its load suddenly and build a steep débris slope, which the physiographer calls an alluvial cone. But in the conditions at the base of the Sierras the process is more gradual, and the result is not a cone, but a wide-sweeping fan of mountain-born waste, stretching far over the lowlands. There are so many streams and so close together that the fans blend and make a continuous gentle slope of waste. The climate of the valley is dry, but there are perfect conditions for watering, for here are never failing streams, and a land surface of just the right form for easy and universal distribution of the waters.

Like the Atlantic border, the Pacific shore line shows proof both of greater uplift and greater submergence of the land than now. That submergence was once greater appears in the sea terraces on the outer border of the Coast Range. Some are low, not more than ten feet above the present surface of the Pacific. And they range up to fifteen hundred feet, marking a time when the Valley of California was a broad and deep gulf. On the other hand, this edge of the continent has been higher than now. Then there was no Golden Gate, and there were no salt water bays behind it. Perhaps we should not say no Golden Gate, for the gap in the mountains was there, and through it the trunk river of California found its way out to the sea. The Golden Gate without San Francisco was like the Hudson in the days when there was no New York and no Manhattan Island, and the sea border was distant some score of miles.

Such is California, framed with mountains, — shall we say a gold frame? — and facing the greatest of seas. With all its variety, it is a simple, knowable country. None has said this better than Professor Josiah Royce, whose mother was an emigrant of '49, and who, in his history of California, has viewed his native country with affectionate appreciation. California is no such labyrinth as many eastern states.

"In most hilly regions, if one climbs to some promising summit, hoping to command therefrom a general view of the land about him, he often sees in the end nothing but a collection of gracefully curving hills similar to the one that he has chosen; . . . he gets no sense of the ground plan of the region. . . . But, in the typical central California landscape, as viewed from any commanding summit, the noble frankness of nature shows one at a glance the vast plan of the country. From hills only eighteen hundred or two thousand feet high on the Contra Casta side of San Francisco Bay you may, on a clear day, see to the westward the blue line of the ocean, the narrow Golden Gate, the bay itself at your feet; . . . you may easily find the distant range of the Santa Cruz Mountains; while to the eastward and northward you may look over the vast plains of the interior valley, and dwell upon the great blue masses of the Sierra Nevada rising far beyond them, and culminating in the snowy summits that all summer long would gleam across to you through the hot valley haze."[1]

The first Spanish occupation of our own or upper California began in 1769, when a group of soldiers and friars, less than a hundred in number, landed at San Diego. Other settlements and missions followed, and are noteworthy, not for spiritual or temporal fruitage, but barely as the first white colonization of California. No permanent institutions grew up, the wealth of the land was not found, and no influence was exerted upon the future. Spanish occupation

[1] "California," in "American Commonwealth," pp. 4-5.

only gave a sentimental background to Californian history. It only seems as if there were a real historical perspective instead of a state coming forth full-fledged in the West. A few old mission buildings give an antiquated flavor to the land, and the names of a hundred towns, rivers, and mountains are mouthed a million times in a day by people who are not even thus reminded that Spain held rule in California for almost as many years as have passed since the American flag was raised above the soil.

Mexico became independent of Spain at length, and this freedom was proclaimed in California in 1822, and from this time the spirit of local independence began to rise ; there was intrigue and strife, and the ferment that led the way to new unfoldings and a larger life. Thus California became "an outlying and neglected Mexican province." This applies to the later years of Mexican affiliation down to 1846. ·

But meantime a wedge was being driven in which would soon separate California from the southern land. For more than twenty years Yankee ships had been calling at California ports for trade, selling at extravagant prices what the lazy and incompetent Spanish-American wanted and had not the wit or industry to make. It is said that he sold hides to the traders, who took them around Cape Horn, had them made into shoes in New England, brought them back and sold them again in California. Hunters and frontiersmen, too, were coming overland year by year and reaching the western coast from across the mountains. California was being conquered in the surest of ways by the settler and the trader. The first

group of Americans established themselves in the
Sacramento Valley in the early forties.

In 1846 the crisis came. Frémont had come to
the valley, and independence was there proclaimed in
June. Early in July a naval force seized Monterey
and San Francisco, the latter then being known as
Yerba Buena. Gold was found in January, 1848, and
the rush to California began. Before the end of the
year 1849 the territory held more than one hundred
thousand people, a rough, miscellaneous, and lawless
population. And yet lawless is too strong a word,
for so many men cannot live together without the
rudiments of society. They crowd each other, and
their contacts are upon matters of such eager interest
to all that there is conflict indeed, but erelong something like systematic restraint develops, a code written
in custom if not in books. And if justice sometimes
lapses into cruelty, it never tortures its victim with
months of delay. Caution is not a cardinal virtue on
the frontier, but sagacity, courage, and instantaneous-
ness win. It is a land of clear skies and life-giving
air; this is a geographic factor. And it is a country
of gold and of a fertile soil, and this is geographic
also. But the call that went out to the people, and
the sort of men that would hear such a call and rush
across the mountains, the "forty-niners," the "Ar-
gonauts," — this is only in part a geographic condition; and who shall measure the resulting Californian
society, or, having measured it, shall single out its
attributes and say, so much is due to a unique geographic environment, and so much is a heritage from
the prairies, from New York, from New England,

Fig. 64. Cape Disappointment Light (on the rock at the right), Mouth of the Columbia River.

from everywhere ?   Ah, but there is the defiant fact about these western societies, they are composite in a way before unknown to history, and they are yet too young to be called historical.   They are like their own Sequoian forests two or three thousand years ago, when most of those trees had not been planted and the patriarchs were saplings.   But, if we choose this analogue, we must remember the size of a Sequoia that is young, say of two or three hundred years.

The history of California has been like that of Colorado, in which mining came first and was soon supplanted by agriculture, with manufacturing industries smaller, but growing.   With these must go an enlarging commerce, and upon all, as a foundation, must be built the structures of the higher life, and all these California has more than begun to achieve in her fifty-three years of statehood.   She has been able to attain so much because she was the first Pacific state, because her natural riches are so great, and because she has been peopled by sturdy and prompt men picked from every state in the East ; it is a civilization not grown from the soil, but transplanted.

The mineral product of California in 1900 was somewhat more than $30,000,000, but long before that the agricultural output of the state had begun to exceed $100,000,000 a year, and, so far as minerals are concerned, Colorado had taken the lead in the race.   Mining is a sober and normal industry, one among others, in California to-day, and such it will always remain.   Not half so important would the finding of new gold bonanzas be as is the discovery of petroleum, for in her poverty of fuel the state's greatest lack has lain.

Two schools, the greatest in the Cordilleran country and ranking with the eight or ten greatest universities of the East, have grown up within a single generation, — the Stanford University, with perhaps the richest educational foundation in the world, and the University of California, with its three thousand students, its generous public support, and its magnificent situation upon the western slope of the Berkeley Hills, looking out across the bay upon San Francisco and through the Golden Gate.

California is the most densely populated state west of the Great Plains, and yet dense is not the word; for less than ten people, on the average, dwell within a square mile, and the state has but ten towns of more than ten thousand people, and but four which exceed twenty-five thousand. Of these Oakland is but a suburb of the metropolis. Sacramento has a little less than thirty thousand, a modest development due to its seat in a fertile valley, and to its standing as the capital of the state. With manufactures in their beginning, and a comparatively undeveloped commerce, there has not been occasion for large cities.

California has a singularly unbroken coast line. There are other harbors, but that of San Francisco is unrivaled in magnificence. Great as the city is, it may become vastly greater as its state grows, and especially with the piercing of the Isthmus. And yet in all these prophecies the Columbia River, and especially Puget Sound, must not be overlooked;

for the United States has three western gates, and a splendid state with its greatest cities has come into existence about each of them.

California has such an enormous extension of sea and mountain that a fourth gathering of people and products should perhaps be added, not strictly maritime, nor far from the sea, Los Angeles, with its hundred thousand people in 1900, and having more than doubled its size in the previous ten years. Every interest of southern California, fruit, grain, petroleum, minerals, and the seeking of health — all have contributed to the growth of what is to-day the second city of the Pacific coast. The history of California is in the years to come, but the foundations are laid, not in gold, not in wheat, nor in oranges, but in character. "Life there is a little fresher, a little freer, a good deal richer, in its physical aspects, but for these reasons, possibly, more intensely and characteristically American. . . . It is the most cosmopolitan of all the states of the Union, and such it will remain. Whatever the fates may bring, the people will be tolerant, hopeful, and adequate, sure of themselves, masters of the present, fearless of the future." [1]

Oregon and Washington may stand together, for in their lands and their history, in their past and in their future, they have much in common. Oregon was once the inclusive name of the Northwest, taking in Idaho and a part of Montana. As with California, so with Oregon, our title to the lands came originally through Spain; but while the more

[1] David Starr Jordan, in *Atlantic Monthly*, 1898.

southern state fell, like her own fruit, into our hand, the Northwest was a bone of prolonged and stubborn contention with Great Britain. Here the beaver and the other fur-bearing animals were the makers of American history — a phase of our origin that deserves far more attention than it has had in these brief pages. There is no room for the story, but only for the gist of it. The Hudson Bay Company, rich,

Fig. 65.   Astoria.

grasping, powerful, and organized like an empire, was the agent of the mother country. If it could build forts enough, keep the woods full of its trappers, monopolize the trade of the savages, and persuade every Rocky Mountain emigrant that the road, or rather the trail, westward was impassable, then Oregon would become British territory.

In 1810 John Jacob Astor began his persistent and memorable attempt to plant a town at the mouth of the Columbia, doing it in the interests of the fur trade and of Americanism. In 1813 the trial had come to failure, and the British had run up their flag upon Fort George. But with the passage of another generation knowledge of the Northwest had increased and permanent settlers had welded the territory to the United States.

So majestic is the music of Bryant's line, "Where rolls the Oregon," that one might almost wish that even Columbia had not become familiar to our ears. But no poet could now write the words which follow, — "and hears no sound save his own dashings." The St. Lawrence, the Mississippi and its confluent waters, the Colorado, and the Columbia — these are the four great rivers of the United States, and but one of these, the greatest, is wholly within our domain. The Columbia reaches its long fingers widely among the Cordilleran Mountains, northward into the British provinces, eastward by the Snake River over all of Idaho and among the Rocky Mountains of Montana, and southward by the Willamette and other streams over most of Oregon. Although the waters of the trunk stream completely cross Washington, and only wash Oregon on its northern border, the river is the commercial highway of the Southern rather than the Northern state. This comes from the possession by Washington of Puget Sound, whither the railways tend and where most of the cities are built. Astoria, now a prosperous town, long after Astor's failure to effect a permanent settlement, stands at the mouth of the river in the extreme northwest corner of Oregon, while Portland, the third city of the Pacific coast, is on the Willamette a few miles south of its junction with the Columbia, and more than a hundred miles from the sea. But the water is deep and forms one long harbor, like the Thames. The lower Columbia is like the lower Delaware, Potomac, or Mississippi in bounding states.

Here the Coast Range and the Cascades are like the Coast Range and the Sierras in the south, and between them the Willamette flows northward like the San Joaquin. Here is the garden of Oregon, where the soil is rich, moisture abundant, transportation easy, and institutions have been maturing for two generations. It has been no part of our plan to offer catalogues of material resources; yet it is not easy to study these budding empires even from a distance without marveling at their riches and giving the imagination freedom as one thinks of the unfoldings of the coming hundred years.

Minnesota has wheat and forests and iron and the lakes; Iowa has wheat and corn and cattle; New England has mills and the sea; but Oregon has the sea and wheat and cattle and fruit and forests and the fisheries of the Columbia, gold, silver, nickel, copper, tin, and if she has yet only the beginnings of manufacture, she has power. The Willamette falls forty feet at Oregon City, but twelve miles above Portland, affording one million horse-power. Several years ago some of this energy was first turned into electricity and carried down to Portland. Two counties, as long ago as 1895, had yielded $25,000,000 in placer gold, and a quarter of a billion feet of lumber was cut each year. The disintegrated lavas of the Snake River plains are pastured, or where possible watered and plowed, and the people are calling for a

canal between the oceans.   Said Senator Mitchell of
Oregon : "We want, our interests demand, and we
must and will have at no distant day a ship canal
across the Isthmus of Nicaragua.   The interests not
only of Oregon, but of the Pacific coast, of the whole
nation, and of all the civilized nations of the globe
demand it. . . .   Give us the Nicaragua Canal, and
we will then stand erect in every element which con-
stitutes independent commercial supremacy."   These
are but sober words, and they are a good sample of
western honesty, directness, and strength ; and they
are nearer fulfillment, putting Panama in place of
Nicaragua, than they were in 1895.

Indeed, if there be a quality which breeds in western
air, it is quick decision and the instant application
of energy to the matter in hand.   To wait, to weigh,
to hesitate and do nothing — these are qualities or
habits that seem to have been lost in crossing the
Mississippi River.   One writer asserts that the West
is excessively individualistic, that no man regards
another, but seeks for himself and walks alone.   Another tells you of the coöperative habits of the Northwest, the readiness with which men receive ideas, form
projects, and put shoulders side by side under the
burden.   It would be a waste of time to debate the
issue.   Both views are true ; and there is ready and
fearless coöperation because every man feels adequate
in himself, he has large resources, he can therefore
gain something from his neighbor, and spare something for him.   He knows that three and three are
not so great as three times three.

Three young women, sisters, from Portland, were

FIG. 66. Seattle.

studying music in Munich. To the observation that their parents must be lonely, their rejoinder was that it might be a relief at home to have them gone. They were honest, vigorous, refined, and true; they were going home after a year or two, by way of Japan. The West is the cosmopolitan part of America. A thousand miles is a short excursion, and across the continent is not an undertaking. Men who could not change their horizon without homesickness did not go west; they are independent of distance, they are accustomed to looking up to find their mountains, and their children are born into their wide, free life.

We may stop again to wonder at a land of unbounded wealth, opening on the greatest of oceans, and yet peopled from across mountain and desert. But it was a choice of prairie schooner or Cape Horn, until now man has made his own geography, and reads and smokes and sleeps and dines himself across the continent in five days. But if railroads had come seventy years sooner, we should not have had Lewis and Clark and the other heroes of western exploration. The West has her great men and great events, and a hundred years from now they can be read as history and not as magic; there will not be so much kaleidoscope effect; the events of the nineteenth century will not seem so dazzling, but just as wonderful.

Almost everything, perhaps all, that can be said of Oregon is equally true of Washington. The physical conformation is the same in its important features. The Coast Range becomes the Olympic Mountains. The Cascades reach northward to the British line,

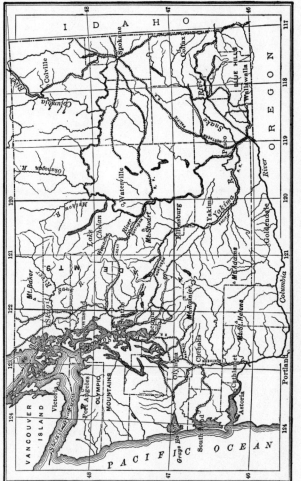

OUTLINE MAP OF THE STATE OF WASHINGTON

surmounted by the most splendid of the volcanic peaks, Rainier. The Willamette Valley is replaced by the Puget Sound Basin, and the river by the sound. And beyond the Cascades are the Columbia plateaus and the wheat fields and Spokane. There is abundant coal and almost every other thing that the under earth affords. And the soil bears nearly everything that will grow in any temperate latitude. The climate is softened by the warm Pacific, and the

FIG. 67.   Golden Gate at Sunset, from the Campus of the University of California.

wharves along the sound are the gateway of the Northwest; they open the way to Alaska, and they confront the Orient.

Even an Easterner will not long study this land of swift and large achievement before his pen will speed over the page, and he will share the glow in which great cities have grown in a generation, and lines of commerce have been run out over the world. Four of the lines of railway that cross the continent can shift their loads by these wharves. Not one, but a dozen harbors or more, in these still and retired waters, invite commerce, and there is room for more cities than Seattle, Tacoma, and Everett.

What nature has denied to the Pacific coast, it would not be easy to tell. In coming days she will be commercially independent of the East, and will have her own communication with all the world across the seas. Whether the New York of the West will be by the Golden Gate, or on the Willamette River, or on the borders of Puget Sound, this writer will not incur enmity by predicting; but he need be no seer who sees cities like those of the Atlantic standing under the western sun.

CHAPTER XI

GEOGRAPHY AND AMERICAN DESTINY

We cannot look on the freedom of this country in connection
with its youth, without a presentiment that here shall laws and
institutions exist on some scale of proportion to the majesty of
nature. — EMERSON.

IN our steady march westward we have rested
upon one region after another, each having some
natural unity, and developing, in more or less clear
fashion, a type of life. It remains to see what general views are possible and to ask whether the past
and present point in any simple and clear way to the
future. At each step we have assured ourselves that
geographic influences are real, but real as they are,
they cannot be narrowly defined or be given in
quantitative terms.

Racial tendencies, whatever their source, are
always obscuring or swerving the lines drawn by
nature. There is no better example of both our
principle and its limitations than our motherland.
No historian doubts that Great Britain owes much to
her isolation. She has suffered no real invasion since
the Norman conquest. In earlier centuries there
were invasions enough, but when a measure of defensive unity had been gained, the Channel was too
much for the would-be conquerors from the mainland. And a recent writer has pointed out that the

feudal forty-day period was quite inadequate for English military service on the continent, and that this condition, in the time of Henry II, led to more stable military provision.   Thus both from the defensive and offensive point of view, the " silver streak " wrought for England's greatness.   Within the island, geographic facts are quite as ruggedly real.   From the earliest days to the last blood shed on Scottish soil, invasions stopped at the base of the Highlands. The Celt remains in his own mountains.   Almost every square mile of England is within easy distance of navigable waters, her deep-set estuaries, or the canals crossing her lowlands.   The growth of industry and the transfer of political influence and of population to the north of England tell in no faltering way the power of natural conditions.   But there is no certainty that other than the many-fibered English race would have made Great Britain.

Spain gives useful comparison if we can group the facts fairly.   She, too, has isolation.   Less than half her northern boundary follows the Pyrenees, and all the rest on every hand is sea, — the Bay of Biscay, the open Atlantic, and the Mediterranean.   Once a great seagoing people, she now, with all her coastline, might almost as well be in the heart of the continent. Portugal stands athwart two of her largest streams, with far less geographic excuse for national independence than Wales or Ireland, or the Scottish Highlands.   Much, however, as we may ascribe to the difference between Saxon and Latin, there are geographic differences which qualify the one great fact of isolation.   Even the Pyrenees are a less effective barrier than a belt of salt water, and it was late in modern history before the boundary rested on their crest. And Spain is lofty in her interior provinces, arid, and cut up by mountains, and her rivers are not tidal. Spain is not much like the low, fertile, and accessible plains of England. It was a saying of Henry IV that if you enter Spain with a small army, you are defeated; if you go with a large army, you are starved.

In Holland is a people who, by their earliest traditions, were a stern and sturdy stock. For centuries they have fought out the sea under leaden skies, built up their civilization, and sailed the seas of the world. And yet the Dutchman settles in South Africa far from any shore, becomes a farmer, and to all appearance forgets the ocean. Such facts are perplexing, and make us think that the principles of organic evolution, interpreting all the facts of ethnology, history, and geography, can alone in the end give us truth.

When we look back upon the history of America, we see one fact of overshadowing importance: it is this, — that a wide ocean separated an advanced civilization and a relatively dense population from a wide, rich, and almost unoccupied continent. This is the mainspring of American destiny. The discovery of the New World was coincident with conditions of discontent and internal pressure in the Old. There followed the unique transfer of a highly developed civilization, in a short time, to a far-distant and isolated land. New ideas needful for human progress had germinated and made a certain growth, as in the cramped spaces of a nursery. They were suddenly transplanted to open grounds far away. All that a change of environment can induce came to them; and thus we see American social and political ideas growing and fruiting in a free field, maintaining continuity with the old through heredity and frequent reinforcement from the ancient sources, but free from repression, and unfolding in the unsullied atmosphere of a " reserved " continent, if we may adopt the pregnant phrase of Horace Bushnell.

American history is the story of the modern overflow into this New World. We have followed the French up the St. Lawrence and down the Mississippi, and the Spaniard along the shores of the Gulf; and we have seen the Englishman in the narrow land between the sea and the Appalachian Mountains. Not because of geographic opportunity, but by virtue of qualities that inhered in his race, he reached northward and southward, dispossessing his Latin neighbors, and poured at length across the barrier, and swept the valley of the Mississippi. Westward to the Mississippi the land was covered in claim by the ancient colonies, but the claim had to be made good by the wilderness men of the Ohio Valley. The Louisiana Purchase, in 1803, first made the United States a continental nation, giving foothold on the Gulf, and carrying the frontier to the Rocky Mountains. The purchase of Florida, in 1819, widened our domain on the Gulf of Mexico, and the annexation of Texas, in 1845, still further increased our southern shore-line and gave us the Rio Grande. Then, in 1846, we leaped to the Pacific by the settlement of the long-drawn Oregon dispute, and two

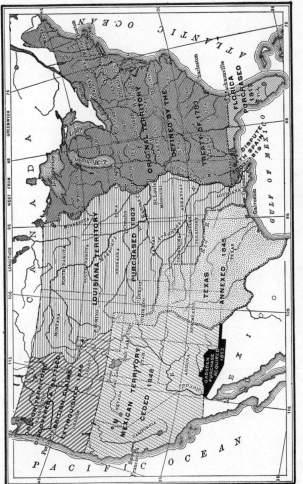

Expansion Map of United States

years later, in 1848, we gained our normal place on the Pacific by acquiring California. The Gadsden Purchase, in 1853, rounded out our territory, when expansion rested until the acquirement of Alaska and the island possessions of recent years.

There is meaning in this westward direction of our growth. It began in the simple reason that the discoverers lived on the eastern shore of the Atlantic, and were obliged to find the new continent from the East. And there was advantage in this for the progress of empire. America is open to the East. Its Atlantic border is lined with deep-set bays and innumerable harbors, from Labrador to the far South. The Laurentian waters open to the heart of the continent. To this same broad basin the Mohawk furnishes a separate gateway. The Gulf of Mexico opens on the east, making, with the Caribbean, the American Mediterranean, bordered by the great island group of the Western Hemisphere. From the Gulf the broad prairies of the Mississippi Valley lead to the Rocky Mountains, and merge with the plains of the Great Lakes.

A nation founded in the East could reach out and hold the Pacific, with support at every point. It is doubtful whether a state planted on the Pacific could have bound the wide Atlantic slope to itself. Vast as the destinies of the Pacific may be, the history has observed a normal order. The center of empire may lie west of the Appalachians, but it is east of the Rocky Mountains. Whatever the unfoldings of future generations, when a New York rises on the Pacific, and every arid plateau is watered to the utmost, we still could not imagine Massachusetts and Ohio as tributary to a national capital in some Cordilleran state.

When the currents of Old World life had crossed the New, with speed unparalleled, and had reached the Pacific, new conditions came into being, conditions still so new and so near that we cannot now see them in true proportion. The pent-up Old World of the modern centuries has filled the New, and this New World is beginning to react on the Old. This novel and wide relation was unpredicted and perhaps unpredictable before 1898. Since that date the return wave has crossed the seas with bewildering swiftness, and swept the ancient shores with surprising power. The American diplomatist and the agent of the American manufacturer only give local expression to this vast recoil of the New World on the Old, while behind is the all-embracing influence of American democracy upon the social and political evolution of the ancient continents. No man, in these conditions, should essay prophecy.

No more can be done than to mark the trends of the past, and these can be seen only in short perspective, or to follow the lines of the present, as well as we can, and see how far they are likely to run into the future. Professor R. H. Thurston has emphasized the fact that the graphic curves which may be drawn, on the basis of the past, to represent national progress, are not likely in the near future to suffer any abrupt change of direction,[1] and this will be true

[1] R. H. Thurston, "Trend of National Progress," *North American Review,* Vol. CLXI, p. 297.

without much reference to good or bad times, or so-called "crises." And the result will be the more trustworthy the larger the forces and the greater the masses of men taken into the reckoning.

Applying this principle, we can select our natural resources for consideration : our variety of soil, our diversities of climate, and minerals of every useful kind. We have only made a beginning in the use of our coal and iron. These and other mineral bases of our material prosperity can be relied on for long periods. Or we may take those purely geographic conditions of wide plains and inland waterways as related to domestic transportation, and our position between two oceans as relating us to the commerce of the world, and we find these to be fixed facts, with a stable relation to our place in the world.

The character of our people is to be taken as a datum for future expectation. Whatever the American type is, it is a fairly fixed and trustworthy quantity. We need not make any claims for geography here, though geographic influences may have been dominant, lying too far back on the ancestral grounds of Europe and Asia for us to trace them.

If we were trying the rôle of the prophet, we must take account of the ultimate moral type, as possibly affected by growing luxury, or by large strains of new immigration, but to this question our theme does not bid us. Nor can any man predict the revolutions that may arise from new and unforeseeable applications of energy, with swift and radical results upon our social order.

If we come back to the surer ground of the immediate past, we may discuss with a sense of certainty the decline of sectionalism in the United States, as related to geographic conditions.   And this is coming to pass notwithstanding the fact that our country abounds in geographic centers and in regions of strong physical individuality.   In truth, such diversities are more felt in the early days of national history.   The dweller on the New England shore was likely to be a fisherman, but modern conditions have made him, for the greater part, something else. The early inhabitant of the Western mountains was almost sure to be a miner or a stock raiser, but now he is as often a merchant, a professional man, or a farmer. The power of primitive controls is lost, or it is absorbed in the more mature and general trends of an older life.   A few tons of coal are now enough to overcome the Appalachian barrier, and it is from this point of view, apparently, that a recent writer [1] treats the Appalachians lightly, as if they were no barrier. They do not now stop or turn aside the movements of men and commodities, but they still interpose a peculiar belt of climate, soil, field, and forest between the Atlantic and the Mississippi, and their influence in early days was enormous.   Geographic influences are no less real because they blend with other types of control in the maturity of society.

In an early chapter of this volume we have taken New England as a region of enough geographic unity to stand by itself, but individuality does not mean isolation.   In the single matter of gaining a miscel-

[1] Rev. H. B. George in "The Relations of Geography and History," p. 284.

laneous population, New England has shared the fortunes of the rest of the country. Massachusetts has contributed her Puritan sons to every middle and western state, and has to-day about eight hundred and fifty thousand foreign-born persons. Of these a quarter of a million are Irish, one hundred and thirty thousand are French Canadian, not far from thirty thousand each are German, Italian, Russian, and Swedish, and the rest are from almost every country of Europe and Asia. New England cannot sit peacefully behind the Berkshires and ignore the problems that face other sections of the Republic. It has surrendered or modified its agriculture, focused its foreign trade in a single port, shared its fishing and its cotton mills with other sections, and has felt in all ways the pulse of a common life.

Especially is the geographic unity of our country having its way in the common life that is now rapidly growing as between the North and South. The passing of slavery has removed the only insuperable obstacle to social and economic union. The colored race, indeed, remains, but no longer presents the unattacked and depressing problem of ten years ago. The growth of varied tillage of the soil, the building of railways, manufactures in the southern Appalachians, the development of cities, the rising of Gulf commerce, the influx of Northern capital, and the pressure of common national motives, have gone far to banish all harsher differences between North and South. Intercommunication, common business interests, common national ideals, — these are the watchwords, and they have no larger or finer expression

than in recent movements in Southern education, led
by the executives of great Southern schools, and fostered by that beneficent body grown out of the best
and most deeply patriotic sentiment of South and
North, the Southern Education Board. Mr. P. A.
Bruce does not hesitate to say, in view of the revolution that has been enacted since the war, that "if
the only object the Federal authorities had in view in
prosecuting the war of 1861–1865 had been to estab-
lish the complete unification of the civilization of the
Southern States with the civilization of the Northern,
they could not have accomplished that purpose more
successfully." [1]

We have already dwelt enough, perhaps, on the
fast-coming unity of the South and the old West,
along the Mississippi River, through the continuity
of the prairies, favorable lines of transportation to
common ports, and the absence, since 1865, of a
divisive social system.

With equal emphasis may we claim the unity of
the East and the West. It is now some years since
Professor Turner showed that the "West" is not a
place, — it is only a stage of progress, exhibited now
in the upper Mississippi, now in the Rocky Mountains, and now on the Pacific coast. The new is
constantly becoming the old, under the transforming
power of time, of ready intercommunication, and of
absorbing social and national ideals. A Western man
has been defined as an Eastern man who has had
some additional experiences. Every contact with so-

[1] Mr. Philip Alexander Bruce, in the *Contemporary Review*, Vol.
LXXVIII, 1900.

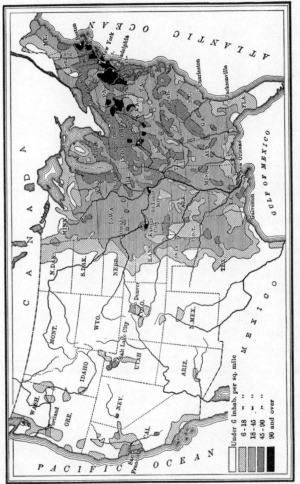

POPULATION MAP OF UNITED STATES

called Western life in its more settled phases will convince one of the truth of this definition.   In large measure, prairie, plain and plateau were directly peopled from the East.   Great cities have grown up among the farms of the Mississippi Valley.   Minneapolis, Denver, and Portland are far older than their years.   Following the first blunders of settlement and tillage, the Middle West has adjusted itself to conditions, has grown forehanded, has ceased to be discontented, and is no longer, therefore, the sworn social and political enemy of the East.

In every state of the Cordilleran mountains mining has become a more sober industry ; mining camps are cities with brick buildings and modern conveniences ; the herder and cowboy find their claims limited by the rights of the irrigator and plowman, and railroads have brought remote mountain valleys into union with the centers of life.   Property rights are the same recognized things as in the East, and the schools and churches offer to settled societies the same guarantees of progress and perpetuity that are found in the oldest commonwealths east of the Mississippi River.

The decline of sectionalism is apparent if we compare the Farthest East and the Farthest West ; the supposedly staid New England with the new societies beyond the Sierras and the Cascades, in a land where precedents are thought to count for little.   So recently as 1896 a brief writing appeared in the *North American Review*, bearing the title, " Two Republics or One ? "   It is not easy to believe that an argument professedly based on current conditions could, in seven years, become so antiquated.   The East and West are

out of sympathy upon the questions of money. " The
two sections are apart on almost every vital principle." The two sections are divided on the tariff.
The inland West does not care about a navy. The
East has no interest in the problems of irrigation.
The West no longer feels the ancestral ties that once
bound it to the Atlantic states. Most of this reads
curiously in 1903, and two republics meeting along the
Mississippi River seem little other than a vagary of
insanity. Far more true to the general trend was
a word of Mr. Bryce, written several years earlier,
" Even the Pacific states, which might have seemed
likely to form a community by themselves, are being
drawn closer to those of the Mississippi basin."

In fact, the very diversities that have shown themselves in our geography, and in the sources and
character of our population, have promoted our unity.
They have favored interchange and mutual depend-
ence; have kept alive wholesome discussion, and
we have had in them, as we shall always have in
greater or less degree, the actions and reactions which
are essential to a true organic life.

There is perhaps no better example of the general
awakening and social integration than is furnished in
the southern Appalachians. These are no longer a
remote and private ground. In an earlier chapter we
have had glimpses of the beginnings of their curious
life. Then the wilderness closed around this land of
mountain and forest for a hundred years. Surrounding life progressed, until that of the mountains
became almost fossil. Now, however, the novelist
has revealed it to the world. Railways have pierced

the country; iron and coal are exploited; cities are
growing, and forests and water power have become
matters of national concern.   All the processes of
social unification are in full operation, and two millions of people of pure American stock, if we may so
call it, are soon to be assimilated to modern conditions.   Asheville is already as well known as Springfield or Duluth; a school of forestry exists there in
the heart of the Southern mountains.   Knoxville sees
every summer a gathering of hundreds, if not thousands, of Southern teachers, and such schools as Berea
College introduce into the very heart of this secluded
domain the appliances and culture of modern life.

We might truly call these processes of social unification continental, for the Provinces of Canada will
all be virtually, if not formally, linked in destiny with
the parts of the American Union.

Reference has been made to the comment of Mr.
Bryce on the East and the West.   His observations
deserve to be still further recalled.   Our country, in
his view, is monotonous, and excessive in its sameness.
The Mississippi plains are larger than the western
half of Europe, bearing what could scarcely "be
called a hill."   There is more uniformity for a thousand miles than could be found in a journey of
a hundred miles in Europe.   The dweller on the
prairies must travel hundreds of miles in order to see
a different kind of landscape.   Professor Shaler has
emphasized this physical unity of our continent in his
argument that we have no isolated grounds fitted to
be the cradles of diverse races.   Bryce does not
ascribe a sole or unbalanced influence to geographic

conditions, but truthfully gives due weight to all the
conditions of our developing civilization, the mobility
of our population, the diffusion of common ideas by
reading, our swift growth, and ready means of communication.

Other English writers have made like comments
upon the homogeneity of our life, and their impres-
sions, as outside observers, have peculiar interest.
Professor Freeman is one of these, and he marks the
differences between parts of our Union as hardly
so great as may be seen in passing from England to
Scotland. And his word, it should be added, was
spoken twenty years ago. But Frederic Harrison,
writing just two years ago, puts the case even more
strongly : " The American world is practically 'run'
by genuine Americans. In one sense, the United
States seemed to me more homogeneous than the
United Kingdom. There is no state, city, or large
area which has a distinct race of its own, as Ireland,
Wales, and Scotland have, and of course there is
nothing analogous to the diverse nationalities of the
British Empire. From Long Island to San Francisco, from Florida Bay to Vancouver's Island, there
is one dominant race and civilization, one language,
one type of law, one sense of nationality. That race,
that nationality, is American to the core." [1]

We may add to our review two further considera-
tions, both comparatively new in development, and
now beginning to be reckoned at their real value.
We are now ceasing to be a country with a frontier.
The isolation, the absence of laws and settled usage,

[1] *Nineteenth Century*, Vol. XLIX, 1901, pp. 914–915.

the tense struggle with Nature,—these belong largely
to the past, and every region is come to more settled
conditions.   We must now assimilate, and use our
resources intensively.   Society has no ready outlet for
its turbulent elements, and the stream of our life is
turning on itself to mingle with the broad sea of
Americanism.   Adjustment to geographic conditions,
variety of occupation, stable conditions of industrial
and social life,— such are the phrases now properly
descriptive of America.   Added to these internal
conditions, the common pressure of new foreign problems and relations has had its share in welding diverse
elements into a national unity.

Wholeness, with individuality and variety, are
working as the half conscious, but not less real or
precious ideals of our people, and we may look hope-
fully to a blending of the elements of our Americanism, like an antique Persian carpet, with colors ever
themselves, never lost, more glorious with age, but
perfect in their harmony.

Mr. Frederic Harrison has been quoted as saying
that this country is "run" by the typical American,
but what, or who this is, is at least an open question.
A widely observant student of the East and West
recently averred in the hearing of the writer, that
your typical New Yorker was born either in Ohio or
in Jerusalem, and any analysis of names honorable in
civic and business life in America would show a generous quota of Germans, Irishmen, Scandinavians,
and Hebrews.   How long has your foreigner been
in America, is the question you cannot omit.   If he
came when a boy, he is "Americanized."   If his

father came, and he is only of foreign extraction, it is fair to assume that only in name is he to be referred to European stock. If, indeed, an Old World visage cling to him, it will be the misleading garb of a spirit belonging to the Western Hemisphere. All this points to an immensely effective capacity for assimilation, in our atmosphere, by the early group of Americans who have continued to give color and direction to our civilization.

It has, however, been well urged by Roosevelt[1] that these early Americans were not the single, unmingled race that they are often taken to be, that not English alone, but Dutch, German, Irish, Scandinavian, and Huguenot came also. Latter-day immigration has scarcely made us a more heterogeneous people. Whatever unity we possess, it is not unity of original stock, save as that stock was, in the main, a Teutonic compound from Northern Europe. The backwoodsmen of the Appalachians were of mixed ancestry, — Scotch-Irish, English, German, Dutch, Huguenot, and Swede; yet they had become American in speech, thought, and character, long before the Continental Congress assembled.

Union of races may indeed have given virility to our stock, but it is no new thing in the history of the English peoples. Far more important is the fact that America was first occupied by picked men. The Old World was sifted in the unconscious search to find men that were fit to build a new one, — men with convictions, daring endurance, and self-trusting strength. That such a process of selection has proceeded from

[1] "Winning of the West," Vol. I, pp. 38–39.

first to last, holding not only of the original colonists, but largely of those men who in the last two generations have fled from narrow lands and strong governments, need not be doubted. It is easy to pass a false verdict on the steerage. The same faces, ten years later, tell a truer story of innate capacity and of the molding power of America.

Beginning thus, often despite appearances, with the selected elements of Old World life, we may then assure ourselves that our political and social institutions, combining with wide areas of field and forest, have afforded more free and spontaneous conditions for vast multitudes of the common people than the world has before seen. The greatness and variety of our land has challenged the best powers of men, who, in common equality, and spurred by hopeful ambition, could make the most of our resources. Here comes in again the fact of a "reserved continent," ready to be swiftly overrun, precisely at the time when energy is being used in all modern ways, and by selected men, forced out by the exigencies of an Old World, and lured by the opportunities of the New. Nor can it be overlooked that political freedom and geographic riches have often been vitalized by deep moral and religious ideals, and by widely diffused education. Indeed, all these factors are so entangled in their activity that we may well despair of orderly analysis.

With a sure sense of the future, Washington and his contemporaries saw that the stability and wealth of the Republic were bound up with the possession of the old Northwest, and this led to the building of roads and soon to the Erie Canal. The Louisiana Purchase, in its turn, became an equally imperative step in expansion, and the logical sequence of this was Oregon and California and an outlet on the Pacific Ocean. The prairies and great plains invited the swift construction of railways, and railway surveys to the Pacific followed almost at once upon the extension of our title to its shores. It was the unique opportunity for civilization to overrun a continent in two generations. It had not happened before, and it cannot happen again. Other large lands remain to be civilized, but none of them is so nearly empty of human populations as North America, and none is so well placed and well fitted for a high type of society.

Such opportunity, opening so swiftly and compelling men to grapple with large problems, has reacted on American character, producing alertness, faith, insight, and inventiveness. Retaining a useful measure of ancestral conservatism, the American has followed the lead of new conditions, in the swift evolution of a political system, and in conquering a fresh continent with adequate tools of industry. An American army never failed to furnish men to do the needed thing on the instant. A mill could be set running, a bridge built, a locomotive repaired, or a city governed, the moment that military necessity presented itself. Without boasting, it may freely be said that the conditions of American life during the past century have favored versatility and swift achievement.

Not long ago a cartoon showed Uncle Sam turning the citizen mill. Great drops of sweat were falling from his face, but the mill did not stop, nor did the endless supply of rough and uncombed immigrants cease to pass forth as well-clothed and intelligent men and women to join the ranks of our citizenship. Swift, sure, and unremitting — such is the process of Americanization. Bald statements concerning the sum of foreign population in our cities, New York, Cincinnati, Chicago, or Milwaukee, are startling; and they are misleading if the pervasive leaven of our American land and our Americanism is forgotten.

The only disturbing element in the problem is the decline of the Teutonic stream and the growing numbers of Slavs and Latins. But we are in no immediate danger, and the policy of more rigid restriction is yet open to us.

This strenuous internal history seems to have been fitting us for some larger rôle in the affairs of the world. Exploiting our own continent and dominating the Western Hemisphere, we seem to have been destined for a recoil of power upon the world at large. From the point of view of resources and national wealth, we can now see in Alaska what must have been sealed even to Seward, in his purchase, forty years ago. Hawaii followed, after a long period, an unconscious stepping-stone to that great base which we now hold in Asiatic waters. Meantime we have come into normal relations to the American Mediterranean, in our acquisition of Porto Rico and our affiliation with the free people of Cuba.

The next step in American expansion is the opening of the canal across the Isthmus. Like Suez, Panama will be a critical point in history. The Red Sea and Black Sea routes controlled the commerce of the East and the destinies of Southern Europe for centuries, until modern sailors passed the Cape of Good Hope. Then the Mediterranean ports declined, and England came to her commercial heritage. She opened Suez, and then ceased, as one of her own economists has shown, to be the distributing center of Europe, although she retained her financial supremacy. What results the new canal will have for New Orleans, or New York, or San Francisco, it might require a seer to say, but that they will be large, and that they will enhance the wealth and promote the commercial dominance of the United States there can scarcely be doubt.

We have seen how naturally the improvement of the Mississippi River will lead to close commercial relations between the central parts of the Union and the nations of the East. And the new ships of the Pacific will also place the Andean lands of South America, as well as New Zealand and Australia, at short range with the American farmer, merchant, and manufacturer.

The geographic conditions for American growth seem to have been perfect. At a critical time in the history of European thought and life, a sturdy people needed a new field. That field was opened to them by the voyagers of the fifteenth and sixteenth centuries. It was entered from the Atlantic side, and opened so freely on those waters as to insure swift occupancy and a single dominion from ocean to ocean. It had the widest variety of surface, soil, and climate, and was fitted, or can be fitted, to produce nearly all that human comfort and intelligence can crave. The land is large enough to support an enormous population, and still produce a surplus for the markets of the world. The very largeness of American problems has helped to make a people able to solve them, and that people now finds itself fronting the two great oceans, where, more easily than any other nation, it can reach out and touch every part of the world. These conditions, in their entirety, are unique in history. They are largely geographic in their character, and they only need the perennial support of the basal moral qualities to insure to our country unfailing leadership among the nations.

CHAPTER XII

GOVERNMENT STUDY OF OUR DOMAIN [1]

ONE hundred and six years ago George Washington urged upon his countrymen to " promote, as an object of primary importance, institutions for the increase and diffusion of knowledge; in proportion as the structure of government gives force to public opinion, it is essential that public opinion should be enlightened."

The American government has been faithful to these counsels. Presidents, cabinet officers, legislators, and officers of the army have lent their influence, have organized and supported institutions through which America has made her contribution to pure and applied science.

In a single chapter we cannot traverse this field of public activity, but we can take a bird's-eye view. Familiar as some phases of this work are, most American citizens fail to appreciate its vastness, and the splendid history by which it has grown to its present proportions. We may begin with the Geological Survey, which may safely be called the greatest institution of its kind in any land. It is not

---

[1] The pages that follow were first presented before the Oneida Historical Society at Utica. It has not been thought needful, in revision, to remove all traces of the style suited to public address.

exactly true to say that the Survey was founded in 1879, for more or less geological work had been done under the patronage of the government throughout the century. The diaries of Lewis and Clark contain geological notes, and are, in the main, devoted to the geography of the Western wilderness. To nearly the same date belong the explorations of Major Pike; Major Long's expeditions followed, as we have seen, in 1819 and succeeding years; Schoolcraft went to the sources of the Mississippi in 1832; Captain Bonneville's work was done in the years 1832–1836. All these explorers did something with the geology of their routes.

The first formal geological work under federal patronage was done by Featherstonhaugh in 1834–1835. Such surveys were sporadically undertaken as the years passed, down to 1867. Sometimes they were under one, and sometimes under another department at Washington. Often the geologist was a mere appendage to boundary or other surveys, and he must catch his knowledge and gather his specimens on the run, since his was not the main purpose of the expedition. Such are the geological studies pertaining to the Pacific Railway surveys in the years following 1850.

In 1867 something more formal was undertaken. It is not our purpose to give details, but suffice it to say that for the next dozen years we hear of the Wheeler Surveys, the Survey of the Fortieth Parallel under Clarence King, the Hayden Surveys, and the Powell Surveys. Bulky, and in some cases splendid, volumes and atlases show the fruitfulness of that period.   Noteworthy were the explorations and studies of the daring veteran of the Civil War, one-armed, determined, versatile, creative Major John Wesley Powell, patriot, geographer, geologist, ethnologist, who a few weeks ago finished one of the greatest scientific careers ever achieved by an American.

But these numerous surveys crossed lines and clashed, with needless expenditure, and fell short of the best public service.   Largely through Powell they were superseded, and the geological work of the government was reorganized in 1879 by the founding of the present survey.   The best geologists were called into its service, far-reaching plans were adopted, and the financial affairs of the survey were handled with such thoroughness that a few years later the books of the organization were subjected to an unfriendly examination without raising a breath of suspicion.   The result has been a steady growth in annual appropriations, which in late years have amounted to about one million of dollars.   And now the work required by the new irrigation legislation has been intrusted to it, greatly enlarging its financial responsibility and increasing the personnel of its service.   And may I add in this connection that I believe this to be no scheme for the aggrandizement of the West at the expense of the East?   Some study of irrigation problems has convinced me that conflicting water rights as between contiguous states render federal supervision imperative.   And our Eastern public may rest assured that under the administration of the United States Geological Survey not one dollar of public money will be misappropriated.

The first thing that a civilized government does is to map its domain. The results are often rough and incomplete, and hence we find that the oldest and most enlightened peoples are still perfecting these graphic delineations of their territory. The Survey has a department of topography which is constructing a map of the entire country.

FIG. 68. The Smithsonian Institution, Washington, D.C.
See page 348.

In most of these maps we find a scale of one inch to the mile, and contour intervals of twenty feet, and one familiar with such maps soon comes to feel that in using one of them he is taking a bird's-eye view of the country. The scale and the contour interval are varied to suit different purposes and types of topography, but the principles are the same for all.

In New York, as in some other states, the expense is
equally shared by the state and the Geological Survey.   More than one-half of New York has now
been surveyed, and in a few years we shall have a
complete map of the Empire State — a boon to every
enlightened citizen, and especially to every student
of geography in our schools.   Massachusetts, Rhode
Island, Connecticut, and New Jersey have for some
years had their maps complete.   Much has been
done among the southern Appalachians, in the Mississippi Valley, and in the Far West, though something
like two-thirds of our dominion remain yet to be
covered.

Such a map serves as a base map for all purposes,
but the Survey needs it especially for the delineation
of the geological formations.   Many geological parties
are every year in the field.   The government geologist
goes out during the summer and autumn in the
Appalachians, in the Rocky Mountains, among the
wastes of the Great Basin, the canyons of the Colorado, the lava plains of the Northwest, or the mountains of California, and returns with his specimens
and his note-books in the beginnings of winter, and
sits down in his office in the Survey building at
Washington to work up his results and prepare them
for publication.   His specimens are put into the
hands of specialists, his negatives are turned over to
the Survey photographer, his maps are drawn and
engraved, laboratories are at hand for needed exami-
nations, and expert authorities on all geological questions can be consulted at a moment's notice.   The
Survey is a hive of scientific industry, and it should

minister to the pride of every citizen that such a body of experts is making known the resources of the United States.

But we are not to think of the Survey as a mere exploiter of our mineral wealth. It is much, but not all, that we have means for the study of coal, oil, iron, clay, gold, silver, copper, and scores of other substances that are of use to man. We have, however, an engine for the increase of knowledge, in the field of pure science. The physical and the organic evolution of North America is a problem of great interest, and our resources cannot readily be exploited without attention to these more strictly scientific inquiries. Nor should any citizen desire to restrict the spending of government funds to a bare searching out of economic materials. Rather does he rejoice that pure and applied science go hand in hand, and he learns the great principle that the abstract scientific conclusion of to-day may contribute beyond measure to human wealth and comfort to-morrow.

We are sure to hear the story, if Nansen, or Peary, or Abruzzi, or Hedin returns from laborious exploits in the North or East; but year after year, members of the Survey, usually young men, often graduates of Harvard, Columbia, Johns Hopkins, and other schools, are achieving most important results in Alaska, and the public hears little of their daring, their endurance, and their devotion to science. We are so far away that we do not appreciate the wilderness of mountain and plain in that far Northwest still unknown to civilized man. Some reconnoissance work has also been done in the Philippines, which are to be,

for years to come, one of our most important fields
for geographical and geological research.

Let me refer again to a single department of the
Survey, that of Hydrography. Its field is the water
supply of the United States. Nearly every year it
requires a large volume of the Survey reports to
record its work. The flow of most of the important
rivers of the United States is measured. In one of
the recent reports, that for 1899, you will find maps,
with tables and diagrams of flow, for the Mohawk,
the Hudson, and the Croton, along with many others
throughout the East and West. It is to this Bureau
of the Survey that the federal operations in irrigation
have been intrusted.

Our notice of the Geological Survey may close
with a reference to its publications. A professor in
an English university once said in substance: The
reports of your Survey are to us an envy and a despair, — so sumptuous are they, and distributed with
such liberality. Here they are, the maps sold at
mere nominal rates, the splendid annual reports —
given to you through application to your Congress-
man, as are also the bulletins. Then come the more
formal volumes, the monographs, sold practically at
what it costs to print them; and finally, the folios,
each one exhibiting the geography and geology of
the area of a single atlas sheet, fully described and
illustrated. The Survey is administered as a bureau
of the Interior Department, under the Secretary of
the Interior.

When we take up the work of the Department of
Agriculture, we are introduced to a bewildering array

of scientific activity. We can only touch here and there.

We are quite familiar with the ordinary work of the Weather Bureau, which is administered by the Department of Agriculture. But certain undertakings of the Bureau are not so well known. For example, it maintains a flood service, and by means of reports from a large number of flood stations upon certain important rivers, as the Ohio and Mississippi, is able to make predictions of great value to life and property. The Bureau is also extending its operations effectively over the West Indian region and the north Atlantic, even to European shores, and now, with the aid of wireless telegraphy, there is scarcely any limit to the efficiency with which storm warnings can be furnished along our coasts and to outgoing vessels. The Secretary of the Department of Agriculture, in his report for 1900, affirms that the great storm which devastated Galveston was forecast for eight days before it reached the Texas coast, during a course of two thousand miles, and that no craft plying on open waters of the Gulf of Mexico suffered disaster.

The Bureau of Animal Industry deals with the inspection of meat and of animals imported and exported. It thus has a close relation to the health of our people, and this in some most important fields, as, for instance, tuberculosis. An inspector has even been stationed in Great Britain, to relieve the danger and financial loss incurred in importing high-bred cattle that might be infected. Dairy products offer another sphere for this bureau. The Division of

Chemistry is occupied in the study of food adultera-
tion and the composition of foods. National legislation is fostered, looking toward co-operation with the
state governments for the same end. The sugar-beet
industry is somewhat dependent on this division for
its progress in this country. Problems in practical
chemistry are here solved also for other departments
of the government. Here belongs, for example, the
examination of imported sugars for the Treasury
Department. On the authority of Secretary Wilson,
the services of the Division of Entomology are annually worth more to our people than the entire Department of Agriculture costs.

The Division of Botany is naturally one of the
most important. No part of its work is of greater
interest than its care for the introduction of new
fruits and cereals such as may be adapted to special
areas of soil and climate in the United States. Reference has already been made to efforts to naturalize
the date palm in the hot and dry Southwest.

Much more important, perhaps, is experimentation
with wheats, which, in the Old World, notably Russia,
have become adapted to a semi-arid climate. With a
rainfall of thirteen inches, the lower Volga furnishes
one of the chief wheat areas of the Empire. No one
can tell how much this may mean to the semi-arid
belt of the Great Plains. It may make it worth while
to hold on to some Western mortgages. Kaffir corn
is another of these importations. Examples of important introductions could be much multiplied.

The Division of Biological Survey carries on, in
several states, systematic field work for determination

of life zones.   A special inquiry, important in Texas and other states, relates to the best methods of destroying the prairie dog.   Large authority is given to this division, for the protection of useful birds and the destruction of those that are harmful.   One line of study relates to the food of birds, a knowledge of which is essential to determining their status, whether good or bad.

The Division of Soils has in progress a soil survey of the United States.   The object is to classify and map the soils, with such reference to climate, economic conditions, and special crops, as to make the work of practical value to the farmer.   In 1900 nearly five thousand square miles were surveyed, and the 17,600 copies of the annual report were actively called for.   Operations reached nearly a dozen states.

Directly related to the Department of Agriculture are the Experiment stations which have developed with the Agricultural colleges, and in co-operation with the state governments.   The first station to be established by a state was that of Connecticut, and this came about no longer ago than 1875.   North Carolina followed in 1877, and New Jersey in 1880. National legislation was delayed until 1887, and since that time all the states have joined with the national government in this work.[1]

Perhaps no part of the Department's work is of

[1] Bulletin No. 80, United States Department of Agriculture, 1900, gives a detailed story of the history, organization, publications, and practical results of experiment station work as a whole, and in particular for each state.

more striking interest than that of the Division of
Forestry. In his first message to Congress, President Roosevelt gave authoritative expression to the
public interest in our forests, and to the demand for
their preservation. He urges (and has secured) an
increase of the forest reserves and their management

FIG. 69.   Experiment Station Farm, U. S. Department of Agriculture,
Washington, D.C.   Lettuce Trials in the Foreground.

upon business principles. Our highest sylvan ideals
are nowhere better set forth than by him in these
words: "The forest reserves should be set apart forever for the use and benefit of our people as a whole,
and not sacrificed to the short-sighted greed of a
few."

Silently and almost without observation, during the
few past years, a great science has been growing up,

a great field of professional study and practical effort has opened — I mean Forestry — and I commend it to any young man, a lover of the outdoor world, who is vainly looking for a career. We are now tardily out on the road, along which our friends across the seas have led the way. We have first the forest reserves. Recent additions carry their area up to about ninety thousand square miles, about one-fortieth of our territory, apart from Alaska, or for better comprehension, about twice the area of the Empire State. These reserves will require a permanent force for their care, including a good number of trained foresters. Responsibility is at present too much divided. The General Land Office is charged with the protection of the forests, the geological survey describes the timber, and the Bureau of Forestry in the Department of Agriculture provides plans for forest management. The President advises that all of these functions should belong to the Bureau of Forestry.

But the Bureau also works in the interests of, and in co-operation with, private owners of forests throughout the country. A recent bulletin of the Bureau is devoted to private forestry in the Adirondacks. Working plans were prepared for two large tracts. One is Nehasane Park, belonging to Dr. W. Seward Webb, and the other is Whitney Preserve, about Little Tupper Lake, belonging to Mr. W. C. Whitney. In the case of the latter we have the first instance of systematic forestry by a lumber interest, in the Adirondacks. It is shown that ideal forestry is not always practicable, — that we must be satisfied with

the best results possible under the circumstances,
involving, to be sure, great improvement in present
conditions, and yet maintaining a margin of profit.

Another publication by the Bureau deals with
forest extension in the Middle West. The object
is to show that tree planting will pay. A ten-year
plantation of Catalpa in Kansas now shows a net
value of $197.55 per acre. Great destruction of the
native trees has taken place there, as in Arkansas.
There is large call for fence posts, railway ties, and
telegraph poles, and 90,000,000 railway ties are
needed each year for renewal. The telegraph lines
of this country require every year 600,000 poles.
For these and other needs, 500,000 acres, annually
planted, would not be enough for the Middle West.
The Bureau of Forestry will oversee the work of
planting without cost to the planter.

Another paper deals with forestry in the Appalachians. Here are the finest virgin forests in the
eastern United States. Here it is to be hoped that
current discussion will result in the setting apart of
a great forest reserve, preserving for all our people
the scenic glories of those southern mountains. One
hundred kinds of native trees thrive in these forests
of western North Carolina and eastern Tennessee.
Many areas have suffered from cutting, from fires,
and from grazing. These evils can be checked, and
the high mountain forests can be improved by cutting out the overripe trees. But it is in the Western
forest that the sheep grazer, the shake maker, the
hunter, and the tourist have wrought the most dread-
ful havoc. And it is there that the forest ranger and

FIG. 70. Jefferson Memorial Road, from Charlottesville to Monti-
cello, Va., as it is and as it will be. The upper view shows a sample
section, improved with the equipment brought by the U. S. Good
Roads train, in April, 1902.

the officer of the law are beginning to check the ruthless and destructive hand and preserve the monarchs of a forest, some of whose single trees go back beyond the days of David and Homer.

We do not need to be told that the improvement of rural roads is one of the most vital and important projects now before our people. Here again the Department of Agriculture comes to the front with its Office of Public Road Inquiries. Its general object is to disseminate scientific information and advice, and thus enter into helpful co-operation with good-roads people everywhere. It supports for this purpose an expert in each of several sections of the country. These experts are to lecture, to report on local conditions, to send road materials for examination; in short, to be an intermediary between the office and the people. Machinery has been set up or testing such materials, and the work is done free of charge, on certain conditions, for any section of the country. Improved road machinery is carried to various points and sample roads are constructed, thus affording most valuable object lessons to the people. We are beginning, in the way of laboratory tests, to do what France has done for a generation, and we may hope in the near future to have, at least along some main lines of travel, such roads as every traveler is familiar with in the more advanced countries across the seas.

We close our notice of this magnificent department with a reference to its publications. Let me remind you that it issues a monthly list of publications, a small pamphlet, and that upon your request your

name is put upon a list for the regular reception of
this catalogue. You can then find the titles that
interest you, and learn whether they can be obtained
by donation or by purchase. Between two and three
million copies of the various publications were issued
in 1900.· This shows an enormous extension of the

FIG. 71. Laboratory and Hatchery of the United States Fish Commission, Woods Hole, Mass.

department's influence. A volume which cannot fail
to be prized by all who love horticulture or care for
rural affairs in general is the year-book of the department, varied and rich in contents and finely
illustrated.

This is perhaps a suitable place to add the United
States Fish Commission to our roll of great government instruments of research. Not only fresh and

salt water fishes, but marine foods of all kinds belong to its sphere. The report for 1899, taken at random as a sample, discusses the propagation and distribution of food fishes, and has chapters on the fisheries of Porto Rico, of the South Atlantic and Gulf states, and of the state of Washington and adjacent waters. Abundant maps and pictures adorn the pages of such volumes, often passed by as the lumber of the Government Printing Office by readers who have no idea of their riches. Other reports deal with other fields and phases of this industry, and are at once of high scientific and practical value.

No more striking event has ever taken place in the growth of education for the people than when a well-born Englishman, James Smithson, wrote, in 1826, these words, " I bequeath .the whole of my property to the United States of America to found at Washington an establishment for the increase and diffusion of knowledge among men." He elsewhere said, referring to the purpose that ruled his life : " The best blood of England flows in my veins; on my father's side I am a Northumberland, on my mother's I am related to kings; but this avails me not. My name shall live in the memory of man when the titles of the Northumberlands and the Percys are extinct and forgotten."

This sounds like prophecy. He was wise in his selection of an object, one which fills a larger place in human thought with every year, and in his choice of a place — the capital of the greatest of nations. Gifts of half a million dollars for research and education fall like raindrops in these days, but if we remember the date, and the influence of that young Englishman's gift, we must perhaps call it the largest of its kind in history.

It has co-operated with and vitalized scientific work of other government departments and all our higher institutions, and there is scarcely an important library in the world which does not regularly receive Smithsonian publications and send us in return its own. It early became the custodian of the National collections, and has carried the National Museum forward to its present development. Under its care the Bureau of Ethnology studies the vanquished and vanishing races of this country, and through it are published and disseminated each year the reports of the American Historical Association.

The War Department makes a contribution to the knowledge of our country, which is as conspicuous as it is little known to most citizens. This it does through its engineer department of the United States Army, which constantly details a large force for various forms of engineering work. The engineers' report for 1900 filled eight large volumes, giving in bare outline the enterprises carried forward. There is now increased demand on this branch of service, for the construction of roads and bridges, and for sanitary engineering in Cuba, Porto Rico, the Philippines, and in China. The engineers direct the United States Engineer School, make river and harbor improvements, and construct fortifications. The California Debris Commission belongs here, charged to protect and control the rivers, and empowered to license or forbid hydraulic mining operations, through

which rivers have been silted up and fields ruined.
The lighthouse service and the improvement of the
Yellowstone National Park are other items of the
engineers' duties.   All these forms of work add to
our knowledge of the geography and geology of our
country, and some enterprises have been of vast use
to science, though the prime object has been inland
navigation.

The early surveys of the Mississippi and its delta,
by Humphreys and Abbott, afforded data which have
been used by geologists and quoted in text-books the
world over, for many years.   And, in later years, we
have the Mississippi River Commission publishing
its remarkable series of large scale section maps of
the river and its lowlands, the Missouri River Commission doing a similar work for that great stream,
and the United States Lake Survey accomplishing for
the Great Lakes what the United States Coast Survey
does for all our marine borders.

Here, as in agricultural experiment work, the tech-
nical schools of the land supplement the work of the
government, and prepare men for the public service.
To name but a single example, Cornell University
offers a variety of courses in hydraulic engineering, and the great gorge and waterfalls on the north
border of its campus give it a unique equipment, a
hydraulic laboratory, in which experimentation is carried on, both by students, and in solving problems
offered by hydraulic projects in this and other lands.

The Coast Survey is one of the most honorable
scientific organizations in the United States.   It has
had continuous activity since the year 1832.   We

FIG. 72. Hydraulic Laboratory of Cornell University.

are all reasonably familiar with its general purpose to facilitate safe navigation of the marginal seas. To this end it sounds the waters along our coasts, and constructs charts, tide tables, and coast pilots. As the marginal coast lines and sea bottoms are suffering ceaseless changes, so the work of the Coast Survey is never complete. And in the realm of pure science, perhaps no government institution has contributed more to the world's knowledge. Much of our knowledge of the sea as a whole is due to its labors. More than any other agency, it has given us precise information about the Gulf Stream, information that is as far removed from ancient exaggerations on the one hand, as it is from current writings on the "Gulf Stream Myth."

The Coast Survey has accomplished much in the field of deep-sea exploration, thus sharing honors with Alexander Agassiz of the *Blake* and other expeditions, and with Sir John Murray of *Challenger* fame. Captain C. D. Sigsbee is known as the commander of the sunken battleship *Maine*. He deserves to be as well known and honored as the author of a portly Coast Survey volume, bearing the title " Deep Sea Sounding and Dredging." Inquiry would show the large contributions to science in America made by modest, highly trained officers of the army and navy.

If you cross 17th Street from the War Department in Washington, you may enter a low, dingy, and insignificant building, once a private residence, and find at his desk in an upstairs room, the chief of an important government establishment. Assistants

and messengers constantly appear for directions, and
depart, and when your turn comes, you will receive the
courteous attention of the chief of the United States
Hydrographic Office, which day and night reaches
out its arm to gain and impart information, over the
remotest seas. We may call its business the survey
of the ocean. Or, perhaps, we may better define it
as the clearing-house for our knowledge of the sea.
It seeks all marine and nautical information, home
and foreign. Facts are communicated from the
vessels of the navy, which thus find a large field of
usefulness in time of peace. Also from all cable
steamers of national and private ownership, giving
soundings from all parts of the world; from all similar offices of foreign nations, with which correspond-
ence and exchange are constant; from all sea-going
vessels, for any ship captain is expected to report
discovery of shoals, islands, or other unknown or
changed conditions of the sea. Data are often furnished by the United States Fish Commission, as, for
example, through the study of warm and cold currents off the New England coast, for their effects on
the movements of schools of fishes. Slips are supplied to mariners to be inclosed in sealed bottles and
dropped into the sea at various points, bearing the
request that finders will transmit them to the office
in Washington, giving the latitude and longitude of
the point of recovery. Many of these returns come
in after curious voyages across all seas, journeyings
which tax the imagination. But they add to our
knowledge of the movements of the sea. Those
abandoned hulks known as " derelicts " are often

reported as they are sighted by some vessel, when pursuing their weird voyages, with no steersman but wind and wave, and their lonely paths up and down the weary wastes of ocean have thus been charted and made known.

And the work of diffusion of knowledge thus gained is equally wide-reaching. Charts of depths, shoals, currents, buoys, and lights are published, and the work of correction is never done. Sailing directions are printed, with light lists and coast pilots. Branch offices are maintained, especially in all the greater maritime cities. Notices to mariners are issued every week, and sent to newspapers, shipping companies, and all foreign hydrographic offices. Thus the sea is less a wilderness, the mariner knows its highways, shares his experience with all brother sailors, and receives theirs in return. It gives one a new sense of the compactness of the world, and brings home with vividness and power the growth of social unity among all men.

Mr. Carnegie has founded an institution in Washington for the promotion of research. He has endowed it with ten millions of dollars. We think it is a splendid gift. And it is, but the income from this great principal is small, almost trivial, by the side of the sums spent every year in scientific work by the various departments and bureaus which have come under our review. And this institution is deliberately planned to supplement and work in harmony with the federal establishments.

The map work of the Geological Survey is of direct interest to every citizen of the United States.

Soil survey, forestry, good roads, new fruits and grains, and the prevention of insect ravages are interests that touch every farmer in our domain, and, in more or less direct ways, all our people. The same is true of the Weather Service. The reclamation of the arid lands has a vital relation to the wealth of the whole country, and the methods of irrigation devised in the West of necessity, will in the end be of great commercial value in Eastern agriculture. The mountains give up their treasures, the wealth of Alaska and of distant islands will be won, and the deepest and most distant seas will yield their stores of knowledge, and become, in reasonable measure, safe and homelike for the seafaring people of all nations.

INDEX

357